MERLEAU-PONTY AND METAPHOR

MERLEAU-PONTY AND METAPHOR

JERRY H. GILL

HUMANITIES PRESS
New Jersey ▼ London

First published in 1991 by
Humanities Press International, Inc.,
Atlantic Highlands, New Jersey 07716, and
3 Henrietta Street, Covent Garden, London WC2E 8LU

© Jerry H. Gill, 1991

Library of Congress Cataloging-in-Publication Data

Gill, Jerry H.
    Merleau-Ponty and metaphor / Jerry H. Gill.
      p. cm.
    Includes bibliographical references and index.
    ISBN 0–391–03713–7
    1. Merleau-Ponty, Maurice, 1908–1961—Contributions
in theory and use of metaphor. 2. Metaphor. I. Title.
B2430.M3764G54 1991
194—dc20   90–22765
                                                    CIP

British Library Cataloging in Publication Data

A CIP record is available for this book from the British Library.

Printed in the United States of America

for

THE McGINNIS CLAN

with fond memories

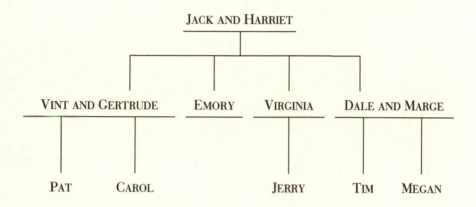

JACK AND HARRIET

VINT AND GERTRUDE   EMORY   VIRGINIA   DALE AND MARGE

PAT   CAROL   JERRY   TIM   MEGAN

CONTENTS

PREFACE

I want to take this opportunity to thank those who have in various ways contributed to this study of metaphor in the philosophy of Merleau-Ponty. My major graduate professor at Duke University, Wm. H. Poteat, is responsible for my initial interest in and understanding of Merleau-Ponty's thought. Years later my student, Jill Fritz-Piggott, did an excellent pilot study of Merleau-Ponty's use of metaphor in a lengthy term paper. More recently my wife, Mari Sorri, focused on the epistemological significance of the notion of embodiment in her Master's Thesis on Merleau-Ponty's philosophy. She also read and made many helpful suggestions for the improvement of the present manuscript. Finally, I received specific and useful direction, especially with regard to format and style, from the editorial readers at the Humanities Press. To each of these people I am extremely grateful, and I trust they will find the following study interesting and valuable.

INTRODUCTION

Since the turn of the century Western philosophy has been divided into three main camps or movements. European thinkers have developed the existentialist and phenomenological tradition, while British and to some degree Scandinavian thinkers have followed the analytical path initiated by Locke, Hume, and Kant. At first America made its own contribution through the pragmatism of C. S. Peirce, William James, and John Dewey. By midcentury, however, American thought was dominated by the other two traditions, especially by the empiricist analysis advocated in Britain.

Unlike previous eras in philosophy, the twentieth century has not been characterized by much, if any, conversation among its dominant traditions and perspectives. Each of these schools of thought has been content to talk almost exclusively to itself, with an occasional potshot fired across the Channel or the Atlantic. Each developed the conviction that its own way of doing philosophy was the only one worth pursuing, and thus by the middle of this century each had pretty much stagnated in its own parochialism.

At that point in time two thinkers arrived on the scene, one in France and the other in England, who initiated a quiet yet pivotal revolution in the way philosophy is understood and practiced. In spite of the fact that both of these philosophers arose within established and essentially insular traditions, and thus spoke the language and addressed the problems thereof, each started a tradition that today is less provincial and more fruitful. Although many of their immediate successors have failed to see the revolutionary character of their thought and thus continue to carry on their work as if their predecessors had not existed, there are indications that this is beginning to change. (See especially Gier, *Wittgenstein and Phenomenology*, and Mays and Brown, *Linguistic Analysis and Phenomenology*.)

One of these seminal thinkers was Ludwig Wittgenstein, whose writing gave rise to two dominant yet opposing currents within the analytic tradition. In his *Philosophical Investigations* he stressed the necessity of shifting the focus of philosophy away from abstract propositional analysis and toward everyday speech as a vital part of the intentional behavior and form of life shared by human beings as they seek to carry out their common

xi

tasks. He saw this form of life as constituting a vast and ever-developing network of overlapping and criss-crossing "language games," each tied in its own way to specific physical and social activity. Understanding and meaning are thus seen as a function of the *use* to which a particular linguistic expression is put within a concrete and purposeful *context*. The influence of Wittgenstein's more profound insights and emphases is slowly but surely spreading throughout the West, significantly altering the way such diverse disciplines as theoretical science, anthropology, literary criticism, and theology conduct themselves. (For example, consider Kuhn, *The Structure of Scientific Revolutions*, Geertz, *The Interpretation of Cultures*, and Rorty, *Philosophy and the Mirror of Nature*.)

The other seminal thinker is Maurice Merleau-Ponty, a follower of the father of phenomenology, Edmund Husserl. Far from being simply a devotee, however, Merleau-Ponty developed a particular emphasis within his phenomenological analysis that may permanently alter the course of Western thought. (See especially his *Phenomenology of Perception*.) Like Wittgenstein, Merleau-Ponty advocated the shifting of philosophical attention away from abstract intellectual analysis and toward the concrete, as it is experienced by all human beings, including philosophers. More specifically, Merleau-Ponty's focus was on the unique *embodied* character of human existence, together with its implications for speech, sexuality, science, and culture, including politics and art. Merleau-Ponty was convinced that the fundamental error of Western thought has been its almost universal insistence on understanding human thought and life as if they were disembodied realities. This emphasis on the necessity of the body in all human meaning and cognition has begun to make itself felt in an extremely wide variety of fields of study beyond professional philosophy, such as psychology, aesthetics, natural science, theology, and artificial intelligence. (For example, consider Gibson's *Perception of the Visual World*, Arnheim's *Visual Thinking*, Polanyi's *Knowing and Being*, Dreyfus's *What Computers Can't Do*, and Nelson's *Embodiment*.)

In addition to their mutual concern for making the concrete character of human life, thought, and speech the central focus of philosophical activity, Wittgenstein and Merleau-Ponty share a common commitment to the impossibility and unimportance of grounding the human search for knowledge in any absolutely certain point of departure. Both agree that such "foundationalist" concerns not only give rise to the specter of skepticism, but pale in the light of pragmatic effectiveness and the self-corrective character of our cognitive activity, whether at the practical or theoretic level. Moreover, both Wittgenstein and Merleau-Ponty stress the uniquely *linguistic* character of human existence. For them speech is not something optional and arbitrary; it is the very matrix by means of which we are woven into the fabric of human life and thought. Language does not simply picture or mirror the world and/or our thoughts; rather, it is through our participation in the speaking community that we come to inhabit the world and to think as we do.

There is one other major common aspect of the philosophical posture advocated by Wittgenstein and Merleau-Ponty, and it is this that I wish to take up in the present study. In spite of the fact that neither has much if anything to say about the nature and role of metaphor in the development and practice of human language, both of these highly significant thinkers not only theorize about speech in ways that carry deep and far-reaching implications for the metaphoric mode of expression, but more than any other important philosopher, they both *philosophize* by means of metaphor. That is to say, both Wittgenstein and Merleau-Ponty, as anyone familiar with their writings can attest, seem to be incapable of expressing their insights apart from the prolific use of metaphorical images. They literally *think* metaphorically.

These mutual and combined emphases on the pivotal nature of both language and metaphor, both in theory and practice, place these two philosophers at the forefront of a field that has come to serve as the bridge that may well unite not only differing schools of thought within philosophy, but whole disciplines that previously had little to do with one another. This fresh point of departure for contemporary inquiry is generally designated "hermeneutics" and pertains to the study of meaning, understanding, and interpretation. (Among the many important works here, see Palmer's *Hermeneutics*, Gadamer's *Truth and Method*, and Panikkar's *Myth, Faith, and Hermeneutics*.) Since such concerns lie at the center of nearly all, if not all, theoretical activity, hermeneutics provides an excellent way to refocus traditional epistemological and methodological issues in a way that incorporates and integrates a wide range of thinkers and disciplines. In addition, the work of Wittgenstein and Merleau-Ponty thereby becomes especially significant.

Moreover, their specific use of metaphor, as well as the particular nature of their perspectives on language in general, places these two thinkers at the heart of the contemporary discussion of the nature and role of metaphor, a discussion that dovetails nicely with the current interest in hermeneutics. Concretely, the insights of Wittgenstein and Merleau-Ponty have called into question the traditional placement of metaphoric speech at the periphery of linguistic activity. They both concur with highly influential literary thinkers that the metaphoric mode is primordial, rather than ancillary to the rest of language. (See especially Barfield, *Poetic Diction*, and Wheelwright, *Metaphor and Reality*.) A significant number of important philosophical thinkers within both the analytic traditions (see Black's *Models and Metaphors* and Johnson's *Philosophical Perspectives on Metaphor*) and the phenomenological traditions (see Gadamer's *Philosophical Hermeneutics* and Panikkar's *Myth, Faith, and Hermeneutics*) have devoted a great deal of attention to the importance of metaphor to all human expression. Many of these thinkers have been directly influenced by Wittgenstein and/or Merleau-Ponty.

Some years ago I did a rather thorough study of Wittgenstein's works (*Wittgenstein and Metaphor*), with an eye both to his *use* of metaphor in expressing his own insights and to the implications of his *thought* for a theory of metaphor and the nature of philosophy. In the present work I shall be aiming at the same thing for the works of Merleau-Ponty. Although a great deal has been written about his philosophy, next to nothing has been done to trace his use of metaphor in the presentation of his thought. It is this important lack which I am seeking to overcome, for like Wittgenstein, Merleau-Ponty uses the metaphoric mode profusely, and as I hope to show, it forms the very axis of his understanding of both language and philosophy.

At this point it may prove helpful to anticipate the conclusions drawn in Chapter 6 concerning Merleau-Ponty's position on the crucial connection between metaphor and philosophy. This could be useful in the context of other interpretations of Merleau-Ponty's philosophy. In short, my overall claim is that previous discussions of Merleau-Ponty's writings have ignored the pivotal role of metaphor in seeking to explain the content of his philosophy and extract it from its medium. Thus a great deal of the significance of his thought is lost and/or distorted in such interpretations. Let me briefly indicate how this is in fact the case.

Merleau-Ponty's most radical claim pertains to the irreducible and far-reaching mediational character of the somatic dimension of human existence and cognition. Moreover, he explicitly develops the crucial parallel between our physical embodiment and the incarnational quality of linguistic meaning in and through the essentially metaphorical nature of speech. In spite of this obvious connection between human and linguistic embodiment in Merleau-Ponty's philosophy, most if not all of his interpreters have neglected its exploration. This is true of the general, more introductory accounts of Merleau-Ponty's work, such as John Bannon's *Philosophy of Merleau-Ponty*, Thomas Langan's *Merleau-Ponty's Critique of Reason*, and Remi Kwant's *Phenomenological Philosophy of Merleau-Ponty*. It is also true of the more thorough treatments of Merleau-Ponty's thought.

In Monika Langer's very helpful *Merleau-Ponty's "Phenomenology of Perception,"* for instance, one finds a sound sensitivity to the radical, somatic thrust of Merleau-Ponty's philosophy of language, but absolutely no mention of the nature and role of metaphor. She says, for example, that according to Merleau-Ponty,

Authentic speech *is* the presence of thought—not its garment, but its body. . . . In speech, as in music or painting, it is successful expression which brings a new significance into being and opens up new possibilities for our experience. (pp. 59–60)

Nevertheless, while Langer seeks to extract the various aspects of Merleau-Ponty's philosophy from his own concrete and ubiquitous metaphors, she makes no acknowledgment of their presence.

Similarly, in his most interesting summary of Merleau-Ponty's philosophy of language in the foreword to *Consciousness and the Acquisition of Language*, James Edie discusses the philosopher's remarks on the role of metaphor without mentioning or in any way exploring the creative and thoroughgoing use of metaphor within Merleau-Ponty's works themselves. Such an oversight clearly indicates a failure to recognize not only the importance of metaphor in Merleau-Ponty's philosophy of language, but its significance for philosophy as a whole.

And consider Richard Zaner's *Problem of Embodiment*, which examines and critiques Merleau-Ponty's philosophy in some detail without giving attention to the fundamentally metaphorical character of his mode of expression in relation to his philosophy of language. Not only does Zaner fail to trace the implications of the notion of *embodiment* for linguistic meaning, but he never deals with the actual, recurrent metaphors by means of which Merleau-Ponty expresses his philosophy. This failure surely contributes to Zaner's tendency to interpret Merleau-Ponty's understanding of phenomenological method as a continuation of the traditional metaphysical perspective, which distinguishes the world from an objective description thereof.

The same can be said, albeit inversely, with respect to Langan's interpretation of Merleau-Ponty's philosophy as "idealist" (*Merleau-Ponty's Critique of Reason*, pp. 169ff). The failure to appreciate the mediational quality of embodiment, in which the intangible is experienced and known in and through the tangible, especially as it is focused in the inherently metaphorical character of language, leads directly to the dichotomy between the "objective" world and the "subjective" knower, thus forcing a choice between an other-worldly, transcendental metaphysics and a worldly, reductionist one. Merleau-Ponty, by means of his understanding of the embodied nature of both cognition and speech, avoids this dilemma. An appreciation for the role of metaphor, both in Merleau-Ponty's theory and in his practice, goes a long way toward preventing mistakes of this sort.

The focal point of Kwant's interpretation of Merleau-Ponty's philosophy, in *From Phenomenology to Metaphysics*, is that there is a fundamental difference between his early and later thought. He contends that while Merleau-Ponty was primarily interested in epistemology in *Phenomenology of Perception*, in *The Visible and the Invisible* his interest shifted to metaphysics.

Without going into the pros and cons of this thesis, it can safely be suggested that attention to the role of metaphor, in both his use and discussions thereof, would underscore the methodological continuity within the entire corpus of Merleau-Ponty's writings. The whole point of the embodiment theme, whether in reference to existence or speech, is to stress the symbiotic character of the relation between knowing and being. The function of metaphor in Merleau-Ponty's work does not constitute a major theme in Kwant's analysis.

Perhaps the most thorough, and in this sense the most helpful, discussion of Merleau-Ponty's overall thought is to be found in Samuel Mallin's *Merleau-Ponty's Philosophy*. Even here, however, one searches in vain for any mention, let alone exploration, of the place of metaphor in either Merleau-Ponty's methodology or his theory of language. Although Mallin correctly points out (p. 186) that Merleau-Ponty is in agreement with the later Wittgenstein and other "ordinary language" philosophers in stressing the pragmatic and open-textured character of "authentic speech," he never comes to grips with the way Merleau-Ponty's own meaning is incarnated within his metaphorical mode of expression. Thus Mallin, like other interpreters, seeks to extricate and explicate Merleau-Ponty's message from its medium, thereby denying his most fundamental insight.

Finally, consider Richard Lanigan's *Speech Act Phenomenology*. The stated aim of this book is to provide a critique of the analytical account of speech acts offered by J. L. Austin, John Searle, and H. P. Grice, by way of bringing to light a more comprehensive theory based on the phenomenological insights of Merleau-Ponty. Once again, however, nowhere in his highly abstract and somewhat cumbersome account of speech act theory in general and of Merleau-Ponty's understanding of language in particular does Lanigan provide any treatment whatsoever of the role and nature of metaphor. Merleau-Ponty's ideas are presented as so much content quite distinct from its metaphoric formulation, in spite of the fact that he himself clearly denies the very possibility of this separation. Indeed, the very notion of "speech act" itself was developed in order to call attention to the inextricable manner in which thought, speech, and behavior are interwoven in human life.

Hopefully this brief survey of the lack of scholarly attention to what is clearly a crucial feature of both Merleau-Ponty's practice and theory sets the stage for the explorations comprising the following chapters. The role and nature of metaphorical speech and thought are, indeed, central to Merleau-Ponty's philosophy and have for too long a time gone untreated. It is time something was done to rectify this situation, and so I offer the following investigations as an initial effort in this direction.

The following explorations are divided into two parts. In Part One I shall locate and sketch the main contours of the major metaphors by means of which Merleau-Ponty develops and presents his philosophy. The emphasis will be on those expressions that occur most frequently and at the crucial junctures in Merleau-Ponty's major works. I shall offer no initial or definitive account or definition of the term or concept of metaphor. To do so would not only involve a presentation and treatment of many of the basic questions at issue among contemporary philosophers, but it would conflict with Merleau-Ponty's own view of how understanding and meaning arise out of the give-and-take of actual discourse. If the reader has come this far into the present study of the term *metaphor*, he or she will have no difficulty grasping its meaning as it emerges within the following discussions. The general meaning of the term, as indicated by the title of this book itself, provides a sufficient point of departure.

Part One will consider Merleau-Ponty's works in three phases or stages. The first will deal exclusively with his first major book, *Phenomenology of Perception*. Here I shall begin by calling attention to the metaphors he uses to describe both the empiricists' and rationalists' inability to account for perceptual experience. The primary difficulty here is their common assumption that such experience is reducible to sensations in and operated on by the disembodied mind. Next I shall focus on those metaphors by means of which he presents his case for the centrality of the body in all perceptual experience and cognitive activity. This is the heart of Merleau-Ponty's philosophy. Finally, I shall take up the expressions he employs to trace the implications of this somatic fulcrum of understanding for the other major dimensions of individual human existence.

The second phase of the first part will consist of an examination of the metaphors Merleau-Ponty uses in the major essays he wrote between the publication of *Phenomenology of Perception* (1945) and his death in 1961. These essays fall into three main groups: (1) those dealing with various aspects of art and aesthetics, (2) those treating political issues, especially pertaining to Marxism, and (3) those involving the relation between philosophy and the social sciences. Most of these articles have been collected into two volumes published during Merleau-Ponty's lifetime, *Sense and Non-Sense* (1948), and *Signs* (1960). A third volume of essays, *The Primacy of Perception*, which was published in 1964, will also be considered, as will some of the essays in *The Adventures of the Dialectic*, published in 1955. I shall not, of course, be able to discuss every one of Merleau-Ponty's essays, or take up each metaphor that occurs. A sufficient number will be explored to provide a stable and fair overview of the range and slant of his approach to these diverse issues. The focus will be on the metaphors used, and not on his views on the various topics in question. However, since these two dimensions clearly intersect, and even merge, the general drift of Merleau-

Ponty's approach to individual topics and issues will make itself felt in nearly every case.

The third phase of the first part will be concerned with locating and exploring the metaphors used by Merleau-Ponty in the book on which he was working when he died. This unfinished volume was published post-humously (1964) under the title *The Visible and the Invisible*. In this work Merleau-Ponty was seeking to give fuller expression to an elucidation of his particular view of the relation between tangible and intangible reality, and of how philosophy should approach this relationship. I shall identify the metaphors he uses to indicate (1) the various basic philosophical efforts that have distorted this relationship, (2) a more fitting and fruitful approach to philosophical activity, and (3) a fresh characterization of the mystery constituting the connection between the tangible and the intangible dimensions of experienced reality.

In Part Two of the present study I shall move on to an exploration of the ramifications of Merleau-Ponty's use of metaphor for a general theory of language, including the metaphoric mode, on the one hand, and for the nature of philosophical activity on the other. These explorations will again divide themselves into three main headings, each comprising a chapter. In no sense are they to be taken as a final or exhaustive analysis of Merleau-Ponty's views on these broad themes. Hopefully, however, they will provide a useful point of departure for further investigation.

I shall begin my treatment of Merleau-Ponty's general view of language by pinpointing his critiques of what others have said language is (Chapter 4). I shall then focus on what he himself says about language as an extension of embodied gestural activity. The two main aspects of this suggestion are then elucidated in terms of understanding behavior itself as a form of speech and speech itself as a form of behavior. In the former case we can, to invert J. L. Austin's phrase, "say things without words" (*How to Do Things with Words*) while in the latter case we can, as Austin himself put it, "do things with words."

In Chapter 5 I shall zero in on the implication of both Merleau-Ponty's use of metaphor and his overall perspective on the nature of language, with an eye to establishing the pivot point of his entire view of the character of human communication. In contrast to most traditional contemporary views of metaphor, Merleau-Ponty stresses its primordial quality in relation to all other aspects and uses of speech. He also connects the metaphoric to artistic activity in general. Meaning itself, as the heartbeat of human existence, is seen as inextricably bound up with the fabric woven by the metaphoric mode, and as embodied, relational activity. (For two recent and helpful efforts to develop what is an essentially similar perspective, see Johnson's *Body in the Mind* and Sorri and Gill's *Language, Truth, and Body*.)

Chapter 6 is devoted to the extension of these insights into and suggestions for the methodological question of the nature of philosophy. As I see it, Merleau-Ponty finds this metaphilosophical issue resolved by a consideration of the crucial role of metaphor for language in general, and for all efforts to come to grips with the mediational relation between tangible and intangible reality in particular. He critiques both skepticism and dogmatism for presupposing the need to ground meaning and cognition in the theoretical possibility of obtaining a "God's-eye" view of how the world is, quite apart from human involvement and views. On the contrary, Merleau-Ponty contends that the relational character of all experienced reality renders such an assumption impossible and irrelevant.

This relational quality of all human cognition, together with the mediational nature of the relation between the tangible and the intangible, leads Merleau-Ponty to conclude that only the indirect character of the metaphoric mode is suitable for grasping and expressing the subject matter of philosophy. In addition, since cognition and speech arise only within our embodied social context, they depend upon interactive participation in the relational and mediational character of the physical and social environment. Hence, philosophy itself necessitates such interaction, and thus must be understood and practiced as dialogue. It must be seen as an ongoing conversation with both reality and other members of the speaking community who take up its concerns.

It is as a contribution to this continuing conversation that the following study is undertaken and presented. I am, to be sure, much influenced by the depth and power of Merleau-Ponty's posture toward all these issues and developments. Having a point of view in no wise disqualifies one from engaging in honest dialogue. We can only insist that every point of view must seek to be responsible, that is, grounded in experience and open to correction. I have sought to fulfill this obligation in the explorations that follow. It is hoped that they will stimulate the reader to enter into this conversation with criticisms and contributions of his or her own. This surely is the spirit that Merleau-Ponty sought to embody in his own work.

Two final, methodological comments are in order. First, locating and categorizing Merleau-Ponty's metaphors will obviously require a large number of quotations from his writings. Moreover, to facilitate an adequate appreciation of their significance, it will frequently be necessary to quote at some length in order to provide an adequate sense of context. Second, I shall document the location of sources in parentheses at the close of the passage quoted, rather than in notes. This should save the reader the trouble of continually turning to the back of the book in order to check references.

PART ONE

THE USE OF METAPHOR

1

PERCEPTION AND EMBODIMENT

The metaphors in *Phenomenology of Perception* fall into three main categories or centers of focus, roughly corresponding to the stages of Merleau-Ponty's presentation. The first comprises the preface, introduction, and the first three chapters of Part One ("the Body"), and is concerned primarily with questions of methodology. The second, which constitutes the heart of the book, establishes embodiment as the axis of human existence and cognition (Part One, chapters 3 through 6). The third explores the ramifications of this somatic starting point for our knowledge of the world, both physical and social (Part Two), as well as for certain traditional philosophical problems (Part Three). While there is a good deal of overlap and exchange between and among the metaphors used in each of these areas of concern, there is a degree of difference in the vector or emphasis that Merleau-Ponty gives to each. The following presentation will stress these differences, but without in any way intending to suggest either exclusivity or exhaustiveness. My purpose is to allow Merleau-Ponty's major insights and emphases to speak for themselves by highlighting and classifying the metaphors he employs.

POSTURE AND METHOD

In his preface, Merleau-Ponty makes use of three main kinds of metaphor by way of introducing his own understanding of phenomenology, especially as it is related to that of Husserl. It is from this methodological posture that he moves to criticize traditional and modern epistemologies in the early chapters of *Phenomenology of Perception*. The first type of metaphor he deploys is a geographic or environmental one. In the midst of his initial discussion of what phenomenology is, Merleau-Ponty contrasts a descriptive "return to things themselves" (phenomena) to the abstract "scientific schematizations" of modern philosophy in terms of the contrast between our first-hand knowledge of the countryside ("what a forest, a prairie, or a river is") and the derivative study of geography (Preface, p. ix). This particular image is repeated in his in-depth analysis of space, where he contrasts "lived" knowledge of a village's whereabouts to that based on landmarks and compass readings (p. 285).

This environmental metaphor is given a slightly different twist when Merleau-Ponty introduces one of his more dominant notions, that of "the background from which all acts stand out . . . the natural setting of, and field for, all my thoughts and all my explicit perceptions" (Preface, p. xi). This image of field, especially in its electromagnetic sense, is employed frequently throughout Merleau-Ponty's work, often in conjunction with the notion of "horizon." We shall have occasion to return to this theme a bit later on. Here it is sufficient to note that from Merleau-Ponty's perspective both the world and our initial perception of it are "primordial" or given, not in some noetic or apodictic sense, but in a pragmatic or intentional sense. We simply arrive on the scene already involved in it, with "an original past, a past which has never been a present" (p. 242).

Although he occasionally speaks of this primordial setting in terms of "depth" (e.g., p. 266), generally speaking the methodological posture advocated by Merleau-Ponty stresses a geographic orientation rather than the image of geological stratification usually associated with modern foundationalist epistemology. This is especially evident in his use of the metaphor of the world being "revealed where paths of my various experiences intersect, and also where my own and other people's intersect and engage each other like gears" (Preface, p. xx). An extremely concrete example of such intersectional revelation is given near the end of the book, where Merleau-Ponty reflects on his own writing process:

> The paper, my fountain-pen, are indeed there for me, but I do not explicitly perceive them. I do not so much perceive objects as reckon with an environment; I seek support in my tools, and am at my task rather than confronting it. (p. 416)

The metaphor of engaging or meshing gears is not, to be sure, so much an environmental image as a mechanical one, but Merleau-Ponty sometimes uses it in connection with other, more organic images (e.g., pp. 77, 251, 442). At any rate we shall turn to this sort of metaphor more directly when we consider his account of the centrality of the body.

The second main kind of metaphor introduced in the preface to *Phenomenology of Perception* is what might be called a textile one. Merleau-Ponty speaks of "the real as a closely woven fabric" (Preface, p. x), of the body as "the fabric into which all objects are woven" (p. 235), and of language as a dialogue in which our own thoughts and those of another "are interwoven into a single fabric" (p. 354). The primary thrust of this frequently repeated image is to convey the relational quality of all human existence and experience. On the one hand it is connected to the organic metaphors involving "networks" (e.g., p. 456) and "tissues" (e.g., p. 57), while on the other hand it ties in with mechanical metaphors, such as: "What has to be understood, then, is how the psychic determining factors and the physiological conditions gear into each other . . ." (p. 77).

An important aspect of this textile image is brought out in this passage from the preface:

> Reflection does not withdraw from the world towards the unity of consciousness as the world's basis; it steps back to watch the forms of transcendence fly up like sparks from a fire; it slackens the intentional threads which attach us to the world and thus brings them to our notice. . . . (p. xiii)

The notion of threads through which we interactively know and alter the world stands in stark contrast both to traditional philosophical models according to which knowledge is passively yet unerringly received, and to modern philosophy, which begins by completely separating the knower from the world and ends up desperately seeking some way to overcome skepticism. These "threads" connect us with the world, thereby providing reliable if incomplete knowledge, while at the same time distancing us from the world, thereby negating arrogance and complacency. This type of connection is fragile but sufficient.

The adjective "intentional" with which Merleau-Ponty qualifies his notion of threads serves once again to emphasize the interactive character of our existence and cognition. It is by seeking to carry out our intentions in the world that we constitute ourselves as well as our knowledge of the world. We are tied to the world in such a way as not to be able to disentangle ourselves from it, but also in such a way as not to be able to fully control or track it. Moreover, philosophical reflection cannot transcend this threadlike connection in order to know the world "as it is in itself." Only by slackening the threads, that is, by reflecting on them and the world *while and as* we function in the world by means of them, can we gain an understanding of the world and our own place in it. "The body, by withdrawing from the objective world, will carry with it the intentional threads linking it to its surrounding and finally reveal to us the perceiving subject as the perceived world" (p. 72).

The mention of transcendence in the passage where Merleau-Ponty introduces the image of threads is a bit complicating, to say the least. The image of "sparks from a fire," which he borrows from Malebranche (cf. p. 26), would seem to suggest that transcendence is epiphenomenal and transitory at best. At the same time, any mention of glimpsing the transcendent smacks of traditional concepts of "idealism" and/or "realism." The juxtapositioning of these two images, sparks and slackened threads, must be understood within the context of Merleau-Ponty's overall posture, which would seem to suggest a notion of mediated transcendence in which the real is revealed "in and through" our interaction with the solid, not above and beyond it. Sparks are, after all, also a form of fire in their own right. We shall return to this highly significant issue of transcendence in conjunction with our consideration of other images in Merleau-Ponty's writings.

The third major type of metaphor introduced in the preface is that of artistic or creative activity. Merleau-Ponty says, "Philosophy is not the reflection of a pre-existing truth, but like art the act of bringing truth into being. . . . we take up this unfinished world in an effort to complete and conceive it" (p. xx). Thus philosophy's method is both constitutive and cognitive, even as in our everyday life we both contribute to and seek to understand the world in which we find ourselves. "Rationality is not a *problem*. . . . We witness every minute the miracle of related experiences, and yet nobody knows better than we do how this miracle is worked, for we are ourselves this network of relationships" (p. xx).

Later on (p. 150) Merleau-Ponty again says:

> . . . the body is to be compared, not to a physical object, but rather to a work of art. In a picture or a piece of music the idea is incommunicable by means other than the display of colours and sounds. . . .

even though it cannot be separated from such sensory particulars (cf. p. 151). This aesthetic metaphor is frequently used in relation to various literary arts, such as poetry and fiction. There Merleau-Ponty speaks of the relationship between a text and our understanding as similar to our cognitive interaction with the world around us. "[N]ormal functioning must be understood as a process of integration in which the text of the external world is not so much copied, as composed," the sensory parts of which comprise "a formation already bound up with a larger whole, already endowed with a meaning" (p. 9). Even with language itself, "the primary meaning of discourse is to be found in the text of experience which it is trying to communicate" (p. 337).

For Merleau-Ponty's specific application of this artistic metaphor to aesthetic experience and understanding, especially to the work of Cézanne, we shall have to wait until the next chapter. Suffice it to say that at the very outset of his monumental *Phenomenology of Perception*, he has introduced three pivotal images around and between which the dominant currents of his thought will flow in the remaining chapters. Before moving on to their consideration, however, we should locate those images by means of which he organizes his critique of traditional and modern accounts of cognition in the four chapters comprising the introduction to *Phenomenology of Perception*.

In his detailed and critical analysis of the empiricist account of perception and experience as based on the building blocks of individual sensations (or "data"), Merleau-Ponty sees this tradition as establishing the holistic or *gestalten* character of perception. Sensations are, after all, "a formation already bound up with a larger whole, already endowed with a meaning, distinguishable only in degree from the more complex perceptions" (p. 9). To be able to identify and analyze sensations as the parts out of which the larger units of experience are supposedly built, one must first be able to grasp the larger whole of which these sensations are said to be the parts; otherwise they are not "parts," as such, but only indiscriminate and undifferentiated plethora of sensations. "The word perception indicates a *direction* rather than a primitive function" (p. 12). In short, psychological atomism simply will not do.

In the midst of grappling with the particulars of the psychology of perception, and by means of the biological metaphor of pregnancy, Merleau-Ponty introduces the notion that the whole is greater than and prior to its individual parts. At first he speaks of the unity of experience as a kind of "foreshadowing of an imminent order which is about to spring upon us, a reply to questions merely latent in the landscape" (p. 17), as the ground rather than the result of psychological "association" (à la Locke, Hume, *et al.*). He then goes on to argue as well that this experiential unity cannot be caused simply by the activity of the memory on what was initially given as data. He says:

> . . . the cleavage between given and remembered, arrived at by way of objective causes, is arbitrary. When we come back to phenomena we find, as a basic layer of experience, a whole already pregnant with an irreducible meaning: not sensations with gaps between them, into which memories may be supposed to slip, but the features, the layout of a landscape or a word, in spontaneous accord with the intentions of the moment, as with earlier experience. (pp. 21–22)

To borrow the worn-out image of the chicken and the egg, Merleau-Ponty contends that any attempt to account for the holistic character of our experience of the world exclusively in terms of its sensory origins fails to consider the question of the source of these "beginnings" themselves. The mystery of biological generation, represented by the imagery of pregnancy, serves to remind us of the inadequacy of any reductionistic analysis of human life and meaning. Here, again, we seem to be required to speak in terms of having a "past which was never a present," of arriving on the scene already involved in the game being played by those around us. Merleau-Ponty's use of biological metaphors extends far beyond this particular context, as we shall soon discover.

In his critique of empiricism, Merleau-Ponty briefly mentions two other images that involve an environmental metaphor, to which he returns time and again throughout his writing. He speaks of the connection between the past and present arising within "A field which is always at the disposal of consciousness and one which, for that very reason surrounds and envelopes its perceptions, an atmosphere, a horizon . . ." (p. 22). A bit later on he terms this environment the "homeland of our thought" (p. 24). In addition to these images of "field" and "homeland," which we have encountered previously, that of "horizon" comes to play an extremely crucial role in Merleau-Ponty's thought, as it does in the thought of other phenomenologists. A more thorough account of it must, however, be postponed until the next section.

Over against his critique of empiricism, Merleau-Ponty places his critique of rationalism, or what he terms "intellectualism." Not only does this tradition repeat the mistake of viewing the perceiving subject as a passive and static recipient of sensations, but where empiricism was unable to establish any basis for truth (having placed an unbridgeable gap between the knower and the known), rationalism is unable to account for error, since the categories of the mind determine the character and organization of the world we experience. More specifically, Merleau-Ponty scores the intellectualist tradition for reducing perception and understanding to functions of mental "attention" and "judgement," where both are viewed as projecting an interpretive structure on our sensations and thereby creating the unity of our experience.

On the contrary, Merleau-Ponty argues, the gap between the knower and the known is not overcome by endowing the mind with "occult" powers by means of which it constructs its own world (thereby passing "from absolute objectivity to absolute subjectivity," p. 39). Rather, we overcome this supposed gap by virtue of our embodied involvement in and with the world from the very outset of our existence. By means of bodily activity we engage and are engaged by the world, both physically and socially. The images Merleau-Ponty makes use of in the process of introducing this revolutionary epistemological standpoint are somatic in nature. He says that "to perceive in the full sense of the word is not to judge, it is to *apprehend* an imminent sense in the sensible before judgement begins" (p. 35). And again, "Now there is indeed one human act which at one stroke cuts through all possible doubts to stand in the full light of truth: this act is perception, in the wide sense of knowledge of existences" (p. 40).

The tactile apprehension and kinaesthetic action designated in these remarks are the result of the embodied character of existence. In answer to the problem of what makes the sensations of seeing or feeling different from their corresponding concepts, that is, how we get from data and input to experience and knowledge, Merleau-Ponty replies that "reflection shows that there is nothing here to understand. It is a fact that I believe myself to be first of all surrounded by my body, involved in the world, situated here and now" (p. 37). In other words, the body provides an Archimedean point or axis, not an indubitable bedrock, around which perception, experience, and knowledge orbit. Epistemologically, we simply must start here; we must begin, in Wittgenstein's words, "at the beginning and not seek to go farther back."

Merleau-Ponty employs one other metaphor in his effort to correct the inadequacies of rationalism, and at this point he departs from Gestalt psychology as well. In discussing how we come to perceive, indeed, experience some objects as farther away in contrast to others whose features we are able to discern in greater detail, he suggests that there is a "silent language whereby perception communicates with us: interposed objects, in the natural context, 'mean' a greater distance" (p. 48). A bit further on he refers to a "wordless logic" (p. 49). This image of linguistic communication as expressive of the nature of the relationship between ourselves and the world is also one that occurs frequently throughout Merleau-Ponty's writings. In contrast to empiricism, which must explain this relationship as "the product of objective causes," and rationalism, which must explain it on the basis of "demonstrative reasons," Merleau-Ponty is quite comfortable speaking of it (p. 49) as "magical," as known tacitly, though obscurely, and validated by "wordless logic."

In the final phase (Chapter 4) of his introductory examination of the inadequacies of traditional approaches to perception, and thus to experience and knowledge, Merleau-Ponty presents his own alternative point of departure. He does this by returning to two images that he introduced in his preface. The first of these is environmental in nature and is mentioned in the title to the fourth chapter of his introduction, "The Phenomenal Field." The second image is biological or organic. Both will, of course, come up again throughout our explanation of Merleau-Ponty's thought.

The fundamental problem with the traditional treatments of perception is their failure to see the relational or situational character of human experience. Both empiricist and rationalist theories treat the knowing subject and that which is known as an isolated unit, floating passively in a static, hermetically sealed vacuum. The simple fact is, according to Merleau-Ponty, from the outset our very existence and nature are part and parcel of a relational, interactive *field* from which arise both our world and our perception.

> The first philosophical act would appear to be to return to the world of actual experience which is prior to the objective world, since it is in it that we shall be able to grasp the theoretical basis no less than the limits of that objective world. . . . our task will be, moreover, to rediscover phenomena, the layer of living experience through which other people and things are first given to us. . . . This phenomenal field is not an 'inner world'. (p. 57)

Merleau-Ponty goes on to say that philosophy in this sense involves "intentional analysis" (p. 59). He frequently speaks of intentionality in terms of organic images, as "intentional tissue" that provides the "thickness" binding the perceiver and the perceived (p. 53). This biological metaphor presents an active and developing organism whose "inner" and "outer" sides interact with each other more by osmosis than by impact and projection.

> The distinction between the perceptual life and the concept, between passivity and spontaneity is no longer abolished by analytical reflection, since we are no longer forced by the atomism of sensation to look to some connecting activity for our principle of all coordination. Finally, after sense experience, understanding also needs to be redefined, since the general connective function ultimately attributed to it by Kantianism is now spread over the whole intentional life. . . . (p. 53)

Having indicated his own point of departure by the image of an organic membrane or interactive field, Merleau-Ponty is now prepared to locate the heart of human experience in terms of embodiment.

Before moving on to the next section, however, we should again take note of an additional issue that arises in Merleau-Ponty's presentation of his methodological posture. Even as the image of philosophy as standing back while "the forms of transcendence fly up like sparks from a fire" posed the question of the overall status of philosophical reflection, so too does the image of perception and knowledge as arising within a phenomenal field that is always encompassed by a horizon. The difficulty seems to be that it is paradoxical, at best, to speak of reflecting on the world of experience, including the act of reflection itself, and arriving at a complete understanding thereof and thereby. Since the world, as encompassed by a horizon, and our understanding, as an ongoing process, are both by nature unfinished, how can they be known "completely"? To put the question in the vocabulary of Bertrand Russell, are we not here involved in a self-stultifying "paradox of self-reference"?

Merleau-Ponty's answer to this question would seem to be an attempt to redefine the term "transcendence" so as to refer not to some world or knowledge beyond everyday human existence but simply to this self-referential character of all experience and knowing, including philosophy (cf. p. 61). He says that philosophical reflection must consider not only the world and the self, but it must also

> reflect on this reflection, understand the natural situation which it is conscious of succeeding and which is therefore part of its definition. . . . Only on this condition can philosophical knowledge become absolute knowledge, and cease to be a specialty or a technique. (p. 62).

This answer seems only to transfer the problem from the notion of transcendence to that of "absolute" knowledge. Part of the resolution of this framing of the difficulty might lie in Merleau-Ponty's insistence that "the mistake of reflective philosophies is to believe that the thinking subject can absorb into its thinking or appropriate without remainder, the object of its thought that our being can be brought down to our knowledge" (p. 62). On the contrary, he claims,

> A philosophy becomes transcendental, or radical, not by taking the ways by which this is reached, but by considering itself as a problem; not by postulating a knowledge rendered totally explicit, but by recognizing as the fundamental philosophic problem this *presumption* on reason's part. (p. 63)

These remarks would seem to indicate that for Merleau-Ponty what is transcendental or "absolute" about the knowledge gained through phenomenological exploration is qualitative rather than quantitative. It does not "go beyond" human experience; rather, it demonstrates or exemplifies the various features and vectors that constitute human experience.

To put this provisional resolution a bit differently, phenomenological method acknowledges the limitations of philosophical reflection. "The most important lesson which the reduction teaches us is the impossibility of a complete reduction" (p. xiv). At the same time, however, it accredits our ability to carry on the reflective process, even with regard to the process itself, since even second-order activity only confirms and illustrates the very discoveries that it makes. We merely "slacken" the intentional threads, for we cannot set them aside. Merleau-Ponty concludes his introductory section with the confidence that this process will transform "the phenomenal field into a transcendental one" (p. 63). We shall discuss this idea of the transcendental transformation of phenomena again and more thoroughly before we conclude our examination of Merleau-Ponty's use of metaphor.

THE BODY AT THE CENTER

In the first two chapters of Part Two of his *Phenomenology of Perception*, Merleau-Ponty continues his critique of modern thought, now with special reference to mechanistic physiology and classical psychology. The former is presented as reducing human life and consciousness to the functioning of various reflexes and instincts, while the latter tended to view the body as nothing more than the mind's tool for effecting its ideas in the world. Now both the epistemological and scientific aspects of the modern failure to do justice to the complexity and primacy of perception have been documented. This failure stems, in Merleau-Ponty's view, from ignoring the centrality of the body in the very basis and nature of human existence and experience. Against the background of this two-pronged critique Merleau-Ponty presents his own perspective, which places the body at the absolute center of human life and knowledge.

He initiates this presentation through the use of the general image of visual and spatial perspective. "Is not to see always to see from somewhere?" (p. 67). Thus my body not only locates me in the space that I "inhabit," but it provides me with a place from which to see the surrounding world. Vision is "an act with two facets" (p. 68), since it exists and operates between the location of my body in the world and as I alter my location, what was "there" is now here, and vice versa. This notion of perspective applies to time as well as to space, for

> with my immediate past I have also the horizon of futurity which surrounded it, and thus I have my actual present seen as the future of that past. With the imminent future, I have the horizon of past which will surround it, and therefore my actual present as the past future" (p. 69).

Thus, for Merleau-Ponty, the body is the nodal point, the ground or anchor by means of and at which we take up our place in the world, with respect to space and time as much as to physical objects. It is our entry point to or "point of view upon the world" (p. 70). Whenever we fail to acknowledge and remember this we are in danger of reducing our notion of the body to that of other objects, of "objectifying" our own presence and perspective in the world. In this way we inevitably distort our understanding of both human existence and experience. To avoid this danger, "We must discover the origin of the object at the very center of our experience; we must describe the emergence of being and we must understand how, paradoxically, there is *for us* an *in-itself*" (p. 71).

In order further to counteract the tendency to think of the body as simply an object among other objects in the world, Merleau-Ponty employs metaphors of movement. In this way he contrasts the active, intentional character of embodiment with the idea of the body as merely a stimulus–

response structure (cf. p. 79). He speaks of our awareness and knowledge of the world as resulting from our movement toward it, not just from reacting to it.

> In so far as I guess what it may be, it is by abandoning the body as an object, *partes extra partes*, and by going back to the body which I experience at this moment, in the manner, for example, in which my hand moves around the object, anticipating the stimuli and itself tracing out the form which I am about to perceive. I cannot understand the function of a living body except by enacting it myself, and except in so far as I am a body which rises towards the world. (p. 75)

This image of active rather than mere *reactive* movement is continued when Merleau-Ponty introduces the metaphor of the body as vehicle. He says: "The body is the vehicle of being in the world, and having a body is, for a living creature, to be intervolved in a definite environment, to identify oneself with certain projects and be continually committed to them" (p. 82). Here, too, in the terms "intervolved" and "environment" are hints of previously mentioned images. But the notions of project and commitment interject a fresh aspect into our understanding of the character of embodiment, an aspect that might be called a *vectorial* thrust or current. The body "is not some kind of inert thing; it too has something of the momentum of existence" (p. 84).

For Merleau-Ponty there is a certain bipolar character to embodied existence, the self consisting of the interactive dynamic between the body as physical reality and consciousness as intentional reality, situated in and involved with the world. "Man taken as a concrete being is not a psyche joined to an organism, but the movement to and fro of existence which at one time allows itself to take corporeal form and at others moves towards personal acts" (p. 88). This image of alternating movement, somewhat like alternating electrical current, occurs at other points in Merleau-Ponty's explorations as well (cf. pp. 165, 284).

The more positive and direct presentation of Merleau-Ponty's case for the centrality of embodiment is introduced by means of metaphors having to do with the axial or tether-point character of the body in relation to all aspects of our existence. He begins with the notion of "body image" as it arises and reveals itself in our body's spatiality and motility (p. 98), not as the composite result of the conditioned responses of each particular part of the body, but as the purposeful principle of intentional direction that renders such composition possible and actual. "We are therefore feeling our way towards a second definition of the body image: it is no longer seen as the straightforward result of association established during experience, but a total awareness of my posture in the intersensory world . . ." (pp. 99–100).

A bit further on, Merleau-Ponty refers to this body image as a "dynamic attitude directed towards a certain existing or possible task" (p. 100).

By means of this "posture" or "attitude," a kind of intentional equilibrium, we are aware of and insert ourselves into the world. The image of the body seeks to call attention to the integration of our kinesthetic awareness with our embodied motivation that lies at the center of uniquely human experience.

> The word "here" applied to my body does not refer to a determinate position in relation to other positions, or to external co-ordinates, but the laying down of the first co-ordinates, the anchoring of the active body in an object, the situation of the body in face of its tasks. (p. 100)

The images of spatial coordinates and bodily "anchorage" have been employed elsewhere by Merleau-Ponty (cf. p. 144), and it must always be remembered that they are to be thought of in relation to bodily movement in space and time. The center of our existence is always our own body, not as a fixed point in general space and time, but as the axis from which spatiality and temporality are oriented, as we move through them (cf. pp. 247–249).

In this context Merleau-Ponty also returns to the "point-horizon" metaphor in order to clarify both the absolute and the relative dimensions of our embodiment in relation to the world, as well as our knowledge of it.

> The horizon or background would not extend beyond the figure or round about it, unless they partook of the same kind of being as the figure, and unless they could be converted into points by a transference of the gaze. . . . the multiplicity of points or "heres" can in the nature of things be constituted only by a chain of experiences in which on each occasion one and no more of them is itself built upon the heart of this space. And finally, far from my body's being for me no more than a fragment of space, there would be no space at all for me if I had no body. (p. 102)

Thus the vector of space, and that of time as well, always moves *from* our own body *toward* our tasks in the world.

The vectorial quality inherent within this point-horizon image is emphasized once again when Merleau-Ponty likens the unity of consciousness and purposeful activity, which serves as the pivot-point of existence, to a searchlight. He characterizes this embodied integration as "a vector mobile in all directions like a searchlight, one through which we can direct ourselves towards anything, in or outside ourselves, and display a form of behavior in relation to that object" (p. 136). He immediately alters this image to that of an electric arc.

> Cognitive life . . . is subtended by an "intentional arc," which projects round about us our past, our future, our human setting, our physical,

ideological and moral situation, or rather which results in our being situated in all these respects. It is this intentional arc which brings about the unity of the senses, of intelligence, of sensibility and motility. (p. 136)

The result of such vectorial analysis of our embodied relation to space and time is the conclusion that

consciousness is being towards the thing through the intermediary of the body. . . . In so far as I have a body through which I act in the world, space and time are not, for me, a collection of adjacent points nor are they a limitless number of relations synthesized by my consciousness. . . . I am not space and time, nor do I conceive space and time; I belong to them, my body combines with them and includes them. (pp. 138, 140)

Or, to put it more compactly, "My body *inhabits* space and time" (p. 139). This metaphor of dwelling or habitation is not meant to suggest the arbitrary and optional relation between house (as mere residence) and life characteristic of much of modern, Western existence. Rather, it is meant to invoke the more primordial relationship of native land or family home. That this is so is made clear by the fact that at the conclusion of his chapter on bodily spatiality and motility, Merleau-Ponty alters his imagery slightly so as to say, "The body is our general medium for having a world" (p. 146). The notion of a medium in relation to a form of life (as with water and fish, air and birds, etc.) is incompatible with that of a temporary residence.

Having tied the integrated centrality of the body to the world of things, space, and time, Merleau-Ponty moves on to consider two further dimensions of human existence that are equally significant. The first is sexuality and the second is language. Both of these dimensions, though essentially social in character, serve as much to constitute and define our being and situation as they do to express them. And both are elaborated in terms of key metaphorical expressions.

Concerning the sexual dimension of our embodiment, Merleau-Ponty argues that it too is a "form of original intentionality . . . based on an 'intentional arc' . . . endowing experience with its degree of vitality and fruitfulness" (p. 157). Sexual desire, like all other emotions, is inextricably bound up with both physical processes and organs, on the one hand, and highly significant personal and social realities, on the other. It is embodied intentionality that integrates and mediates these symbiotic poles. "In this way the body expresses total existence, not because existence comes into its own in the body. This incarnate significance is the central phenomenon of which body and mind, sign and significance are abstract moments" (p. 166).

This mention of "incarnate significance" brings up a particularly interesting feature of Merleau-Ponty's use of metaphor in the development of his thought. In the present context he speaks of our embodied relations to each other as giving rise to sexuality, even as our embodied relation to physical objects gives rise to spatiality and temporality. In a later passage (p. 320), on the other hand, he uses the image of sexual union to characterize the knowledge that arises from our embodied interaction with the world. In this connection he also introduces the metaphor of communion by way of explaining perceptual knowledge.

> To this extent, every perception is a communication or a communion, the taking up or completion by us of some extraneous intention or, on the other hand, the complete expression outside ourselves of our perceptual powers and a coition, so to speak, of our body with things. (p. 320)

Thus, in a sense, all cognition is essentially carnal knowledge, since our existence is incarnational in character.

Concerning language, Merleau-Ponty contends that it is no mere appendage to human life. On the contrary, speech must first of all be understood as an essential means of becoming and expressing our humanness, "as an instrument of action" (p. 175). Indeed, speech does not mirror the world; rather, it is by means of speech as an extension of ourselves in the world that we come to know as well as alter it.

> When I fix my eyes on an object in the half-light, and say "It's a brush," there is not in my mind the concept of a brush under which I subsume the object, and which moreover is linked by frequent association with the word "brush," but the word bears the meaning, and, by imposing it on the object, I am conscious of reaching that object. . . . for the child the thing is not the known until it is named. (p. 177)

The other side of the coin here is that our thought, like our knowledge of the world, is also embodied in our speech and does not "represent" it. "Thus speech, in the speaker, does not translate ready-made thought, but accomplishes it. *A fortiori* must it be recognized that the listener receives thought from speech itself" (p. 178). In all of this language is seen, in J. L. Austin's locution, as a pattern of "speech acts," as a tool for coming into the human world as well as knowing it and expressing it. It is not altogether clear if these expressions are best understood as metaphors, but they at least border on being so used. This same ambiguity obtains with respect to Merleau-Ponty's most crucial way of speaking of the nature and basis of linguistic activity, namely in terms of gestural meaning.

Herein lies the linchpin of Merleau-Ponty's understanding of the relation between speech and embodiment, and of the centrality of the latter to the former.

> And as, in a foreign country, I begin to understand the meaning of words through their place in a context of action and by taking part in a communal life—in the same way an as yet imperfectly understood piece of philosophical writing discloses to me at least a certain "style". . .

which is the first draft of its meaning. I begin to understand a philosophy by feeling my way into its existential manner, by reproducing the tone and accent of the philosopher. (p. 179)

It is these somatic features of speech, its tones, accents, and gestures encountered in concrete contexts, which serve as the matrix of linguistic meaning. These features, in turn, become internalized within my own bodily existence. As Merleau-Ponty puts it:

I do not need to visualize external space and my own body in order to move one within the other. It is enough that they exist for me, and that they form a certain field of action spread around me. In the same way I do not need to visualize the word in order to know how to pronounce it. It is enough that I possess its articulatory and acoustic style as one of the modulations, one of the possible uses of my body. I reach back for the word as my hand reaches towards the part of me which is being pricked. . . . (p. 180)

Merleau-Ponty continues to speak of linguistic meaning as "a form of gesture in which speech and thought, like consciousness and body, are intervolved, the sense being held within the word, and the word being the external existence of the sense" (p. 182). Thus, "The spoken word is genuine gesture, and it contains its meaning in the same way as the gesture contains its [meaning]" (p. 183). The point here seems to be that intentions and meanings are mediated by the body in gesture and speech in such a way as to be irreducible to mere physicality without being separable from it. We do not normally infer the meaning of an utterance from reflecting on it; rather, we grasp it directly as it is embodied in the utterance, which is imbedded in its context.

The gesture *does not make me think* of anger, it is anger itself. . . . The sense of the gesture is not given, but understood, that is, recaptured upon by an act of the spectator's part. . . . The communication or comprehension of gestures comes about through the reciprocity of my intentions and the gestures of others, of my gestures and intentions discernible in the conduct of other people. It is as if the other person's intentions inhabited my body and mine his. (p. 185)

For linguistic gesture, that is, speech itself, things are essentially the same. In opposition to the traditional contrast between gestures as "natural signs" and speech as "conventional" signs, language is anchored in the natural character of our common feelings, movements, and sounds. Arbitrary signs, as conventions, are a rather late and sophisticated development in language. In short, at the core of speech and linguistic meaning stands our particular form of embodiment, endowing our actions and utterances with significance and at the same time receiving its meaning from them. "The linguistic gesture, like the rest, delineates its own meaning. . . . the meaning inhabits the word, and language is not an external accompaniment to intellectual processes" (pp. 186, 193).

Merleau-Ponty brings to a close his presentation of the centrality of the body by calling attention to the open-textured character of linguistic activity (cf. pp. 193–197). On the one hand, meaning must already fully reside in language, otherwise it could be neither learned nor used to incarnate intentions. On the other hand, not only can an individual speaker or a community of speakers add to and/or delete from language specific terms and meanings, but each specific speech act can serve to twist or fill a conventional utterance with fresh meaning. Perhaps the most forthright case of this is found in the uses of irony. Here the speaker literally says the opposite of what the linguistic conventions would require and expects this move to be understood! Context alone serves as one's guide in such situations. Language is thus organic in two senses of the term. It consists of a vast network of tenuous yet effective relationships and connections ("tissues" and "threads"), and it continually undergoes change and development within the ongoing fabric of human life.

All of this brings us back to the centrality of the body as the mysterious yet pivotal mediator of our intentions, our peculiar way of being-in-the-world.

> The analysis of speech and expression brings home to us the enigmatic nature of our own body even more effectively than did our remarks on bodily space and unity. It is not a collection of particles, each one remaining in itself, nor yet a network of processes defined once and for all—it is not where it is nor what it is—since we see it secreting within itself a "significance" which comes to it from nowhere, projecting that significance upon its material surrounding and communicating it to other embodied subjects. (p. 197)

This image of mystery, of "enigmatic secreting," is an important feature in Merleau-Ponty's treatment of linguistic activity, and we shall encounter it again when we turn to a more comprehensive discussion of the implication of his use of metaphor for the theory of language in Chapter 4.

CIRCLES OF MEANING

Having established the body as the axis of human existence and experience, at roughly the midpoint of *Phenomenology of Perception* Merleau-Ponty is ready to begin his exploration of the dimensions of meaning that flow through and around this axis. It is possible to understand these dimensions as a series of ever-expanding concentric circles emanating outward from the embodied self toward the world. Traditionally, especially in modern philosophy, the sequence assumed in such patterns begins with the self, as a conscious monad, and moves on to the reality of the "external," physical world, and deals with the problem of "other minds."

It is highly significant that Merleau-Ponty does not follow this pattern in his expectations. Rather, as the sequence of chapters in *Phenomenology of Perception* indicates, he begins with an account of the embodied self's sense experience and spatial awareness, and then moves on to a consideration of our encounters with physical objects and other persons. Finally, in the last part of his book, he takes up self-knowledge (the *cogito*) in relation to temporality and freedom. Thus he begins with the world and progresses toward the self, rather than the other way around.

The significance of this reversal lies in the notion of mediational awareness as it emerges from Merleau-Ponty's account of the role of the body in cognition. As should be clear from our discussion thus far, just as our body provides our entry-point or intentional vehicle into the world, it also serves as the bearer of meaning and knowledge of the world to us. Our body mediates our awareness of physical and social reality in relation to sensory experience in space. In turn, it is our awareness of and interaction with things and other persons that mediate our awareness of ourselves. Thus our self-knowledge is further from the embodied center or axis of our existence than is our knowledge of physical and social reality. We work backwards, as it were, from and through our embodied vantage point, developing first an awareness of the world and then, through it, an awareness of our selves.

The metaphor that Merleau-Ponty uses as the basis for his understanding of this mediational and developmental pattern is, once again, a biological one. In the first sentence of Part Two, he says: "Our own body is in the world as the heart is in the organism; it keeps the visible spectacle constantly alive, it breaths life into it and sustains it inwardly, and with it forms a system" (p. 203). In addition to the obvious sense in which the heart functions as the center of our physiological existence, thereby paralleling the role of the body in our cognition, there are at least two additional aspects of this metaphor that merit special attention.

The first of these is suggested by the phrase above, "forms a system." The fact is, of course, that the heart does not simply lie inertly at the center of the body, but interacts with its other parts and organ, such as arteries, veins, and lungs, to form a dynamic system that sustains life. Even flag poles, centerpieces, and cornerstones, to say nothing of axles, pistons, and riverbeds, though inorganic, interact with their respective environments in such a way as to form a "system" of significance.

In the same way, the body works with the various features of physical and social reality to form the systems of meaning and knowledge we know as "the world." In other words, the world is constituted by means of the body's intentional activity, just as our bodies consist of the systems provided by the heart's connective interactions.

A second aspect of this metaphor that bears special mention is that the heart is, after all, *part* of the body. That is to say, the very systems the heart and other parts of the body form in order to sustain the life of the whole organism also sustain the heart itself. The heart, too, needs oxygen and nutrients, and in a sense it pumps these vital elements to itself. Here, again, it can be said that the body likewise contributes to its own existence and significance by means of its interconnective activity with and in the world. The body is part of the world, even and especially the physical world, but at the same time it is that which provides or "renders" the world for us.

> The thing, and the world, are given to me along with the part of my body, not by any "natural geometry," but in a living connection comparable, or rather, identical, with that existing between the parts of my body itself. (p. 205)

Merleau-Ponty's overall point, as stated in the title of his introduction to Part Two, is that our "theory of the body is already a theory of perception." This works both ways. If we have a theory of the body that sees it merely as an object among other objects in the world, whether reductionistically or dualistically, we shall inevitably develop theories of perception and cognition that begin by separating us from the world and each other, and then complain that we cannot overcome solipsism and subjectivism. If, on the other hand, we begin by acknowledging the centrality of the body, both to the nature of our being in the world and to our knowledge thereof, we are enabled to develop theories of perception and cognition that are both realistic and fruitful. Such is Merleau-Ponty's claim.

> If, then, as we have seen to be the case, the body is not a transparent object, and is not presented to us in virtue of the law of its constitution, as the circle is to the geometer, if it is an expressive unity which we can learn to know only by actively taking it up, this structure will be passed on to the sensible world. The theory of the body image is, implicitly, a theory of perception. We have relearned to feel our body; we have found underneath the objective and detached knowledge of the body that other knowledge which we have of it in virtue of its always being with us and of the fact that we are our body. In the same way we shall need to reawaken our experience of the world as it appears to us in so far as we are in the world through our body, and in so far as we perceive the world with our body. But by thus remaking contact with the body and with the world, we shall also rediscover ourself, since, perceiving as we do with our body, the body is a natural self and, as it were, the subject of perception.

In dealing with sense experience, Merleau-Ponty returns to many of the basic metaphors used in his earlier discussions. The images of field and horizon (pp. 216–217), pregnancy (p. 235), fabric (p. 235), and corporeal merging (p. 238) all come into play by way of stressing and demonstrating the essentially relational, as opposed to the atomistic character of perception. Once again, the emphasis is on the organic quality of the body's interaction with the world. There are, at the same time, two fresh metaphors introduced at this point that require our attention.

The first occurs in the midst of the treatment of the relation between the sentient and sensible, or perceptual and conceptual, dimensions of experience. Merleau-Ponty compares this relationship to that between the sleeper and sleep itself.

> Sleep comes when a certain voluntary attitude suddenly receives from the outside the confirmation for which it was waiting. I am breathing deeply and slowly in order to summon sleep, and suddenly it is as if my mouth were connected to some great lung outside myself which alternately calls for and forces back my breath. . . . In the same way I give ear, or look, in the expectation of a sensation, and suddenly the sensible takes possession of my ear, or my gaze, and I surrender a part of my body, even my whole body, to this particular. . . . (pp. 211–212)

Merleau-Ponty elaborates this mysterious interaction by likening it to a religious sacrament, whereby grace is mediated, through the elements of wine and bread, to those who are inwardly prepared. As he has said elsewhere, "sensation is literally a form of communion" (p. 212). This same sense of mystery is present in relation to the rest of the body. Both breathing and the beating of the heart are to some degree controlled voluntarily, and yet at the most basic level they just "take place"; why our heart beats, why we breath is not the same sort of question as why blood flows or air fills our lungs.

The second image introduced in the discussion of sense experience may not actually be a metaphor, only a "borderline case." Nonetheless, such cases are themselves instances of the very sort of interactive corporeal merging Merleau-Ponty is exploring. Furthermore, it is possible to construe all metaphors as borderline cases; perhaps that is their very essence! At any rate, the image I have in mind is that of "synaesthetic" perception. In spite of the fact that both physiologists and psychologists nearly always study the various senses as independent of one another, we do not experience them in this atomistic manner.

> Synaesthetic perception is the rule, and we are unaware of it only because scientific knowledge shifts the centre of gravity of experience, so that we have unlearned how to see, hear, and generally speaking, feel, in order to deduce, from our bodily organization and the world as the physicists sees it, what we are to see, hear, and feel. (p. 229)

The plain fact is that we experience the world with and through all of our senses simultaneously and, indeed, *inter*dependently. Only by means of special experimentation or unfortunate accident are we afforded the opportunity to rely exclusively on one or two sense organs. Touch, sight, hearing, smell, taste, and even kinaesthetic equilibrium, all work together in what Merleau-Ponty calls "synergy" (p. 232) to construct what we know as perceptual experience. The unity of the senses arises from the integrated and intentional character of our embodiment and their interactive and constitutive participation in physical and social reality.

In treating our knowledge of the spatial aspect of the world, Merleau-Ponty generally relies once again on metaphors already introduced, such as those of axis (pp. 247, 249), body image (p. 250), engagement (p. 251), and depth and thickness (p. 266). There are, however, two or three important and heretofore unintroduced images that figure in this discussion. Merleau-Ponty begins by suggesting that far from being a kind of static "ether in which all things float. . . . We must think of space as the universal power enabling them to be connected" (p. 243). A bit further on, in an analysis of spatial depth, he argues that variations of perspective and size mediate our experience of depth in the same way as specific activity within a concrete context mediates a person's intentions. "Convergence and apparent size are neither signs nor causes of depth: they are present in the experience of depth in the way that a *motive*, even when it is not articulate and separately posited, is present in a decision" (p. 258).

These two metaphors, of power and motive, come together in the concept of motility in Merleau-Ponty's examination of our knowledge of space. It is as we act and move in relation to the world that we come to experience it as spatial, and the same embodied participation gives rise to our experience of temporality as well. In spite of the "logic chopping" of philosophers who continually revive Zeno's paradoxes, we all experience and cognize movement and thus space and time, at "square one" of our existence, even as we wrestle with the concepts thereof. Moreover, apart from any motion, including the continual though generally unnoticed vibrations of our eyeballs, we would not be able to perceive at all, and thus could not be said to experience the world "humanely."

> My eye for me is a certain power of making contact with things, and not a screen on which they are projected. The relation of my eye to the object is not given to me in the form of a geometrical projection of the object in the eye, but as it were a hold taken by my eye upon the object. (p. 279)

Merleau-Ponty sprinkles his account of movement with various appropriate metaphors. He speaks of things coexisting "in space because they are *present* to the same perceiving subject and enveloped in one and the same temporal wave" (p. 276). Again, he says: "I do not have *perceptions*, I do not posit this object as beside that one, along with their objective relationships, I have a flow of experiences which imply and explain each other simultaneously and successively" (p. 281). Finally, he likens perception to a *journey* through a city, in which the particulars are experienced as an integral part of the whole, not as discrete entities. "Just as we do not see the eyes of a familiar face, but simply its look and expression, so we perceive hardly any object" (p. 281).

Within this context, Merleau-Ponty takes up our experience and knowledge of physical objects and other persons. The metaphors he uses for this task, as well as the general points he makes, are by now quite familiar. Thus, our discussion of these images and emphases will be considerably briefer. For instance, with respect to our experience of natural objects, he speaks of them as cognized within a "network or system" (p. 301), as the result of our being "at grips with the world" (p. 304) within the "organization of a field" (p. 138), as grasped by "the gaze" (pp. 310, 317), as finding "an echo within me" (p. 316), as "a coition . . . of our body with things" (p. 320), and so on. The one new metaphor employed in this context is that of our cognition of things in the natural world being a function of our "taking up" a specific posture toward, or abode within, physical reality (pp. 311, 317, 319, 326). Here again, intentional action and embodied participation are the main emphases.

With respect to our knowledge of "other selves and the human world" (Part Two, Chapter 4), Merleau-Ponty uses many by now familiar metaphors in order to show that we do not engage in inferential reasoning, beginning with our own individual self-consciousness, to arrive at the reality of "other minds." Rather, from the outset we experience ourselves and others as "situated in an intersubjective world" (pp. 335, 357). In a word, we are mutual participants in a "permanent field or dimension of existence" (p. 362). Thus in order to flesh out the contours of the inter-subjective character of our natural, though social, life, Merleau-Ponty reuses such images as "dialogue" and "woven fabric" (p. 354), "vortex" of meaning (p. 353), or another person's "gaze" (p. 351). He concludes that

> our relationship to the social is, like our relationship to the world, deeper than any express perception or any judgement. It is as false to place ourselves in society as an object among other objects, as it is to place society within ourselves as an object of thought, and in both cases the mistake lies in treating the social as an object. (p. 362)

One of the dominant images employed in this examination of our experience of the physical as well as the social worlds is that of linguistic communication. More pointedly, Merleau-Ponty specifically says, "There is one particular cultural object which is destined to play a crucial role in the perception of other people: language" (p. 354). So both literally and metaphorically, speech serves as the instrument of significance within human experience. And as we have seen in the previous section of the present chapter, linguistic activity, both physically and figuratively, is anchored in gesture and embodiment. A consideration of the full import of Merleau-Ponty's understanding of language will have to wait until Chapter 4 of the current study.

In Part Three of *Phenomenology of Perception* Merleau-Ponty turns to a consideration of our knowledge of our own selves. He places his reflections within the context provided by Descartes' famous *cogito*, relying on his previous analysis of human experience as embodied to counteract the dualism and ultimate skepticism inherent in Descartes' approach. In general, it is safe to say that Merleau-Ponty expresses his dissatisfaction with, and his own correction of, Descartes' view in terms of metaphors we have already discussed. The main problem he sees is that Descartes, and a large part of modern philosophy that has followed him, separates the knower from the known in the very act of perception, assuming that cognition pertains exclusively to *mental* activity. In fact, however, that perceptual cognition is through and through a *relational* reality, a symbiotic, bipolar interaction in which the knower and the known are mutually interdependent. The moment Descartes separated the former from the latter, in order to ground knowing in something absolute, he destroyed the every character of knowing itself.

All of this follows fairly naturally from the relational metaphors Merleau-Ponty has used throughout his examination of perception. In this context he stresses that perceptual cognition is something that is *done*, as an act, something that is *lived*, performed, and so on. (cf. especially pp. 382–383). Perception is clearly something that takes place in a "field" in which the perceiver moves as the "axial point" in relation to all that is encountered therein, and which is encompassed by an ever-changing, though always present "horizon." Moreover, it is the human body that provides this fulcrum, since it is the medium through which we affect and are affected by the world. The body, in short, is the "intersection" at which the knower and the known encounter each other. Thus, when Descartes' knower is assumed to be a disembodied consciousness, this notion collapses in upon itself and loses touch with the world. Merleau-Ponty sums it up in the following paragraph:

> If the subject *is* in a situation, even if he is no more than a possibility of situations, this is because he forces his ipseity into reality only by actually being a body, and entering the world through that body. In so far as, when I reflect on the essence of subjectivity, I find it bound up with that of the body and that of the world, this is because my existence as subjectivity is merely one with my existence as a body and with the existence of the world, and because the subject that I am, when taken concretely, is inseparable from this body and this world. The ontological

world and the body which we find at the core of the subject are not the
world or body as idea, but on the one hand the world itself contracted
into a comprehensive grasp, and on the other body itself as a knowing-
body. (p. 408)

Thus it is that self-knowledge, far from being the foundation of our
knowledge of the world and other persons, as with Descartes, is for
Merleau-Ponty that which arises from participatory interaction with these
dimensions of our embodied existence. Moreover, the full explication of our
knowledge of our selves, as with that of the world and others, always lies
beyond our present cognitive powers. That is to say, in the words of
Michael Polanyi, "we always know more than we can say." Cognition is
bounded by our perceptual horizon, which is both unlimiting and limiting;
it is unlimiting in that it moves as we move, yet it is limiting in that we are
always aware that something lies beyond it. Indeed, it is only within such
cognition that knowledge is possible at all.

Merleau-Ponty frequently speaks of this aspect of cognition as having a
"transcendent" character (cf. pp. 364, 369, 376, 392). As this way of
speaking raises issues that go beyond the immediate concerns of the present
chapter, a discussion of them will be postponed until the final chapter,
which will deal with Merleau-Ponty's view of the nature of philosophy in
general. Suffice it to say at this point that the sort of transcendence he has in
mind is clearly distinct from that generally associated with the rationalism
and/or idealism of traditional philosophy. At the same time, he does insist
that a flat reductionist account of perception and cognition is as far from the
truth as any form of dogmatism (cf. pp. 363–365, 374–376, 397). We shall
return to such matters in due time.

Finally, Merleau-Ponty rounds out his treatment of self-knowledge with
a relatively brief discussion of temporality and freedom. While this discussion can be said to follow from the images and analyses developed in the
previous chapters of *Phenomenology of Perception*, we do encounter a few
fresh metaphors in these two last chapters. In dealing with the experience
and concept of time, Merleau-Ponty contends that it is not helpful to think
of it as a river that flows through our lives, independent of and preexistent
to our relationship to it. We do not "observe" time as it goes by us; rather,
it comes into being as a function of our embodied interaction with the
world. "Time is, therefore, not a real process, not an actual succession that I
am content to record. It arises from *my* relation to things" (p. 412).

A bit farther along, Merleau-Ponty says: "Let us no longer say that time
is a 'datum of consciousness'; let us be more precise and say that consciousness deploys or constitutes time" (p. 414). And again:

It is in my "field of presence" in the widest sense—this moment that I
spend working, with, behind it, the horizon of the day that has elapsed,

and in front of it, the evening and the night—that I make contact with time, and learn to know its course. (pp. 415–416)

These images of "field and horizon" are by now quite familiar. That of "deployment," while not unrelated to previously employed images of intentionality, is rather striking in its application to our experience of time. It is reinforced by Merleau-Ponty's reference to Husserl's speaking of having the past "in hand" and reaching toward the future (p. 417).

It is the "thickness of the pre-objective present" (p. 433), the past that was never a present, that constitutes the starting point of "explanations" of human behavior, "and at the same time the basis of our freedom" (p. 433). These words form the bridge between Merleau-Ponty's examination of time and his discussion of human freedom in relation to causality and determination. His overall point here is that the philosophical confusion that has surrounded this topic is dissolved when we adopt the perspective provided by placing the body at the center of understanding of experience and knowledge. "I am an intersubjective field, not despite my body and historical situation, but, on the contrary, by being this and this situation through them, all the rest" (p. 452).

Thus freedom must be defined in relation to both our activity in the world, as against determinism, and the causal factors comprising our situation, as against extreme indeterminism.

If freedom is to have *room* in which to move, if it is to be describable as freedom, there must be something to hold it away from its objectives, it must have a *field*, which means that there must be for it special possibilities, or realities which tend to cling to being. (p. 438)

In this way Merleau-Ponty brings his familiar phenomenological images to bear on these traditional difficulties.

In another place he employs a slightly different metaphor in making essentially the same point.

I am free in relation to my being in the world, free to make my way by transforming it. But here once more we must recognize a sort of sedimentation of our life: an attitude towards the world, when it has received frequent confirmation, acquires a favored status of us. (p. 441)

This "sedimentation" functions at one and the same time as that which determines our actions and that by means of which we determine ourselves. In short, we both choose and are chosen, and only when we begin by acknowledging the bipolar, interactional character of our experiential situation can we resolve the controversy of free will.

Merleau-Ponty concludes his discussion of freedom, and *Phenomenology of Perception* as well, by applying his analysis to class analysis. A direct consideration of his reflections on social philosophy will be presented in the next chapter. Here we only note that he is intent on affirming the insights of both Sartre's existentialist analysis and Marx's economic determinism. We shape ourselves and our destinies while we are shaped by factors beyond ourselves.

> I must, therefore, in the most radical reflection, apprehend around my absolute individuality a kind of halo of generality or kind of atmosphere of "sociality". . . . My life must have a significance which I do not constitute; there must strictly speaking be an intersubjectivity; each one of us must be both anonymous in the sense of absolutely individual, and anonymous in the sense of absolutely general. Our being in the world is the concrete bearer of this double anonymity. (p. 448)

This image of "halo" or "atmosphere" is made more forceful by casting it in terms of the contrast between abstract, determining forces and concrete, individual decisions.

> What makes me a proletarian is not the economic system or society considered as systems of impersonal forces, but these institutions as I carry them within me and experience them; nor is it an intellectual operation devoid of motive, by my way of being in the world within this institutional framework. (p. 443)

> What then is freedom? To be born is both to be born of the world and to be born into the world. The world is already constituted, but also never completely constituted; in the first case we are acted upon, in the second we are open to an infinite number of possibilities . . . it is impossible to determine precisely the "share contributed by the situation" and the "share contributed by freedom." (p. 453)

This completes our survey of the images used by Merleau-Ponty in his first major work. In the next chapter we shall consider his use of metaphor in his many essays between this early work and the conclusion of his career. The essays will be taken up topically, rather than chronologically, and special attention will be given to similarities and differences between them and the *Phenomenology of Perception*, with respect to the specific metaphors employed. A further comparison of these images with those used in Merleau-Ponty's final work, *The Visible and the Invisible*, will be undertaken in Chapter 3.

2

EMBODIMENT AND
CULTURE

The metaphors identified in the previous chapter fall roughly into three main categories. First, there are those drawing on the notion of environment, expressed in images of geography (field, horizon, perspective), geology (layers, "above," "beneath"), spatiality (atmosphere, depth, axis), and habitation ("inhabit," "lived," intersection). Second, there are those drawn from organic life, using images of biology (tissues, diffusion, coition), physiology (organs, motility, body image), and generation (pregnancy, growth, systems). Third, there are those taken from human creative (techñ) activity, specifically images of art (painting, music, poetry), mechanics (gears, anchors, vehicles), textiles (fabric, threads, patterns), and language (speech, echoes, writing).

With these metaphors and categories in mind, we can now turn to the essays written during the years between *Phenomenology of Perception* and *The Visible and the Invisible*, with an eye to locating any significant shifts in the images by and through which his thought developed. The following explorations will focus on three main themes within these essays: aesthetics, politics, and culture. Once again, while the emphasis will be on metaphorical expressions, Merleau-Ponty's approach to philosophy will also be revealed in the process. Indeed, it is the merging of content and form, of thought and style in Merleau-Ponty's work that renders a study such as the present one both interesting and important.

SOMATIC AESTHETICS

Merleau-Ponty's reflections on the arts are concerned with their ontological and cultural ramifications, as well as their perceptual and epistemological aspects. Thus his essays have a broader scope than did his *Phenomenology of Perception*. Nonetheless, many of the metaphors used in the early work reappear in his shorter and later writings as well. In this section we shall discuss his treatment of paintings, novels, and films.

One of Merleau-Ponty's more well-known essays is "Cézanne's Doubt." The overall theme here is the relationship between an artist's life and his or her work. He concludes that "it is true both that the life of an author can teach us nothing and that—if we know how to interpret it— we can find everything in it, since it opens onto his work" (*Sense and Non-Sense*, p. 25; hereafter *SNS*). The image of "opening" runs counter to the temptation to conclude that an artist's works follow deterministically from specific causal factors in his or her life, and/or that the life itself is "overdetermined" or closed by genetic and environmental factors. Such *post facto* explanations are consistently denied by Merleau-Ponty. "If Cézanne's life seems to us to carry the seeds of his work within it, it is because we get to know his work first and see the circumstances of his life through it, charging them with a meaning borrowed from that work" (p. 20).

The metaphors used in these remarks, of "opening," "seeds," and electrical "charges," follow the earlier environmental and biological images. The relation between causal factors and freedom, essentially similar to that presented in *Phenomenology of Perception*, is also expressed in familiar, if paradoxical images.

> Two things are certain about freedom: that we are never determined and that we never change, since, looking back on what we were, we can always find hints of what we have become. It is up to us to understand both these things simultaneously, as well as the way freedom dawns in us without breaking our bonds with the world. (p. 21)

Within the context of this discussion of freedom and artistic creation, Merleau-Ponty also addresses the relationship between art and reality. Relying once more on tactile imagery, he says:

> Art is not imitation, nor is it something manufactured according to the wishes of instinct or taste. It is a process of expressing . . . that is, to grasp the nature of what appears to us in a confused way and to place it before us as a recognizable object—so it is up to the painter . . . to objectify, project, and arrest . . . to recapture the structure of the landscape as an emerging organism. (p. 17)

Here it is important to note the term "emerging." This image suggests that the reality in question is not yet finished and requires our interaction for its own completion.

This completion is accomplished indirectly, "incarnationally," not by trying to reproduce the reality in question, but by allowing its intangible qualities to be mediated in and through its tangible ones. Speaking of his desire to paint a still life described by Balzac, in which a set table was said to be "crowned with blond rolls," Cézanne himself is quoted as saying,

> All through my youth I wanted to paint that, that tablecloth of new snow. Now I know that one must will only to paint the place-settings rising symmetrically and the blond rolls. If I paint "crowned" I've had it, you understand? But if I really balance and shade my place-settings and rolls as they are in nature, then you can be sure that the crowns, the snow, and the excitement will be there too. (p. 16)

These remarks dovetail nicely with those in the preface of *Phenomenology of Perception*, where the philosophical task is likened to that of art, "the act of bringing truth into being . . . the act whereby we take up this unfinished world in an effort to complete and conceive it" (p. xx). Both philosophy and art are involved in what might be termed an activity of "co-creation" in cooperation with the structural possibilities inherent within the world itself. Apart from our interaction, the world remains inert and mute, while apart from its presence we have no arena within which experience can take on substance and shape. The results of this "co-creation" are the various dimensions and cross-currents of what we call "reality."

In terms of the epistemological dynamics involved in aesthetic awareness, Merleau-Ponty begins by contrasting Cézanne to the Impressionists, in whose works objects become "submerged in the atmosphere and lose their proper weight" (p. 12). The primary concern or thrust of Cézanne's work was to rediscover the natural object within our sensory impressions. "By remaining faithful to the phenomena in his investigations of perspective, Cézanne discovered what recent psychologists have come to formulate: the lived perspective, that which we actually perceive, is not a geometric or photographic one" (p. 14). Here again the notion of "lived perspective" figures in Merleau-Ponty's reflections. It is the axis or standpoint from which both the artist and the artistic prehender encounter the world in nature and in the work of art, respectively.

This encounter involves, even with respect to painting as a visual art, a fully synaesthetic perceptual awareness on the part of the prehender.

> The lived object is not rediscovered or constructed on the basis of the contribution of the senses; rather, it presents itself to us from the start as the center from which these contributions radiate. We *see* the depth, the smoothness, the softness, the hardness of objects. . . . (p. 15)

Here, too, we find Merleau-Ponty once more employing the image of a somatic axis around which the particular features of perception arrange themselves, and from which they take on their meaning. Moreover, the "lived object" only arises within the field provided by the "lived experience"—and vice versa!

The essay "Eye and Mind" was one of the very last things Merleau-Ponty wrote. It is particularly interesting to notice the similarities, especially in terms of the metaphors used, between it and the book on which he was working at his death, *The Visible and the Invisible*. These will be discussed in the next chapter, when we turn our attention to that volume. Here we shall focus on how Merleau-Ponty applies the images he introduced in *Phenomenology of Perception* to artistic endeavor in general and to painting in particular.

Against the backdrop of Cartesian dualism, which would completely separate the eye and the mind as being of two distinctly different "metaphysical substances," Merleau-Ponty seeks the point of connection between them. Since it is obvious that perception and thought are inextricably interrelated, there must be a place where they intersect and unite. Unsurprisingly, he locates this axial connection in the human body, which both sees and is seen, both thinks and perceives.

> Visible and mobile, my body is a thing among things; it is caught in the fabric of the world, and its cohesion is that of a thing. But because it moves itself and sees, it holds things in a circle around itself . . . they are incrusted into its flesh . . . the world is made of the same stuff as the body . . . vision happens among, is caught in, things—in that place where something visible undertakes to see, becomes visible for itself by virtue of the sight of things; in that place where there persists . . . the undividedness of the sensing and the sensed. (*The Essential Writings of Merleau-Ponty*, p. 256).

There are familiar metaphors here: "fabric," "center," "cohesion." In addition, however, the incarnational image is given a fresh twist (to which we shall return in the next chapter) with the introduction of the term "flesh," as well as connecting by means of it the body and the material world as being of the same "stuff." Not only does Merleau-Ponty find consciousness situated in the body, but he finds the body situated in the world of things as well. This, then, is why the eye and the mind should not, indeed cannot, be separated; each is part and parcel of the body, which extends itself in two directions or dimensions simultaneously, toward consciousness and toward the physical world. "Since things and my body are made of the same stuff, vision must somehow take place in them" (p. 257).

Other familiar images are used in this essay to speak about the crucial significance of the body. It is said to "deploy itself," to "radiate from a self," to be an "intertwining of vision and movement," and to be "both natal space and matrix" for the soul and every other existing space. What particularly interests Merleau-Ponty in this essay is the way in which the body, placed and moving in space, unites the mind and visual perception into truly human vision. To see is not simply to be exposed to sensory data; rather, it involves the intentional grasping of and interaction with the world. Thus we see with the whole body, not just with the eye, in the same way as we think with our body. "There is no vision without thought. But *it is not enough* to think in order to see. Vision is a conditioned thought; it is born 'as occasioned' by what happens in the body; it is 'incited' to think by the body" (p. 269).

This view of vision is what stimulates Merleau-Ponty to take the art of painting seriously. "It gives visible existence to what profane vision believes to be invisible . . ." (p. 259). In painting, the mystery of the unity of eye and mind that characterizes our particular form of embodiment is displayed and focused, as it were, in miniature. Moreover, the possibility of prehending the mystery of Being itself, the "invisible" that is mediated in and through the visible world, is prefigured in paintings as well. In portraying depth as a "third dimension" the painter exemplifies and demonstrates the hierarchical yet mediational structure of reality, since the meaning or depth of existence can only be revealed in and through its other, more prosaic dimensions. "Once depth is understood in this way, we can no longer call it a third dimension . . . if it were a dimension, it would be the *first* one . . ." (p. 275).

In the next chapter we shall pursue this image of "the invisible in and through the visible" more thoroughly. At this point we can only note that Merleau-Ponty sees painting as providing a clue, not only to the purpose and meaning of art, but also to what elsewhere, as we shall see, he refers to as the difference between "vertical and horizontal transcendence." Here he uses the image of seeing through water as a parallel case in point:

> When through the water's thickness I see the tiling at the bottom of the pool, I do not see it *despite* the water and the reflections there; I see it through them and because of them. If there were no distortions, no ripples of sunlight, if it were without this flesh that I saw the geometry of the tiles, then I would cease to see it *as* it is and where it is. . . . (p. 277)

The dimensions of existence cannot be isolated from each other, whether at the perceptual or metaphysical level, since they can only be known—and thus only be real—as interrelated and interacted with.

Merleau-Ponty also gives attention to the art of creative writing, especially that of the novel, in order to develop the connections between it and his own understanding of human experience and meaning. In addition, he is expressly interested in the parallels between the arts and phenomenological philosophy. Thus in his essay "Metaphysics and the Novel," Merleau-Ponty contends that since the advent of phenomenology as a mode of analysis, metaphysics no longer needs to be "superimposed" upon human existence, including the arts.

> From now on the tasks of literature and philosophy can no longer be separated. When one is concerned with giving voice to the experience of the world and showing how consciousness escapes into the world, one can no longer credit oneself with attaining a perfect transparence of expression. Philosophical expression assumes the same ambiguities and literary expression, if the world is such that it cannot be expressed except in "stories" and, as it were, pointed at. (*SNS*, p. 28)

Once again we must postpone a thorough discussion of these broader issues until the final chapter of the present volume.

In this essay Merleau-Ponty provides a fascinating and profound examination of Simone de Beauvoir's novel *L'Invite* by way of illustrating the above insight. He does this, unsurprisingly yet revealingly, by means of many of the same metaphors he used in *Phenomenology of Perception*. The main character, Françoise, experiences the world with herself at the axis; she says that the center of Paris is always where she is. Merleau-Ponty presents his analysis of her doings and being in the following terms:

> There is an infinite horizon of things to grasp surrounding the small number of things which I can grasp in fact. (p. 28) . . .
> It is I who bring into being this world which seemed to exist without me, to surround and surpass me. I am therefore a consciousness, immediately present to the world, and nothing can claim to exist without somehow being caught in the web of my experience. (p. 29)

The romantic crisis in Françoise's life forces her to realize that "there are situations which cannot be communicated and which can only be understood by living them. . . . For the first time she has the feeling of being her body, when all along she had thought herself a consciousness" (p. 33). When she becomes ill, Merleau-Ponty sees this as a temporary solution. "She has withdrawn from the human world where she was suffering into the natural world where she finds a frozen peace. As ordinary language so well expresses it, she *took* sick" (p. 34). He concludes that Françoise's struggle with the difficulties of a *ménage à trois* only reveals the deeper truth that "The immediate lives even of two people cannot be made one; it is the common tasks and projects that make the couple. The human couple is no more a *natural* reality than the trio" (p. 135).

Individual human existence is, of course, no different, "because others are the permanent coordinates of our lives. Once we are aware of the existence of others, we commit ourselves to being, among other things, what they think of us, since we recognize in them the exorbitant power to *see us*" (p. 37). Merleau-Ponty does not draw nihilistic conclusions from this fact, as many other contemporary thinkers are wont to do. Even though our having been "cast into the world without being consulted . . . makes us feel like *strangers* at the *trial* to which others have brought us" (p. 38), life is worth living and morality exists if we choose them to be so.

> One would do better to pay less attention to the unusual situation of the three characters in *L'Invite* and more to the good faith, the loyalty to promises, the respect for others, the generosity and the seriousness of the two principals. For the value is there. It consists of actively being what we are by chance, of establishing that communication with others and with ourselves for which our temporal structure gives us the opportunity and of which our liberty is only the rough outline. (p. 40)

This way of conceiving of human responsibility and freedom, as well as the images used to express it, remind one of Merleau-Ponty's discussion near the close of *Phenomenology of Perception*.

In addition, one detects certain traces of Camus, Kafka, and Sartre in the passages. Although he does not give any detailed attention to the two former writers, he does discuss Sartre's work on more than one occasion. Acknowledging the many difficulties and shortcomings in Sartre's views, Merleau-Ponty defends him against Christians, Marxists, and "artists" alike for being an artist who "considers man's value to be his imperfection" ("A Scandalous Author," *SNS*, p. 44) and honestly portrays humanity as such in his writings. Moreover, Merleau-Ponty agrees with Sartre that the aim of art is to render abstract values concretely in the warp and weft of everyday reality. "The problem is to instill that radical freedom, which is the negation of humanity as a given species and which is an appeal for a self-created humanity, into human relations and to transmute it into history" (p. 46).

In his essay, "Indirect Language and the Voices of Silence," Merleau-Ponty again explores painting and writing, this time by comparing and contrasting them to each other. It should be noted in passing that much of what he says in this essay bears directly on his views of the nature of language in general and of metaphor in particular. The discussion of these two important themes will be taken up in Chapters 4 and 5, respectively. Here we shall confine our discussion to what is said about the arts of painting and writing, as well as to the images by means of which it gets said.

After proposing a fundamental reversal of our most commonly accepted understanding of language, a proposal essentially similar to that made in *Phenomenology of Perception*, Merleau-Ponty sets out to explore its implications for artistic expression. It should be noted that here again we find him using such familiar images as the "fabric of speech," "linguistic gesture," "intersectional meaning," and "transforming pregnancies." This organic, indeed somatic view of linguistic activity leads him to the conclusion that speech can never be direct or precise, that it is always characterized by an "open texture" and a multiple significance that both limit it and are the source of its power. "Now if we rid our minds of the idea that our language is the translation or cipher of an original text, we shall see that the idea of a *complete* expression is nonsensical, and that all language is indirect or allusive—that it is, if you wish, silence" (*Signs*, p. 43).

From this foothold, Merleau-Ponty goes on to distinguish between the empirical and the creative uses of language, arguing that the former "can only be the result" of the latter (p. 44), since it is impossible to begin speaking with directness and precision; we must always begin with indirectness and ambiguity, moving, if we wish, toward increased explication. In a sense, the more explicit it becomes, the more meaning we crowd out of an exploration; the greater the articulation, the less gets said. Against this background, Merleau-Ponty designates both the creative writer and the painter as those who leave as much unsaid, "between the lines and the words," as they say. Such artists work in the "second-order language in which signs once again lead the vague life of colors, and in which significations never free themselves completely from the intercourse of signs" (p. 45). Like a weaver, the creative artist "works on the wrong side of his material. He has to do only with language, and it is thus that he suddenly finds himself surrounded by meaning" (p. 45).

The other side of the coin here is that writers and painters have as much to do with silence as they do with expression. For it is in what is not expressed that we find the greatest significance within their works. Merleau-Ponty suggests that we must therefore seek "to uncover the threads of silence that speech is mixed together with" (p. 46) if we are to grasp the meaning of artistic expression. His overall conclusion (cf. pp. 80–83) is, of course, that things are no different when it comes to common, everyday discourse, as distinguished from the chit-chat of "dangling conversations" and "small talk." Authentic speech is always "pregnant" with richer meaning than meets the ear. Moreover, the same holds true for authentic philosophical language; it, too, speaks in a way that suggests what it cannot explicitly say.

The foil Merleau-Ponty uses to probe the indirect and silent voices of artistic expression is Malraux's *The Voices of Silence*. His overall theme is that far from presenting things and events "as they are" in their empirical flatness, and just as far from discovering transcendent character "above" or "behind" their mere appearance, the creative artist sets them before us, already situated in relation to the interconnections comprising the world and in such a way as to intimate or mediate their wider significance. Both painters and writers, when successful, are said to "impregnate" their works with meaning in such a fashion that the latter "sinks into it and trembles around it like a wave of heat" (p. 55). Therefore, "the accomplished work is thus not the work which exists in itself like a thing, but the work which reaches it viewer and invites him to take up the gesture which created it and, skipping the intermediaries, to rejoin, without any guide other than the movement of the invented line (an almost incorporeal trace), the silent world . . . henceforth uttered and accessible" (p. 51).

Unsurprisingly, Merleau-Ponty submits that it is by means of and according to the principles of human embodiment that the artist and the prehender are capable of participating in this dialogue of "lateral or indirect signification" (p. 76). Human intentions are both real and expressed through bodily interactions in the world.

> We would not do anything if our body did not enable us to leap over all the neural and muscular means of locomotion in order to move to the goal. Literary language fills the same kind of office. In the same imperious and brief way the writer transports us without transitions or preparations from the world of established meanings to something else. And as our body guides us among things only on condition that we stop analyzing it and make use of it, language is literary (that is, productive) only on the condition that we stop asking justification of it at each instant and follow it where it goes, let the words and all the means of expression of the book be enveloped by that halo of signification that they owe to their singular arrangement, and the whole writing veer toward a second-order value where it almost rejoins the mute radiance of painting. (p. 78)

Language and meaning are related as body and mind;

> neither is primary nor secondary. . . . There is no subordination between them. Here no one commands and no one obeys. What we *mean* is not before us, outside all speech, as sheer signification. It is only the excess of what we live over what has already been said. (p. 83)

Throughout this presentation, Merleau-Ponty makes use of his usual metaphors, especially those having to do with woven fabrics, intersections, and organic functions. There are, however, two differences worth noting, one pertaining to the image of indirection and the other to that of silent voices. The former is, to be sure, simply a modification of the broader figure of motility in space, but here Merleau-Ponty stresses the "lateral" movement of aesthetic creation and awareness. Whereas heretofore he has spoken of meaning accomplished "in and through" particulars, he here speaks of it as achieved in "roundabout" fashion. "What one too deliberately seeks, he does not find" (p. 83). The lateral approach, both in creating and in prehending significance, whether artistically or existentially, is always the most effective approach.

The second metaphorical divergence worth special mention here incorporates the notion of silence into the "meaning of meaning." Not only is silence heard here, as the background against which voices are identified and understood, but it penetrates the very texture of language itself. Since speech not only does not consist of continuous sound, but often is deliberately withheld in order to make a point, silence plays an integral part in meaning. Moreover, since all speech carries the potential for a large if not infinite number of improvisations and convolutions, what is left unsaid often speaks more loudly than what is said. All of this applies with special force to discourse about what Merleau-Ponty refers to as "horizontal transcendence," a topic to which we shall return in Chapter 6.

Finally, a brief consideration of Merleau-Ponty's application of his approach and insights to the art of film will round out this section of the present chapter. In an essay entitled "The Film and the New Psychology," given as a lecture in 1945, Merleau-Ponty outlines the similarities between Gestalt perceptual theory, the technical dynamics of filmmaking, and his own epistemology. His first point concerns the holistic, as opposed to the atomistic, structure of perception, and thus of meaning itself. "[W]e should think of it not as a mosaic but as a system of configurations. Groups rather than juxtaposed elements are principal and primary in our perception" (SNS, p. 48).

Second, perception is said to have a synaesthetic unity rather than being the compiled result of five individual senses. Through the unity of our body we grasp and interact with wholes with all of our senses simultaneously and interdependently.

Third, according to Merleau-Ponty, we perceive other persons as persons from the outset, but not by drawing inferences from sensory data about "other minds."

> Since emotion is not a psychic, internal fact but rather a variation in our relations with others and the world which is expressed in our bodily attitude, we cannot say that only the signs of love or anger are given to the outside observer and that we understand others indirectly by interpreting these signs; we have to say that others are directly manifest to us as behavior. (p. 53)

Merleau-Ponty affirms the art of film, with its use of montage, cutting, sounds, and dramatic dialogue, as highlighting these particular somatic principles, in much the same way as other creative artists use the raw materials of events and characters, or colors and shapes, to mediate a wider meaning.

> Movies, likewise, always have a story and often an idea . . . but the function of film is not to make these facts or ideas known to us. . . . The meaning of a film is incorporated into its rhythm just as the meaning of a gesture may immediately be read in that gesture: the film does not mean anything but itself. The idea is presented in a nascent state and emerges from the temporal structure of the film as it does from the coexistence of the parts of a painting. (p. 57)

In addition to his usual images, such as "gesture," "gaze," "incarnation," "incorporation," "systems," and "bonds," Merleau-Ponty speaks of the "melodic unity" and "finer-grained" reality of film in this essay. These images are particularly appropriate to the medium under discussion, since they partake of the actual technical dynamics involved. In addition, Merleau-Ponty suggests that the parallels between cinematic technology and phenomenological analysis result from the fact that "the philosopher and the moviemaker share a certain way of being, a certain view of the world which belongs to a generation wherein modes of thought correspond to technical methods" (p. 59). Both of these enterprises are concerned "to make us *see* the bond between subject and world, between subject and others, rather than to *explain* it . . . to make manifest the union of mind and body, mind and the world, and the expression of one in the other" (p. 58). As should be clear by now, this same general correspondence applies as well to the relationship between Merleau-Ponty's philosophy of the primacy of embodied perception and the creative activity of writers, painters, and filmmakers.

THE BODY POLITIC

In the previous section we found a strong common thread running throughout Merleau-Ponty's application of his images and insights from *Phenomenology of Perception* to various aspects of artistic endeavor. Many of the same metaphors reappeared and those that were freshly introduced were of a piece with the organic, incarnational, and participatory character of these in his major early work. As we turn our attention now to his specifically political essays, the most striking thing about them is the relative absence of metaphor. Here the language is much more direct and analytical, and generally when figurative images do occur they tend either to be those of the common garden variety or to be borrowed from the vocabulary of other writers, especially that of Marx.

When Merleau-Ponty does employ metaphors of his own in this context, they are, to be sure, quite familiar and appropriate to the somatic posture he takes up in *Phenomenology of Perception*. In fact, since most of his political writings are primarily involved with various aspects of Marxist thought, it is easy to see the lines of connection from the one to the other. There is a "this-worldliness" about the orientation of both Merleau-Ponty and Marx, a common concern for material reality and human action, that obviously drew the former to the latter. At the same time, however, it is also possible to discern Merleau-Ponty's gradual disenchantment with Marxism, especially as developed and applied in Russia and France, during the years between World War II and his death in 1961. The following pages will trace this drift in his political thought.

Merleau-Ponty's early political writings were primarily engaged in explaining and defending the main motifs of Marxist philosophy. In "Concerning Marxism" he frames his remarks in terms of a critique of the writings of an erstwhile neo-fascist thinker, Thierry Maulnier. Here he seeks to distinguish between those who would explain Marxism as a reductionist and rigid formula for the future and those who would discern its "central intuition." "The greatness of Marxism lies not in its having treated economics as the principal or unique cause of history but in its treating cultural history and economic history as two abstract aspects of a single process" (*SNS*, p. 107). It should be noted that Merleau-Ponty's understanding of Marxism was quite "humanistic" from the outset. This is a bit surprising, since the early, more humanistic writings of Marx were not generally known in the West until after World War II.

When describing what he takes to be the "central intuition" of Marx, Merleau-Ponty makes use of metaphors that have become his stock in trade. He says that

> Marxist materialism consists in admitting that the phenomena of civilization and concepts of rights have an *historical anchorage* in economic phenomena . . . it is not a separate order to which the other orders may be reduced: it is Marxism's way of representing the inertia of human life. (p. 108)

These images of "anchorage" and "inertia" fit well within the general emphasis on embodiment developed in Chapter 1. In fact, Merleau-Ponty even states that Marxism's chief assertion is "that there is an incarnation of ideas and values" (p. 108) in the material conditions of human existence.

He pinpoints the direct parallel between the Marxist understanding of the relation between "substructure" and "superstructure" and his own views on the relationship between the body and the mind. In each case the latter is mediated by the former without being reducible to it.

> But economic life is at the same time the historical carrier of mental structures, just as our body maintains the basic features of our behavior beneath our varying moods; and this is the reason one will more surely get to know the essence of a society by analyzing interpersonal relations as they have been fixed and generalized in economic life than through an analysis of the movements of fragile, fleeting ideas—just as one gets a better idea of man from his conduct than from his thought. (p. 108)

Thus cultural life and economic life are reciprocally interdependent or bipolar aspects of human society.

> Production of the material conditions of life is not the foundation of human history, but neither is it the passive, disgraced servant; it is securely installed in this history, exerting a continual, powerful influence upon it, determine it and determined by it—*on equal footing*, as it were. (p. 112)

Here again we see the somatic bent of Merleau-Ponty's philosophy in his use of images drawn from the dynamics of reality and movement. Human nature and society are not abstract, static conditions, but living organisms on the move in the world. This much of his thought is clearly parallel to Marxist dialectic.

In the essay entitled "Marxism and Philosophy," Merleau-Ponty sought to clarify the paradoxical fact that Marxist philosophy is openly hostile to philosophy itself. He admits that "there are passages in Marx with positive overtones" (*SNS*, p. 127), in which Marx would seem to be seeking the reduction of all philosophical questions to scientific ones, à la Auguste Comte. On the other hand Merleau-Ponty insists that the heart of Marx's thought involves a "concrete human intersubjectivity" (p. 129) in which we define "man as a being who 'suffers' or 'senses', that is, a being with a natural and social situation but one who is also open, active and able to establish his autonomy on the very ground of his dependence" (p. 130). Thus Marx is seen as anything but a scientific determinist, subsuming every aspect of human life, including philosophy, under abstract formulas and laws.

In Merleau-Ponty's view Marx was only against "speculative" philosophy, which inevitably expresses itself as "ideological mystification." He sees Marxism as in agreement with existential or phenomenological philosophy, in which

> knowledge finds itself put back into the totality of human praxis and, as it were, given ballast by it. The "subject" is no longer just the epistemological subject but is the human subject who, by means of a continual dialectic, thinks in terms of his situation, forms his categories in contact with his experience, and modifies this situation and this experience by the meaning he discovers in them. (p. 134)

Thus Marxism and phenomenology stand together against the idealism and subjectivity of traditional philosophy by emphasizing the concrete intersubjectivity of human existence.

Even in 1945, however, in his essay, "For the Sake of Truth," Merleau-Ponty was careful to distance himself from doctrinaire Marxism. After insisting that we can no longer do with a "Kantian politics" that ignores consequences, or a "skeptical politics" that pretends to have no presuppositions, he goes on to admit as well that we can no longer have

> a proletarian Marxist politics along classical lines, because this politics has lost its grip on the facts. Our only recourse is a reading of the present which is as full and faithful as possible, which does not prejudice its meaning, which even recognizes chaos and non-sense where they exist, but which does not refuse to discern a direction and an idea in events where they appear. (p. 169)

In the midst of these ambiguities, however, Merleau-Ponty continued to affirm his commitment to Marxism, qualified though it is.

In short, pursue what is, in effect, the policy of the Communist Party. Reconstruct with the proletariat: for the moment there is nothing else to do. Only, we will play this waiting game without illusions about the results to be hoped from it and without honoring it with the name of the dialectic. (p. 171)

By the mid-1950s the distance between Merleau-Ponty's political thought and that of Marxism had grown much wider. The essays in his book *Adventures of the Dialectic* reflect his deep disappointment with the implementation of Marxist thought in Stalinist Russia and postwar France, especially as it was expressed in the latter case through the writings of his colleague, Jean-Paul Sartre. In his "Crisis of the Understanding" Merleau-Ponty couches his critique in a consideration of the thought of Max Weber. After providing an account of Weber's work and method as a philosopher of history, along with an acknowledgment of his tendency toward idealistic liberalism, Merleau-Ponty concludes by praising Weber's insistence on the self-critical character of all real knowledge and viable theory. The honesty inherent in self-criticism leads to what Weber termed "the ethics of responsibility," wherein one is able and willing to stand apart from one's own tradition or political party and say, in the words of Martin Luther, "Here I stand, I can do no other" (*Adventures of the Dialectic*, p. 28). Merleau-Ponty ends the essay with the lament, "There were Marxists who understand this, and they were the best" (p. 29).

Merleau-Ponty's split with Jean-Paul Sartre over the viability of the Communist Party in postwar France was essentially a matter of different philosophies on the nature of the human situation. As is clear from his essay, "Sartre and Ultrabolshevism," Merleau-Ponty came to see Sartre's position as fundamentally that of atomism, in which each center of consciousness is isolated and alienated from the others, as well as from history and the world. He brings the full force of his own somatic epistemology, as expressed in metaphors of embodiment, to bear on the solipsism of Sartre's thought in the following lengthy passage, which I feel constrained to quote in full:

It is always through the thickness of a field of existence that my presentation to myself takes place. The mind is always thinking, not because it is always in the process of constituting ideas but because it is always directly or indirectly tuned in on the world and in cycle with history. Like perceived things, my tasks are presented to me, not as objects or ends, but as reliefs and configurations, that is to say, in the landscape of praxis. And just as, when I bring an object closer or move it further away, when I turn it in my hands, I do not need to relate its appearances to a single scale to understand what I observe, in the same way action inhabits its field so fully that anything that appears there is immediately meaningful for it, without analysis or transposition, and calls for its response. If one takes into account a consciousness thus engaged, which is joined again with itself only across its historical and worldly field, which does not touch itself or coincide with itself but rather is divined and glimpsed in the present experience, of which it is the invisible steward, the relationships between consciousnesses take on a completely new aspect. For if the subject is not the sun from which the world radiates or the demiurge of my pure objects, if its signifying activity is rather the perception of a *difference* between two or several meanings—inconceivable, then, without the dimensions, levels, and perspectives which the world and history establish around me—then its action and all actions are possible only as they follow the course of the world, just as I can change the spectacle of the perceived world only by taking as my observation post one of the places revealed to me by perception. There is perception only because I am part of this world through my body, and I give a meaning to history only because I occupy a certain vantage point in it, because other possible vantage points have already been indicated to me by the historical landscape, and because all these perspectives already depend on a truth in which they would be integrated. At the very heart of my perspective, I realize that my private world is already being used, that there is "behavior" that concerns it, and that the other's place in it is already prepared, because I find other historical situations to be occupiable to me. A consciousness that is truly engaged in a world and a history on which it has a hold but which go beyond it is not insular. Already in the thickness of the sensible and historical fabric it feels other presences moving, just as the group of men who dig a tunnel hear the work of another group coming toward them. Unlike the Sartrean consciousness, it is not visible only for the other: consciousness can see him at least out the corner of its eye. Between its perspective and that of the other there is a link and an established way of crossing over, and this for the single reason that each perspective claims to envelop the others. Neither in private nor in public history is the formula of these relationships "either him or me," the alternative of solopsism or pure abnegation, because these relationships are no longer the encounter of two For-Itselfs but are the meshing of two experiences which, without ever coinciding, belong to a single world.

It is difficult to comment on this passage without lapsing into mere paraphrase, and thereby diluting its power. Suffice it to say that we see here, after over one hundred pages of abstract and technical analysis, the employment of the very same philosophical perspective introduced in *Phenomenology of Perception* to counteract the tendency to turn Marxism into a parody of itself. The images of "thickness," "field," "landscape," "inhabiting," "engagement," "radiation," "dimensions," "perspectives," "perceptual post," "vantage point," "fabric," "linking," "envelopment," and "meshing" are woven together into an amazingly coherent pattern. In addition, certain fresh, though harmonious images, such as those of "divining," glimpsing ("out of the corner of its eye"), "invisible steward," "tunnelling," "crossing over," are intertwined in order to strengthen the overall effect. The incredible concentration of images in this passage compensates considerably for their lack in the main body of Merleau-Ponty's political essays.

This general and growing dissatisfaction with Marxism as practiced in postwar Europe intensified when in his last years Merleau-Ponty turned his attention to Third World politics, especially that of Africa. The brief but forceful essays comprising the third part of his book entitled *Signs* provide something of a blow-by-blow commentary on international developments as they related to Marxism in the 1950s. He takes up, in turn, such issues as the fate and significance of Trotsky, Russian concentration camps, the cold war, de-Stalinization, and imperialist developments in Indochina. Throughout these analyses he remains critical of both Western ideology and reactionary communism. His position to the viability of independence for colonial Algeria, for example, can fairly be described as a "hard-nosed" realism or pragmatism that seeks to avoid the extremes on either side. While this posture may be said to be anchored in his philosophy of concrete personal and social embodiment, the fact remains that when addressing himself to these timely topics Merleau-Ponty does not employ the metaphors so characteristic of his more theoretical works.

While rejecting the immorality and terror, as well as the torture, of French colonization in Algeria, Merleau-Ponty rejected as well the romanticist notion that immediate and complete independence would solve the basic difficulties involved in such situations. He was opposed to France's withdrawal from Algeria because such a move would fail to acknowledge the historical actuality of the interpenetration of cultures. While French policy clearly needed changing, moving toward decolonization, Merleau-Ponty thought it foolish to pretend that Algeria could return to its simple, precolonial state. "I would rather be part of a country which does something in history than a country which submits to it" (*Signs*, p. 336).

When asked whether or not he believed the values of Western civilization to be superior to those of technologically less developed countries, Merleau-Ponty responded:

> Certainly not in respect to their moral value, and even less to their superior beauty, but, how shall I put it, in respect to their *historical* value. . . . This great feverish and crushing arrangement of what is called developed humanity is, after all, what will one day enable all men on earth to eat. It has already made them exist in one another's eyes, instead of each proliferating in his country like trees. They have met in blood, fear, and hatred, and this is what must stop. I cannot seriously consider

this encounter an evil. In any case, it is something settled; there can be no question of recreating archaism; we are all embarked and it is no small matter to have begun this game. (*Signs*, p. 336)

This passage reminds one a bit of Marx's approach to capitalism, acknowledging, even praising it for bringing the world out of the Dark Ages, while at the same time urging us to go beyond it and its evils without succumbing to the temptation to destroy it.

Merleau-Ponty provided something of a preview of this sort of realism in his earlier essay, "A Note on Machiavelli" (1949). He begins with the question, "How could he have been understood?" and proceeds with an account of Machiavelli aimed at exonerating him as a political realist, indeed, as a "humanist." The chief reason he gives for this interpretation is that Machiavelli realized "that in historical action, goodness is something catastrophic and cruelty less cruel than the easygoing mood" (*Signs*, p. 216). He quotes Machiavelli as saying, typically: "The main thing is to keep oneself in power; the means, whatever they may be, will always seem honorable, and will be praised by everyone." A bit earlier, Merleau-Ponty himself says:

> There is a way of affirming oneself which aims to suppress the other person—and which makes him a slave. And there is a relationship of consultation and exchange with others which is not the death but the very act of the self . . . it must be the prince who asks the questions; and he must not, under pain of being despised, grant anyone a permanent authorization to speak frankly. But at least during the moments when he is deliberating, he communicates with others; and others can rally around the decision he makes, because it is in some respects their decision. (p. 215)

The images by means of which Merleau-Ponty envisions such responsible acts of authority are concentrated in the following remarks:

> They awake an echo which is at times immeasurable. They open or close hidden fissures in the block of general consent, and trigger a molecular process which may modify the whole course of events. Or as mirrors set around in a circle transform a slender flame into a fairyland, acts of authority reflected in the constellation of consciousness are transfigured, and the reflections create an appearance which is the proper place—truth in short—of historical action. (p. 216)

A bit further on he says that Machiavelli's "radical humanism" was not unaware of values. "He saw them living, humming like a shipyard, bound to certain historical actions—barbarians to be booted out, an Italy to create" (p. 219).

These images resemble those generally employed by Merleau-Ponty, some incorporating the processes of nature and others the intentional activity of human community and technology. At the same time, however, they do not seem to reflect his usual concern for the fabric or network quality of human relationships. Authoritative political action seems more likely to rend the tissue of the organic whole than to knit and mend it. In other words, one wonders what place is left for democratic processes and accountability within this point of view. It is possible, of course, that Merleau-Ponty (and Machiavelli) is speaking strictly within the context of the chaotic Italy of the Renaissance. It is difficult to know how these remarks might apply to contemporary Third World politics.

He does go on to say:

> Machiavelli was right: values are necessary but not sufficient; and it is even dangerous to stop with values, for as long as we have not chosen those whose mission it is to uphold those values in historical struggle, we have done nothing. . . . History is a struggle, and if republics did not struggle they would disappear. We should at least realize that the means remain bloody, merciless, and sordid. The supreme deception of the Crusades is not to admit it. The circle should be broken. (p. 221)

It is not difficult to hear the strains of Marxism in these remarks, and Merleau-Ponty does identify Marx as having taken up the same problem of the proper relationship between ends and means in the drive to create human community (cf. p. 222). He concludes that even after the Russian Revolution we are still confronted with the same difficult problem (cf. p. 223).

In any case, Merleau-Ponty did consider Machiavelli's "radical humanism" a viable and valuable perspective.

> If by humanism we mean a philosophy of the inner man . . . which replaces political cultivation by moral exhortation, Machiavelli is not a humanist. But if by humanism we mean a philosophy which confronts the relationship of man to man and the constitution of a common situation and common history between men as a problem, than we have to say that Machiavelli formulated some of the conditions of any serious humanism. (p. 223)

To say the least, that evaluation of the traditional enemy of proper political thinking raises fundamental issues that are still struggled with today. Perhaps this is how it must and should be.

BEING HUMAN

A number of the essays written by Merleau-Ponty in the years between *Phenomenology of Perception* and *The Visible and the Invisible* pertain to the relationship between philosophy and the social sciences on the one hand and the nature of religion on the other. The focus of these essays might well be said to be the significance of human efforts to understand the various forms and/or dimensions of what we call being human. The emphasis in some of the essays in question is on the interconnections between the different methodological concerns of sociology and of philosophy, or what today is often termed "the sociology of knowledge." We shall look first at Merleau-Ponty's approach to the issues involved in these concerns, paying special attention to the metaphors that come into play.

In "The Philosopher and Sociology,"Merleau-Ponty addresses himself to the traditional "segregation" between these two disciplines. He insists that this "cold war" must and can be overcome by realizing that each of these endeavors needs the other, that facts and ideas are but two poles of the bipolar process of understanding. The sociologist must remove his/her self-imposed "blinders" to the essentially intersubjective, relational character of all knowing. This is best accomplished through the techniques of anthropology, by means of which we make cross-cultural comparisons and contrasts with our own experience, "throwing this experience in and out of focus" (*Signs*, p. 100) in order to represent it to ourselves. The philosopher must anchor reflective activity in the concrete particulars of everyday life in order to avoid becoming lost in empty abstractions.

Merleau-Ponty uses the development of the philosophy of Edmund Husserl, as it pertains to this issue, as a means of locating the problems involved therein. He traces Husserl's dialectical movement from trying to redefine philosophy as "rigorous science," in order to avoid empty abstractions, through his effort to focus exclusively on the "universal ideas" being experienced, and finally, according to Merleau-Ponty, to his final realization that philosophy can only take place within the *lebenswelt* of actual, everyday personal and social experience. By means of this development we see the resolution of the supposed conflict between social science and philosophy. Moreover, Merleau-Ponty claims that this bipolar character of all knowledge of the human way of being in the world crystallized in the work of de Saussure, especially in his treatment of linguistic activity.

This convergence of the ideas of Husserl and de Saussure results in a philosophy of language that

> is no longer contrasted to empirical linguistics as an attempt at total objectification of language . . . it has become the rediscovery of the subject in the act of speaking . . . language is no longer broken down into elements which can be added up piece by piece; it is like an organ whose tissues all contribute to unified functioning, irrespective of the diversity of their origins and the fortuitousness of their original insertion into the whole. (p. 104)

Understanding, like language, is now seen as a process involving a "community" or "dialogue" of minds which "reanimates and rectifies a genesis which could miscarry without it" (pp. 106–107). Thus, social science cannot place itself outside social experience in the process of seeking to understand it.

Philosophy, likewise, must "reshape" its understanding of itself as an intersubjective perspective, instead of that of an "absolute spectator." Since we are, thus,

> all hemmed in by history, it is up to us to understand that whatever truth we may have is to be gotten not in spite of but through our historical inherence . . . that through it I am grafted onto every action and all knowledge which can have a meaning for me . . . then my contact with the social in the finitude of my situation is revealed to me as the point of origin of all truth. . . . (p. 109)

Thus for Merleau-Ponty, "philosophy is not a particular body of knowledge, it is the vigilance which does not let us forget the source of all knowledge" (p. 110). In this way both philosophy and science are grounded in or orbit around the axis provided by the concrete human world, as lived and experienced in community.

Thus far the images used by Merleau-Ponty in this essay are quite familiar, even predictable. "Field," "organ," "tissue," "miscarry," "fabric," and "grafted" all fit within the environmental, biological, and technological rubrics suggested previously. The image of "vigilance," however, introduces a distinctly human or social emphasis into the account of the nature of cognitive activity. This motif is continued near the close of the essay under discussion when Merleau-Ponty characterized the interaction between individual life and social life in terms of theatrical images.

> The individual drama takes place among *roles* which are already inscribed within the total institutional structure, so that from the beginning of his life the child proceeds . . . to a deciphering of meanings which from the outset generalizes his own drama into a drama of his culture. (p. 112)

At the end of this essay Merleau-Ponty returns to physiological imagery when speaking of the relation between the personal and the social. He speaks of them as "centripetal" and "centrifugal movements," respectively, and claims that it is only through concrete philosophical reflection that these two seemingly contradictory phenomena can be reconciled; factual or scientific investigation alone can only identify them. "Philosophy is irreplaceable because it reveals to us both the movement by which lives become truths, and the circularity of that singular being who in a certain sense already *is* everything he *happens to think*" (p. 113). Human knowledge of human beings doubles back on and is an instance of itself, even as each individual human life both exemplifies and transcends what it means to be human, and philosophy acknowledges and retraces this circularity.

In his essay entitled "From Mauss to Claude Levi-Strauss," Merleau-

Ponty relates this bipolar character of human understanding of being human to another highly significant sociological thinker, Levi-Strauss. He credits Marcel Mauss with "discovering" the "binocular" or double-exposure quality of social knowledge, but Levi-Strauss with articulating it in his theory of "structuralism." Merleau-Ponty interprets the insight that "social facts are neither things nor ideas, they are structures" (*Signs*, p. 117) as dynamic rather than static. In his view the structures by means of which the patterns of individual and social reality unfold themselves are not wooden formulas or rigid archetypes, but are reenactments of or participations in a spiral of signification that is always repeating yet transcending itself.

The knowledge that results from our reflection on these dynamic structures is a synthesis of personal and social reality, "since we live in the unity of one single life all the systems our culture is composed of. We can gain some knowledge from this synthesis which is ourselves" (p. 119). In addition, as we learn other languages, and thereby in some degree dwell in other cultures, we garner additional, even universal or transcendental knowledge. "No longer the overarching universal of a strictly objective method, but a sort of lateral universal which we acquire through ethnological experience and its incessant testing of the self through the other person and the other person through the self" (p. 120). This new cognitive posture, known as "ethnology," constitutes "a way of thinking, the way which imposes itself when the object is 'different,' and requires us to transform ourselves. We also become the ethnologists of our own society if we set ourselves at a distance from it" (p. 120).

Merleau-Ponty offers the example of understanding the nature of myth as an illustration of the difference between "flat" social knowledge and what Clifford Geertz has called "thick description." "To want to understand myth as a proposition, in terms of what it says, is to apply our own grammar and vocabulary to a foreign language . . . let us study its inner articulation . . . its style, its rhythm, and its recurrent themes . . ." (p. 121). This would involve "reciprocal criticism" in which we are as willing to see our own commitment to factual knowledge as a mythology in its own right as we care to understand "primitive" myths. Neither approach can be vindicated over or reduced to the other; rather, we must "take the symbolic function as the source of all reason and unreason" (p. 122).

The metaphors of "structures" and "reciprocity" used in this context are as familiar as they are fitting. The image of "lateral universality," however, is both new and striking. Although it involves the notion of physiological movement, when conjoined with the question of universality or transcendence it takes on special significance. Merleau-Ponty appears to be searching for a way to speak to transcendence that avoids both hierarchical dualism and humanistic reductionism. Sometime he talks of "vertical transcendence" and at other times he speaks the language of mediation, of one dimension in and through the other. Lateral movement and peripheral vision provide excellent images for a post-modern approach to transcendence, and we shall return to this important and complex possibility in the final chapter.

Merleau-Ponty continues his discussion of the relation between philosophy and social knowledge in his essay, "The Metaphysical in Man." Here he applies his notion of the circular, reciprocal character of understanding to the insight of Gestalt psychology and Emile Durkheim. While praising the former for bringing the relational and holistic nature of cognition to the center of the epistemological stage, he is critical of both Wolfgang Koehler and Jean Piaget, for example, for not carrying the revolution far enough. Speaking in terms of the usual dualism between mind and object, Merleau-Ponty accredits Gestalt thought with establishing

> a communication between and a mixture of objective and subjective, and has conceived of psychological knowledge in a new way, no longer as an attempt to break down these typical ensembles but rather an effort to embrace them and to understand them by reliving them. (*SNS*, p. 86)

This way of thinking is connected to de Saussure's approach to linguistics in which language must be seen as surrounding

> each speaking subject, like an instrument with its own inertia, its own demands, constraints, and internal logic, and must nevertheless remain open to the initiatives of the subject . . . always capable of the displacements of meanings, the ambiguities, and the functional substitutions which give this logic its lurching gait. (p. 87)

This image of the asymmetrical, halting, yet powerful animal-like progress of speech, in both its individual and social development, is especially forceful. At one instant, or from one perspective, language seems impossible, while from another it seems eternal and inevitable. The focus of Chapter 3 will be Merleau-Ponty's understanding of language in relation to such images.

Durkheim's efforts to explain religious experience, both personal and social, exclusively in terms of its efficacy on the sociological level are criticized by Merleau-Ponty as merely passing the buck, since the mysterious reality thus exorcized from the concept of religion must now be acknowledged as equally present in the concept of society itself.

> The socialist is not *collective consciousness* but intersubjectivity, a living relationship and tension among individuals. Sociology should not seek an explanation of the religious in the social . . . but must consider them as two aspects of the real and fantastic bond as it has been worked out by the civilization under consideration. (p. 90)

Sociology thus understood is not only not hostile to philosophy and metaphysics, according to Merleau-Ponty, but overlaps with them. In the following passage he uses, once again, the images of the artist, of sedimentation, and of communication to describe this knowledge, which at once is historical and universal.

> All knowledge of man by man, far from being pure contemplation, is the taking up by each, *as best he can*, of the acts of others, reactivating from ambiguous signs an experience which is not his own, appropriating a structure . . . of which he forms no distinct concept by which he puts together as an experienced pianist deciphers an unknown piece of music: without himself grasping the motives of each gesture of each operation, without being able to bring to the surface of consciousness all the sediment of knowledge which he is using at the moment. Here we no longer have the positing of an object, but rather we have communication with a way of being. (p. 93)

Once again we find Merleau-Ponty affirming the essential agreement between philosophical and sociological method, when properly understood. They are not the same enterprise, but two poles of the symbiotic activity of cognition, each requiring and supporting the other. Echoing Kant, Merleau-Ponty puts the relationship thus: "A science without philosophy would literally not know what it was talking about. A philosophy without methodological exploration of phenomena would end up with nothing but formal truths, which is to say, errors" (p. 97). This quotation brings to a close our consideration of Merleau-Ponty's view of philosophy in relation to sociology. We turn next to his application of his philosophy of embodiment to the concerns of psychology.

The majority of Merleau-Ponty's explorations into the connections between his own philosophy of embodiment and the psychological approach to the question of being human center on the insights of Sigmund Freud. Even early on, in *Phenomenology of Perception*, especially in the chapter on sexuality, he expressed a critical appreciation for Freud's work (cf. pp. 158–171). As he did with Levi-Strauss's structuralism, Merleau-Ponty gives Freud's investigations the strong benefit of the doubt, stressing their broad significance while dismissing their specifics as idiosyncratic packaging. "Thus the significance of psychoanalysis is less to make psychology biological than to discover a dialectical process in functions thought of as 'purely bodily,' and to reintegrate sexuality into the human being" (*Phenomenology of Perception*, p. 158).

This same general positive theme is carried on in the essay "Man and Adversity" (1951), where Merleau-Ponty analyzes Freud's treatment of the concepts of instinct and the unconscious. There he argues that the controlling concern of Freud's approach was to break down the traditional barrier between our notions of mind and body by showing how each invests the other with meaning. "With psychoanalysis mind passes into body as, inversely, body passes into mind," by a kind of "osmosis" (*Signs*, p. 229). Merleau-Ponty speaks of this relationship, using his familiar metaphors, as "incarnational" and concludes that for Freud,

> the sexual is our way (since we are flesh, our carnal way) of living our relationships with others. Since sexuality is a relationship to other persons, and not just to another body, it is going to weave the circular system of projections and introjections, illuminating the unlimited series of reflecting reflections and reflected reflections which are the reasons why I am the other person and he is myself. (p. 230)

In "Phenomenology and Psychoanalysis," which was written as a preface for A. Hesnard's book on the importance of Freud's work for the modern world, Merleau-Ponty responds to Hesnard's comments on his own earlier account of Freud in *Phenomenology of Perception*. He sees phenomenology and psychoanalysis as mutually supportive, the former providing the perspective that properly orients the latter, while the latter provides a view of consciousness that "invests the body with symbolic or poetic weight" (*The Essential Writings of Merleau-Ponty*, p. 83). These images, of "investment" and "poetic weight," while not unrelated to the pattern of metaphor of Merleau-Ponty's overall point of view, carry a more human connotation than the majority of his earlier images. That is to say, they are less simply environmental or physiological, or even technological, than those expressions that predominate in *Phenomenology of Perception*. There may be something of a trend in this direction as we come nearer to his most mature thought. We shall return to this question in the next chapter.

In this essay, Merleau-Ponty suggests a fresh reading of his mentor, Husserl, as well as of Freud. At least in his later work Husserl is said to be less "positivist" and "idealist" and more truly phenomenological in his concern to see consciousness and the world as mutually interdependent and constitutive (cf. p. 85). At any rate, Merleau-Ponty concludes that we must

> learn to read Freud the way we read a classic, that is by understanding his words and theoretical concepts, not in the lexical and common meaning, but in the meaning they acquire from within the experience which they announce and of which we have behind our backs much more than a suspicion. (p. 86)

The term "unconscious self," for instance, might thus be used to designate the "intemporal, indestructible element in us . . . so long as we do not forget that the word is the index of an enigma—because the term retains, like the algae on the stone that one drags up, something of the sea from which it was taken" (p. 86). Thus, "Phenomenology and psychoanalysis are

not parallel; much better, they are both aiming toward the same *latency*"
(p. 87). Here, once more, we see the environmental and physiological thrust
of Merleau-Ponty's imagination at work in the very fiber of his philosophy
and its relationship to the work of other modern thinkers.

This same interpretive posture toward the insight of Freud is found in
Merleau-Ponty's early essay, "Cézanne's Doubt." In the midst of discussing the connections between an artist's life and work, he says:

> Unlike the natural sciences, psychoanalysis was not meant to give us
> necessary relations of cause and effect but to point to motivational
> relationships which are in principle simply possible . . . it is like the
> words of the oracle, an ambiguous symbol which applies in advance to
> several possible chains of events. To be more precise: in every life, one's
> birth and one's past define categories or basic dimensions which do not
> impose any particular act but which can be found in all. . . . The very
> decisions which transform us are always made in reference to a factual
> situation; such a situation can of course be accepted or refused, but it
> cannot fail to give us our impetus nor to be for us, . . . the incarnation for
> us of the value we give to it. (*SNS*, pp. 24–25)

Before moving on it should be noted that this notion of an "ambiguous
symbol," couched in the by now expected metaphors of "dimensions" and
"incarnation," will come to play a significant role in the general account of
Merleau-Ponty's overall philosophy of language to be given in Chapter 4.
This is no less true of his specific attitude toward the nature and function of
metaphor, which will be taken up in Chapter 5. In addition, even at this
point, it is worth remarking that the interpretive posture toward Freud that
Merleau-Ponty suggests might well be the most appropriate angle of
approach to take when reading all theoretical thinkers, especially philosophers! As was mentioned at the outset of the present study, it is this
perspective that provides the rationale for exploring Merleau-Ponty's own
use of metaphor as a means of coming to grips with his thought. But more
of this in Chapter 6.

A third aspect of Merleau-Ponty's application of his philosophy of
embodiment to the question of human nature pertains to the place and value
of religion. Although he occasionally expresses dissatisfaction with the
particulars of institutionalized religion (e.g., *Signs*, p. 242), he also resists, as
we have seen, the efforts of the likes of Durkheim and Marx to reduce
religion to the social functions or material conditions of human life. There is
a mystery disclosed and discerned in religious awareness that Merleau-
Ponty, in a variety of essays, insists on recognizing and clarifying within the
purview provided by his own somatic point of departure.

With respect to the long history of conflict and synthesis between
religious and philosophical thought, Merleau-Ponty sees it as inconclusive.

When the two have been opposed to each other, they have been interpreted as mutually exclusive, axiomatic and dogmatic systems of thought. When they have been synthesized, one or the other is subsumed under the categories of the other. Both traditional theology and modern humanism represent a closed posture toward the world and human existence. The true philosopher, in Merleau-Ponty's view, takes an open stance in saying that

> the world is going on, that we do not have to judge its future by what has happened in the past, that the idea of a destiny of things is not an idea but a dizziness, that our relations with nature are not fixed once and for all. That no one can know what freedom may be able to do, nor imagine what our customs and human relations would be in a civilization no longer haunted by competition and necessity. (*In Praise of Philosophy*, p. 43)

After all the moves and counter-moves have been made between religion and philosophy, at least in the West, nothing is settled. The real issue that remains concerns the difference between "this instituted Christianity, a mental horizon or matrix of culture, and the Christianity effectively lived and practiced in a positive faith . . . between Christianity "understood" and Christianity lived, between universality and choice" (*Signs*, pp. 142–143). The traditional interpretation of Christianity, as well as of many other religions, turns on a distinction between "inner and outer worlds and life," but Merleau-Ponty insists that "the Incarnation changes everything. Since the Incarnation, God has been externalized" ("Faith and Good Faith," *SNS*, p. 174). This fundamental change brings the phenomenon of choice out of the "inner" world, as well as bringing the meaning of religion out of the clouds, into the embodied and relational life of human beings.

Displaying a remarkably deep and contemporary understanding of religious expression and meaning, Merleau-Ponty goes on to specify the significance of this incarnational perspective for scripture and sacrament:

> The parables of the Gospels are not a way of presenting pure ideas in images; they are the only language capable of conveying the relations of the religious life, as paradoxical as those of the world of sensation. Sacramental words and gestures are not simply the embodiment of some thought. Like tangible things, they are themselves the carriers of their meaning, which is inseparable from its material form. They do not evoke the idea of God: they are the vehicle of His presence and action. In the last analysis the soul is so little to be separated from the body that it will carry a radiant double of its temporal body into eternity. (*SNS*, p. 175)

This holistic, incarnational understanding of the character of religious symbols and the biological teaching of the resurrection of the body (what St. Paul calls a "spiritual body") is expressed in images that lead both back to our previous discussions of Merleau-Ponty's thought and forward to the exploration of its significance for language and philosophy in general in the chapters comprising Part Two. The references to the parallel complexities of perception, gestural meaning, and mediational vehicles are clearly of a piece with the perspective and images of *Phenomenology of Perception*. At the same time, they entail a particular posture with respect to the metaphorical quality of all speech, especially and including philosophy, a posture the outline of which should now be discernible by the reader, and which we shall begin to fill in after the next chapter.

Exhibiting a position remarkably similar to that expressed by the so-called Death of God movement, more than a decade later, Merleau-Ponty maintains that traditional Christianity has

> not yet understood that God was with them now and forever. The meaning of the Pentecost is that the religion of both the Father and the Son are to be fulfilled in the Spirit, that God is no longer in Heaven but in human society and communication, wherever men come together in His name. (p. 177)

This failure to "complete the Incarnation" has invariably led to its inverse, to the established Church pretending that it speaks authoritatively for God, beyond the limitations inherent in all human claims to knowledge. "And so love changes to cruelty, the reconciliation of men with each other and with the world will come to naught, the Incarnation turns into suffering because it is incomplete, and Christianity becomes a new form of guilty conscience" (p. 177).

Merleau-Ponty goes on to liken the faith associated with such duplicity to that of uncritical Marxism, which because it is "completely devoid of sincerity . . . [is] sheer obedience or madness" (p. 179). In an allusion to Sartre's notion of "bad faith," Merleau-Ponty concludes:

> If commitment goes beyond reason, it should never run either in an explosive, manic sincerity or an unquestioned faith. Instead, it consists of a higher awareness which enables him to determine the moment when it is reasonable to take things on trust and the moment when questioning is in order, to combine faith with good faith within himself, and to accept his party or his group with open eyes, seeing them for what they are. (p. 180)

In his essay "Man, the Hero," which was written in 1948 as the conclusion of *Signs*, Merleau-Ponty depicts the contemporary hero in a way that reminds one of Camus' Sisyphus: neither as the person of ready-made faith, nor as a humanistic Prometheus. Rather, the true hero lives

> at a time when duties and tasks are unclear. He has a sharper sense of human liberty and of the contingency of the future than anyone has ever had before. Taking everything into account, nothing is certain—not victory, which is still so far away, and not other people. . . . But

sometimes—in love, in action—a harmony is created among them and events respond to their will. Sometimes there is a flash of fire, that streak of lightning, that moment of victory . . . that *gloria* which in its brilliance blots out everything else. (p. 186)

The analogy that connects the above analysis of the Incarnation and faith to Merleau-Ponty's understanding of human existence and experience as embodied, though perhaps circuitous, is nonetheless solid. The unity of consciousness and action in the body, as well as the relational and participatory character of our knowledge of the world and others, is parallel in Christianity; God is located at the center of human existence and the world, not above it ("the word became flesh"), and faith is a lived relation of honest interaction with history and persons, as conjoined in society. In both cases, philosophical and theological, the hierarchical dualism and intellectualism of traditional thought and culture have been overcome, at least cognitively. It remains to be seen whether they can be overcome in praxis.

This way of putting the topic of religion, in terms of intersecting dimensions, raises once again the crucial issue of transcendence. Merleau-Ponty himself speaks of his incarnational understanding of religion in relation to the contrasting notions of "vertical and horizontal transcendence" in his essay on "Indirect Language and the Voices of Silence." He sees the heartbeat of the Christian faith as a notion of God that

wants nothing to do with a vertical relation of subordination. He is not simply a principle of which we are the consequences, a will whose instruments we are, or even a model of which human values are only a reflection. There is a sort of impotence of God without us, and Christ attests that God would not be fully God without becoming fully man. . . . Transcendence no longer hangs over man: he becomes, strangely, its privileged bearer. (*Signs*, p. 71)

These images of vertical and horizontal dimensions as a way of speaking of religion and transcendence stem from Merleau-Ponty's orientation within the space suggested by environmental, specifically geographical metaphors. In the end, however, he rejects both as inadequate for being flat and otherworldly, respectively, turning to a mediational model by means of which to depict the relation of transcendence to historical and communal humanity. This mediational motif will play a major role in Part Two, in relation to Merleau-Ponty's views of language, metaphor, and philosophy. First, however, we must turn our attention to the last of the writings comprising the Merleau-Ponty corpus, *The Visible and the Invisible*, and to the metaphors that animate it.

3

THE INVISIBLE WITHIN
THE VISIBLE

The manuscript on which Merleau-Ponty was working when he died was perhaps meant to be his *magnum opus*. It had been given various titles and is seemingly only about half complete. In this manuscript, which has been given the posthumous title, *The Visible and the Invisible*, Merleau-Ponty sought to return to his original point of departure in order to get a firmer fix on the nature of the cognitive processes centered in and emanating from the body. While most of what we have in this book constitutes only the first part of the intended project, it is an extraordinary document indeed. In fact, the last quarter of this manuscript, entitled "The Intertwining—The Chiasm," is very startling, if not a bit overwhelming, in its powerful use of metaphor.

Although he had always expressed his unique insight and perspective by means of figurative images in his previous works, one is hardly prepared for the poetic turn taken by Merleau-Ponty in this final chapter of his last work. This fact is especially fortuitous for a study such as the present one, aiming as it does at a documentation of and a reflection on the place of metaphor in Merleau-Ponty's philosophy. In addition, this increased reliance on metaphor, as he came closer to what he took to be the human way of being in the world, is highly significant in relation to the character of Merleau-Ponty's philosophy in particular, as well as to the entire philosophical enterprise in general. That this is the case will become increasingly clear in the chapters comprising Part Two of the present work. But first we must encounter the invisible within the visible as Merleau-Ponty sought to display them in his most mature effort.

REFLECTIONS ON REFLECTION

The greater part of *The Visible and the Invisible* is devoted to a discussion of the insights and oversights of modern philosophers as they have sought to come to grips with the process and results of human cognition. Along the way Merleau-Ponty interweaves the thread and patterns of his own approach to these issues, making extensive use of the images he introduced in his earlier works. Whereas in *Phenomenology and Perception* he had focused on the limitation and defects of both empiricism and rationalism as accounts of perception in particular, in his last work Merleau-Ponty sought a wider scope with respect to both the problem and proposed solutions. Here the problem is the entire cognitive experience, the subject, the object, and their interrelation, at every level. The epistemological postures under discussion are primarily those of Descartes, Kant, Sartre, and Husserl.

In the middle of his career Merleau-Ponty had edited an anthology containing representative selections from the writings of celebrated philosophers. In his introduction to this volume (published under the title "Everywhere and Nowhere" in *Signs*), he provided a brief survey of classical, medieval, modern, and contemporary Western thought, along with one of Oriental philosophy as well. Although some of the points made in this necessarily short introduction are similar to those he makes in the main part of the *The Visible and the Invisible*, they are far too general to contribute to the more thorough analysis of cognitive postures provided in Merleau-Ponty's concluding effort.

Merleau-Ponty begins *The Visible and the Invisible* by pointing out that although we see and know the world, as well as those realities comprising it, directly and confidently, whenever we set out to explain the nature of this knowing, this knower, and this known, we soon become entangled in a whole host of conceptual difficulties and confusion. The chief reason for this is that we choose the wrong point of departure. His overall aim is to disentangle the epistemological enterprise from these confusions by altering the angle from which it begins. In Wittgenstein's words, his goal is to show the fly the way out of the fly-bottle and thereby allow the way things are to reveal itself. The primary concern of modern philosophy was to question the nature and basis of knowledge, seeking to establish it upon a solid foundation by means of abstract reflection. Thus the first chapter of *The Visible and the Invisible*, which deals with skepticism, Cartesian dualism, and Kantian idealism, is entitled "Reflection and Interrogation." Merleau-Ponty views the interrogation of knowledge by means of abstract reflection as wrong-headed from the outset. Cognitive activity, which in this context he calls "perceptual faith," cannot be understood by pretending that we can stand above or outside of the activity itself. Interrogation can only take place *within* the dialogical or conversational mode, which in its very process shows that meaning and knowledge are possible because they are actual.

The image from which modern critical thought begins and by which it immediately becomes confused is, according to Merleau-Ponty, that of "objectivity," namely seeking to make an object of thought out of the knowing process itself. To objectify is to set the known over against the knower, to separate and hopefully thereby to know better that which is known. Merleau-Ponty's chief objection to this procedure is that it distorts the interactive, bipolar nature of cognitive activity by assuming we know the world through disengaging ourselves from it. Thus the effort to understand understanding itself by stepping back from it constitutes a double distortion.

This distancing procedure is encapsulated in two primary images, or "root metaphors," that give rise to the objectivist perspective, both of which are spatial and passive in character. The first of these is that of rising above that which is to be known, in this case cognition itself, while the second is standing outside of it. Each of these root metaphors yields specific secondary images that have been incorporated into modern epistemological thought. Merleau-Ponty unpacks these various images in his analysis of abstract reflection as a mode of interrogation, revealing their counterproductive nature. An account of these metaphors, along with those that Merleau-Ponty himself proposes as more helpful, is now in order.

Early on in his examination of critical philosophy, Merleau-Ponty speaks of the objectivist perspective as making us feel "capable of hovering over" (p. 13) the object of our common understanding or perception. A bit further along he speaks of this unsituated vantage point as that "of the absolute spectator" (p. 19). He describes this image more thoroughly later as one of "pure vision, in the aerial view of the panorama. . . . High places attract those who wish to look over the world with an eagle-eye view" (pp. 77–78). The advantage of this distancing of oneself, as the knowing subject, from the object to be known would seem to be the minimization of various "subjective" factors that might distort the reality under scrutiny. Thus real knowledge is presumed to be passive, uninvolved with, and thereby unbiased toward the epistemological object.

The paradoxical difficulty with such "high-altitude" thinking is that it produces in itself a distorted view of knowledge, since there can be no knowledge whatsoever once the subject and object have been isolated. Cognition, in Merleau-Ponty's view, is a bipolar, interactive process that can only be dissected at the cost of destroying the very reality one is seeking to understand.

The idea of the subject, and that of the object as well, transforms into a cognitive adequation of the relationship with the world and with ourselves that we have in the perceptual faith. They do not clarify it; they utilize it tacitly, they draw out its consequences. And since the development of knowledge shows that these consequences are contradictory, it is to that relationship that we must necessarily return, in order to elucidate it. (p. 23)

The second major image by means of which Merleau-Ponty identifies the objectivist standpoint that motivates modern epistemological thinkers is that of externality. To be above something is, after all, to be outside of it. Thus critical philosophy is founded on the absolute dichotomy between what is "interior" and what is "exterior." From the perspective of the knower, this translates into the distinction between feelings and observations, while from the side of that which is known, it becomes the difference between introspection and behavior. Real knowledge is viewed as exclusively a function of one's observations of behavior, whether in physics or psychology, thereby excluding all references to "inner" emotions and values.

One correlative image expressive of this objectivist perspective that Merleau-Ponty employs is that of the "harbor" or "abode." Speaking of modern critical thought, and its quest for the comfort of certainty, he says:

This movement of reflection will always at first sight be convincing: in a sense it is imperative, it is truth itself, and one does not see how philosophy could disperse with it. The question is whether it has brought philosophy to the harbor, whether the universe of thought to which it leads is really an order that suffices to itself and puts an end to every question. Since the perceptual faith is a paradox, how could I remain within it? And if I do not remain within it, what else can I do except re-enter into myself and seek there the abode of truth? Is it not evident that, precisely if my perception is a perception of the world, I must find in my commerce with world the reasons that induce me to see it? (pp. 31–32)

This last question carries in it Merleau-Ponty's own answer to the riddles raised by the first two questions. The answer lies neither outside nor inside the knowing subject, but within the give-and-take, the push-and-pull of the subject's participation with the world in constituting reality. There is no final harbor or abode where cognition can be safely anchored, protected from the winds and waves of outrageous skepticism. There is only the coming and going, the tacking and hauling of sailing from one port to the next. The seaworthy vessel cannot be repaired in drydock, but only in the course of the voyage itself, bit by bit as the need arises. This far from ideal process is, nonetheless, both necessary and sufficient.

In a later passage Merleau-Ponty describes this externalizing posture in terms of images of manipulation, such as "forceps" and "microscope." He then contrasts this approach with the images of "hollow and free space," of "resonance," and "porousness," that characterize his own approach to understanding cognitive activity. Reality and truth offer themselves

> only to someone who wishes not to have them but to see them, not to hold them as with forceps, or to immobilize them as under the objective of a microscope, but to let them be and to witness their continued being—to someone who therefore limits himself to giving them the hollow, the free space they ask for in return, the resonance they require, who follows their own movement, who is . . . a question consonant with the porous being it questions and from which obtains not an *answer* but a confirmation of its astonishment. (pp. 101–102)

In his second chapter Merleau-Ponty takes up the contemporary reaction to the foregoing, objectivist point of view, namely the interiorization of knowledge within the knowing subject. This chapter, "Interrogation and Dialectic," focuses on the philosophy of Sartre. After providing a brief summary of the ins and outs of Sartre's analysis of the absolute distinction between nonhuman reality, which exists "in itself," and human reality, which through introspection can be said to exist "for itself," Merleau-Ponty concludes that this dichotomy leaves the knower trapped within a vacuum of negativity. "What was a stumbling block for the philosophy of reflection becomes, from the point of view of negativity, the principle of a solution. Everything really does come down to a matter of thinking the negative rigorously" (p. 63).

Here again, there are two chief images used to communicate the difficulties with this "solution" to the problem of cognition. The first is that of internality, of being "inside" one's self, and the second that of being "behind" and thus cut off from the world.

The so-called pre-reflective *cogito*, which is said to be more fundamental than Descartes' rational analysis of the self, actually implodes or collapses on itself by virtue of its self-stipulated isolation.

> Is it the pre-reflective *cogito* and the reflection that introduces it, or is it a *cogito* that from the depths of ourselves precedes itself, pronounces itself before we have pronounced it, because thought is what we are? The first hypothesis is precluded if I am a nothing; and the second restores to me my emptiness, just when the question is to understand how my life can be opaque for itself. (p. 69)

Not only are we cut off from ourselves by the dichotomy between our own in-itself and for-itself, by our so-called internal self-transcendence, but we are separated from the world by it as well. In his analysis of reality in terms of the absolute distinction between these two modes of existence, in

Being and Nothingness Sartre removes the relational standpoint necessary for any knowledge of the world whatsoever. "I *qua* negativity am always behind all the things, cut off from them by virtue of my status as witness, always capable of suspending my adhesion to the world in order to make of it a thought of the world" (p. 65). Thus, being "inside" ourselves, as the knower, is no better than being "outside" of the world, as the known, since in either case we are disconnected from or "behind" whatever there is to know, including the knowing process itself.

The earlier mention of "porousness," along with the above occurrence of "adhesion", provides something of a cue for Merleau-Ponty's introduction of the metaphoric image which serves as the centerpiece for the entire arrangement of insights in *The Visible and the Invisible*. I have in mind here his image of "the flesh," which becomes that by means of which he pulls together nearly all of his other images and concerns. The first use of the flesh metaphor occurs in the midst of Merleau-Ponty's effort to counteract the negativities of Sartre's introspective and isolationist approach to our cognition of other persons. He says:

> I do not *know* others, in the strong sense that I *know* myself. . . . But my perception of the world feels it has an exterior; I feel at the surface of my visible being that very volubility dies away, that I become flesh, and that at the extremity of this inertia that was me there is something else, or rather an other who is not a thing. (p. 61)

This way of putting things suggests that one of the main features of flesh that Merleau-Ponty seeks to stress is its mediational or "two-sided" character. That is to say, flesh not only serves as the exterior line of demarcation for the individual subject, but it serves as well as the point or veil of connection with the "outside" world. In short, our flesh faces in two directions at once and thereby unites us with as well as separates us from the world of things and persons in which we are situated. Moreover, flesh has a porous quality that allows, even requires, a coming and going through it; by definition, flesh "breathes" or seeps, as well as containing or separating. In this sense, Merleau-Ponty sees the fleshly character of our embodiment as limiting or grafting us to one another as well as providing our individual entry point into the world.

The centrality and power of this rather startling metaphor becomes especially clear in the following lengthy passage, wherein Merleau-Ponty summarizes both his chief objection to Sartre's subjective dialectic and "square one" of his own approach to cognizing human cognitivity. His incorporation of other, already familiar images, such as "horizon," "intersection," and "atmosphere," should be noted:

> The question is whether in the last analysis our life takes place between an absolutely individual and absolutely universal nothingness behind us and

an absolutely individual and absolutely universal being before us . . . or whether every relation between me and Being, even vision, even speech, is not a carnal relation, with the flesh of the world. In this case "pure" being only shows through at the horizon . . . which, between the "pure" being and myself, is the thickness of its being for me, of its being for others . . . at the intersection of my views and at the intersection of my views with those of the others, at the intersection of my acts and at the intersection of my acts with those of the others, makes the sensible world and the historical world be always intermundane spaces. . . . Far from opening upon the blinding light of pure Being or of the Object, our life has, in the astronomical sense of the word, an atmosphere. (pp. 83–84)

Merleau-Ponty makes increasingly heavy use of the image of flesh, which we shall note as we progress in our examination of *The Visible and the Invisible*. Along the way, however, in his critique of the subjectivist account of cognition, he continues to employ his usual metaphors, such as those noted above, as well as those of "vector" and "polarity" (p. 94), "free space" and "resonance" (p. 101), and "cohesion" (p. 88). As has been mentioned, many of these, being organic and/or physiological in nature, are easily combined with the image of fleshiness—and all of these fit comfortably within the broader rubric of embodiment.

In his third chapter Merleau-Ponty turns to a consideration of what he terms the "intuitivist" perspective ("Interrogation and Intuition"), which seeks to go "beneath" rather than "above," "outside," or "behind" the different aspects of cognitive activity in order to ground them absolutely in "essences." In response to this approach, Merleau-Ponty asks:

When philosophy finds beneath the doubt a prior "knowing," finds around the things and the world as facts and as doubtful facts a horizon that encompasses our negations as our affirmations, and when it penetrates into this horizon, certainly it must define anew this new something. Does it define it well or sufficiently by saying that it is the *essence*? (p. 109)

His answer is, of course, No, and his reason is similar to that given in response to the rationalist approach, which sought to "soar above" the particulars of the knowing process in order to understand it better. Such isolation and distancing dissolves the very reality it seeks to grasp.

To put it differently, those thinkers who seek "essential knowledge" through intuition such as Henri Bergson, for instance, end up being as "subjectivist" as those who sought to discover it within the dialectics of self-consciousness. In order to intuit the absolute essence of my reality I would have to

suspend or at least reactivate all the sedimented thoughts with which it is surrounded, first of all my time, my body—which is not only impossible for me to do in fact but would deprive me of that very cohesion . . . without which the essence is subjective folly and arrogance. There is therefore for me something inessential, and there is a zone, a hollow, where what is not inessential, not impossible, assembles; there is no positive vision that would definitively give me the essentiality of the essence. (p. 112)

Once more the reliance on spatial metaphors should be noted. Merleau-Ponty makes ample use of these by now stock-in-trade images throughout his critique of intuitionist thought. He returns frequently to such favorites as "axis" and "dimensions" (p. 114), "environment" and "habitation" (p. 117), "vortex" (p. 119), and "encroachment" (p. 123). In addition, he reinforces these by returning to images involving biological life, such as "latency" (p. 117), "leafing" (p. 119), "osmosis" (p. 123), "pregnancy" (p. 124), and "rootage and foliation" (p. 126). Thus we begin to encounter, as we proceed toward the final chapter of *The Visible and the Invisible*, a progressive buildup, indeed a veritable piling up, of criss-crossing and overlapping metaphors. It is as if Merleau-Ponty's use of the metaphoric mode takes on a momentum of its own as it spirals toward its explosive climax in the final chapter of his last work.

The imagery of the flesh and that of the relation between the visible and the invisible, the two predominant themes of Merleau-Ponty's concluding effort, are brought together for the first time in the midst of his presentation of his own alternative to intuition. He says:

The visible can thus fill me and occupy me only because I who see it do not see it from the depths of nothingness, but from the midst of itself; I the seer am also visible. What makes the weight, the thickness, the flesh of each color, of each sound, of each tactile texture, of the present and of the world is the fact that he who grasps them feels himself emerge from them by a sort of coiling up or redoubling, fundamentally homogenous with them; he feels that he is the sensible itself coming to itself and that in return the sensible is in his eyes as it were his double or an extension of his own flesh. (p. 114)

Merleau-Ponty goes on with this enfleshment motif, speaking of the particulars of our existence in terms of "shreds," "pulp," "rays emitted in the secrecy of my flesh," and concluding: "I experience their solidity from within insofar as I am among them and insofar as they communicate through me as a sentient thing" (p. 114). In this context he speaks, as well, of the nature and function of language, but a discussion of this topic will be provided in the next chapter. The conclusion of Merleau-Ponty's critique of the Bergsonian search for essences beneath the particulars of cognition is that in by-passing the particulars and seeking reality directly, one also by-passes the medium in and through which reality is experienced and known.

> That the presence of the world is precisely the presence of its flesh to my flesh, that I "am of the world" and that I am not it, this is what is no sooner said than forgotten . . . there is this thickness of flesh between us and the "hard core" of Being . . . one forgets that this frontal being before us . . . is second by principle, is cut out upon a horizon which is not nothing, and which for its part is not by virtue of composition. (p. 127)

The question of the most fruitful form of interrogation for philosophy to follow is addressed by Merleau-Ponty at the close of the second chapter, the one dealing with Sartrean dialectics. However, since the gist of his answer is already adumbrated in the images he employs by way of distinguishing his own approach from those that have dominated the modern philosophical landscape, a full discussion of Merleau-Ponty's portrait of the proper philosophical attitude will be postponed until it can be taken up more thoroughly in Chapter 6. He clearly envisions philosophy as following a mode of interrogation that befits the relational and participatory character he attributes to human knowing and being in the world. Therefore, a proper setting for a more thorough treatment of Merleau-Ponty's understanding of philosophical endeavor may well be provided by a brief exploration of the metaphors he introduces in the concluding pages of *The Visible and the Invisible* in order to contrast his own approach to those already discussed.

INTERROGATION AND CHIASM

On pages 100–104 of *The Visible and the Invisible*, Merleau-Ponty turns from the critique of other epistemological postures to depicting the main outline of his own. He does this by means of a number of figurative images, some of them familiar, some of them fresh. We shall take them up in the order in which he uses them, teasing out their individual significance as we go along. Against the backdrop of the image of horizon, creatively depicted in terms of the limits provided by natural trenches rather than cages or fences for animals in the zoo, Merleau-Ponty suggests that above all philosophy is a form of questioning or interrogation. It is neither a form of analysis, à la Bertrand Russell, nor a mystical revelation of the Ultimate, à la the later Heidegger;

> it cannot reconstruct the thing and the world by condensing in them, in the form of implication, everything we have subsequently been able to think and say of them; rather, it remains a question, it interrogates the world and the thing, it revives, repeats, or imitates their crystallization before us. (p. 100)

The sort of questioning inherent in philosophy is not that which allows us to claim we have found, or even to seek "solutions" (p. 102); it does not

> provide answers that would little by little fill in the blanks. The questions are within our life, within our history. . . . Philosophy does not take the context as given; it turns back upon it in order to seek the origin and the meaning of the questions and of the responses and the identity of him who questions, and it thereby gains access to the interrogation that animates all the questions of cognition, but is of another sort than they. (p. 105)

There is, however, according to Merleau-Ponty, nothing secret or silent about philosophy, "what it finds in this returning to the sources, it says . . . it will take its place among the *artifacts* and products of culture, as an instance of them" (p. 102). This raises the question (!) of the nature of the language most appropriate to a questioning enterprise that neither results in silence nor provides specific answers.

> Hence it is a question whether philosophy as reconquest of brute or wild being can be accomplished by the resources of the eloquent language, or whether it would not be necessary for philosophy to use language in a way that takes from it its power of immediate or direct signification in order to equal it with what it wishes all the same to say. (pp. 102–103)

This way of putting the matter clearly seems to call for the very form of speech that Merleau-Ponty has increasingly used throughout the progression of his investigations, namely that of metaphor. Metaphor stands between "direct signification" on the one hand and mystical or poetic silence on the other; like the body and its flesh, metaphorical images partake of both consciousness and matter, of meaning and behavior. In short, the metaphorical mode, as Merleau-Ponty's own philosophy demonstrates, is uniquely capable of serving as the intersection or crucible wherein the different dimensions of experienced reality encounter and interact with one another. The ramifications of this aspect of philosophical interrogation will be discussed more thoroughly a bit further on.

A third aspect of Merleau-Ponty's understanding of philosophy as interrogation is brought out when he speaks in terms of "fundamental interrogation which appears naked in philosophy" (p. 103). In this connection he turns to a passage from Paul Claudel's *Art Poetique*, a passage he quotes elsewhere in his writings, wherein the subtle, tissuelike quality of the connection between the questions of everyday life and those of philosophy are displayed. Here is the passage, as quoted:

> From time to time, a man lifts his head, sniffs, listens, considers, recognizes his position: he thinks, he sighs, and drawing his watch from the pocket lodged against his chest, looks at the time. *"Where am I?"* and,

"*What time is it?*" Such is the inexhaustible question turning from us to the world. . . . (p. 103)

These "fundamental and naked" questions face in two directions at once: they face toward the everyday world and can be given specific answers, but they also face beyond this world toward its *meaning*, and here the "answers" inevitably lead to a further asking of the questions. In a word, the philosophical side or orientation of these questions finds their answers within the very questioning process itself.

Merleau-Ponty comments on the passage from Claudel in the following fashion:

The watch and the map give here only a semblance of an answer: they indicate to us how what we are living is situated in relation to the course of the stars or to the course of a human day, or in relation to places that have a name. But where are these reference events and these landmarks themselves? They refer us to others, and the answer satisfies us only because we do not attend to it, because we think we are "at home." The question would rise again and indeed would be inexhaustible, almost insane, if we wished to situate our levels, measure our standards in their turn. . . . (pp. 103–104)

In other words, at whatever level we ask such questions we do so within an accepted context that provides their answers; and yet when we question this context itself, we can only do so in relation to still another context, *ad infinitum.* Philosophy, in Merleau-Ponty's view, does not provide or even seek the "ultimate context" and/or answers; rather, it simply insists on continually asking the questions, allowing this process itself to constitute its own answer. This would seem to be the significance of the image of philosophy as interrogation.

In the "Working Notes" to the *The Visible and the Invisible*, which are published at the end of the volume, Merleau-Ponty reminds himself of what he wants to say about philosophy as radical questioning in the following words:

Show that philosophy as interrogation (i.e. as disposition, around the this and the world which *is there*, of a hollow, of a questioning, where the this and the world must *themselves* say what they are—i.e. not as the search for an invariant of language, for a lexical essence, but as the search for an invariant of silence, for the structure) can consist only in showing how the world is articulated starting from a zero of being which is not nothingness, that is, in installing itself on the edge of being, neither in the for Itself, at the joints, where the multiple *entries* of the world cross. (p. 260)

This amazing concatenation of images provides an excellent if truncated summary of Merleau-Ponty's view of philosophy as interrogation.

There are three images within this admittedly cryptic passage that merit special attention before moving on. The first is that of a "hollow," which Merleau-Ponty uses more than once. On the one hand, its suggests that backside of a curve, as in the hollow of one's hand, the concave aspect of a figure. His point would seem to be that a hollow, like the "negative space" of which artists speak, is every bit as real as its positive, convex counterpart. On the other hand, this image suggests a natural meeting place or storage place, as a valley between two mountains where rivers and roads intersect, or the trunk of a tree where various articles are lodged. Both of these aspects are congruent with Merleau-Ponty's earlier analyses of the body as the juncture-point of consciousness and the world.

The second image of merit in this passage is that of "joints." In a sense, the joints of our bodies, as distinguished from the bones, are themselves hollows of a specific kind. Whereas traditional philosophical approaches have sought to locate and describe the world and human existence in terms of their "cosmic skeleton," their bones, Merleau-Ponty is recommending interrogation as a technique for allowing the joints between and by means of which the bones are interrelated to be displayed. To put it slightly differently, the value of philosophy, like that of x-ray photographs, lies in its ability, as a negative image, to allow us to see the joints between the substances that comprise the world. In this way philosophy seeks to allow the way the world works to display itself by first subtracting from it the stuff of which it is made.

This way of putting the matter brings us to the third image of special import in this passage. Merleau-Ponty speaks of philosophy as "showing" how the world is articulated, not as "saying" how it is. In other words, rather than explicating the nature and structure of reality, philosophy must seek to allow reality to articulate itself. Just as philosophical interrogation leads not to answers but to further questions, so the "answers" provided by philosophy point indirectly beyond themselves to what, in Wittgenstein's words, "cannot be said, but must show itself." The "hollows" within life and the world, the "joints" of existence and reality, like "team spirit" or "momentum" in an athletic contest, cannot be designated directly, but their reality can be revealed by interrogating the events and behavior animated by them. Such is the function of philosophy in Merleau-Ponty's view.

All of this brings us back to the place of metaphor in philosophical activity. It has been noted that Merleau-Ponty seems to suggest that metaphor, which lies between direct signification and silence, is most appropriate to philosophical discourse. At the very close of his final chapter, "The Intertwining—The Chiasm," in speaking of the nature of linguistic signification, he insists that meaning does not lie on words "like butter on the bread," but comprises the totality of what is said, including how, when, where, why, and by whom it is said. Thus, to speak of meaning "is in our view to form a metaphor. . . . In a sense the whole of philosophy . . . consists in restoring a power, a birth of meaning, or a wild meaning, and expression of experience by experience, which in particular clarifies the special domain of language" (p. 155).

Although he speaks of metaphor several times, it is not sufficiently clear what Merleau-Ponty's position is with regard to it. Moreover, whatever he says about it must be interpreted, as his own view of philosophy necessitates, against the background of his own *prolific use* of it throughout his philosophical writings. There are two additional passages in *The Visible and the Invisible* where he mentions metaphor specifically, and these must be considered in order to come to grips with its relation to his view of philosophy as an interrogative activity. For if the questions asked and the answers given by philosophy are to be indirect in character, to show rather than say how it is with reality, then the role of metaphor would seem to be a crucial one indeed!

In his final chapter Merleau-Ponty speaks of the relation between the body and the flesh of the world by means of a whole host of organic metaphors, such as "ontogenesis" and "pregnancy" (p. 136) and "leaves" and "flesh" (p. 137). He says:

> To speak of leaves or of layers is still to flatten and to juxtapose, under the reflexive gaze, what coexists within the living and upright body. If one wants metaphors, it would be better to say that the body sensed and the body sentient are as the averse and reverse, or again as two segments of one sole circular course which goes above from left to right and below from right to left, but which is but one sole movement in its two phases. (p. 138)

So on the one hand Merleau-Ponty speaks somewhat despairingly about metaphorical speech, while on the other he trades unashamedly in it, both here specifically and in his entire corpus generally.

This seeming ambivalence toward metaphor occurs again in the "Working Notes" section of *The Visible and the Invisible*:

> A "direction" of thought—This is not a *metaphor*—There is no *metaphor* between the visible and the invisible . . . *metaphor* is too much and too little; too much if the invisible is really invisible, too little if it lends itself to transposition. There is no metaphor: 1.) because thought involves a quasi-locality that has to be described . . . locality by elastic tie . . . by investment, and, when all that is said, there is theater of apparition of the other . . . 2.) because . . . a *direction* is not *in* space: it is in filigree across it—it is therefore transposable to thought. . . . (pp. 221–222)

Not only does he here explicitly rely on metaphorical images in the very process of seeming to deny their appropriateness, but the specific reasons he gives against their viability would seem, in fact, to be reasons for their indispensability to philosophical activity. Precisely because metaphor is both too little and too much, because the invisible is also in the visible and can be "transposed" into language, if only indirectly, it is both appropriate and necessary to the talk of philosophical interrogation. To quote Merleau-Ponty himself, from this very passage, metaphorical speech might be said to be the "theater of apparition" within which the invisible acts itself out, or the "filigree" by means of which it inscribes itself across but not within space.

Perhaps we can come closer to a full understanding of the place of metaphor in Merleau-Ponty's interrogative view of philosophy by shifting our attention to a final, major image he employs, namely that of the "chiasm." The title given to the final and most intriguing chapter of *The Visible and the Invisible* is "The Intertwining—The Chiasm." While a direct treatment of the content of this chapter must wait until the next section of our current discussion, some attention to the notion of "chiasm" will prove most helpful to our present concern with Merleau-Ponty's understanding of philosophy as interrogation, especially with respect to his view of the role of metaphor therein. In fact, although this term occurs in the title of Merleau-Ponty's last chapter, he does not use or discuss it at all within the chapter. One finds it used frequently, however, in the "Working Notes" at the end of *The Visible and the Invisible*, and it is to these that we now turn.

Most dictionaries mention two main meanings for the term *chiasm*. The first pertains to the coming together, or intersection of at least two separate entities. Thus the connection with the notion of "intertwining" in the title of Merleau-Ponty's final chapter. The second meaning of the term carries the connotation of reversal, as in the crisis or turning point of a story, or as in the surprising ending or twist in a proverbial saying or joke. Thus the phrase, "Last but not least" and the football coach's remark about his team, "We're not big but we're slow," may serve as brief examples of chiasm. The surprise ending of a Hitchcock film or Shakespearean drama would provide more involved examples.

In speaking about "true philosophy" Merleau-Ponty says that it must "apprehend what makes the leaving of oneself be a retiring into oneself, and vice versa. Grasp this chiasm, this reversal. That is the mind" (p. 199). He goes on to compare philosophy to a work of art, which "can arouse more thoughts than are 'contained' in it, retains a meaning only outside of that context" (p. 199). Here it would seem to be the two-sided or dual-directional character of the mind and philosophy that Merleau-Ponty is concerned with, as in the case of notions like "hollow," "horizon," and "flesh."

Later on, when speaking of the puzzle of the mind, which can be both conscious of itself and conscious of the world and others, he uses the term "chiasm" once more. Our world is private, in the sense that an individual's consciousness is not directly available to others, and yet public, in that we all participate in the same world, are all of the same "flesh." In short, by virtue of our embodiment we are both separate from and united with one another.

> By reason of this mediation through reversal, this chiasm, there is not simply a for-Oneself for-the-Other antithesis . . . that means that there is not only a me-other rivalry, but a co-functioning. We function as one unique body. . . . The chiasm is not only a me = other exchange . . . it is also an exchange between me and the world, between the phenomenal body and the "objective body," between the perceiving and the perceived: what begins as a thing ends as a consciousness of the thing, what begins as a "state of consciousness" ends as a thing. (p. 215)

The crucial point in speaking thus of the person's relation to him- or herself, the world, and others is to focus the simultaneous two–directional movement involved. The embodied person faces and acts in two dimensions at the same juncture of time and space, is both "inside" and "outside" of the body. Merleau-Ponty refers to this as a "double chiasm" (p. 215). As was mentioned above, it is this dual reversibility of human existence and experienced reality that "true philosophy" must grasp. This would seem to require that philosophy itself must take on a dual, and thus chiasmic, character as well. In fact, the very notion of philosophy as *interrogation* carries with it the two-way, vectorial pattern of question-and-answer, of dialogue. All of this fits well within the general scope of the relational, interactive quality of Merleau-Ponty's overall view of both reality and the philosophic enterprise.

Now, returning to the question of what form of language is most appropriate to expressing this dual character of both reality and philosophy, it would seem that only metaphor is adequate to the task. Only with metaphorical images are we able to speak of two realities simultaneously, in two directions and dimensions at once. Moreover, this form of speech frequently involves the sort of shock value or twist indicted by chiasm or reversibility. Not only does the general character of Merleau-Ponty's philosophical writing support this contention, but his specific remarks about language bear it out as well, as was discussed in the third section of the first chapter of the present study. In addition, in the "Working Notes" for *The Visible and the Invisible*, he specifically connects the image of chiasm with speech in a manner that suggests the viability if not the necessity of the metaphorical mode of philosophical activity.

Under the heading of "Chiasm—Reversibility" Merleau-Ponty says:

. . . speech does indeed have to enter the child as silence—break through to him through silence and as silence . . . silence = absence of the word due. It is this fecund negative that is instituted by the flesh, by its dehiscence—the negative, nothingness, is the doubled-up, the two leaves of my body, the inside and the outside articulated over one another—Nothingness is rather the difference between the identicals. . . . (p. 263)

He goes on in this same passage to speak of chiasm as "Reversibility: the finger of the glove that is turned inside out . . . there are two caverns, two opennesses, two stages where something will take place—and which both belong to the same world, to the stage of Being" (p. 263). Not only are these remarks themselves studded with images, they designate precisely the kind of "doubleness," the space between silence and mundane speech, required by philosophy and provided by metaphor.

Finally, on the very next page of the "Working Notes," Merleau-Ponty goes on to speak of this "doubling-up" quality of chiasmic reality and embodiment in terms that suggest the image of the double helix used to model the DNA molecule, the spiral twisting and overlapping that characterizes metaphorical speech. He then returns to the task of depicting philosophy as chiasmic activity: "*What* it says, its *significations*, are not absolutely invisible: it shows by words. Like all literature. It does not install in the reverse of the visible: it is on both sides" (p. 266). Here again we find a connection made between the language most appropriate to philosophy, its words, and that which stands at the intersection between the visible and the invisible, between regular speech and silence.

In this context we should also recall the parallels Merleau-Ponty draws between the arts, especially literature, and philosophy in his essay "Indirect Language and the Voices of Silence." Both must use language, but in a way that keeps its meaning, like a chemical compound, "in solution," neither as mere residue nor as gaseous effervescence. Only in images can this sort of meaning be communicated. We shall return to this topic in greater detail in Chapter 5. The major concern of the present section has been to portray Merleau-Ponty's view of philosophy as interrogation, as developed in the last two chapters of *The Visible and the Invisible*. The ongoing and necessary process of questioning the world about its meaning constitutes a kind of reversibility in both thought and speech, a double spiral of significance best concentrated in metaphorical images.

THE WORD AS FLESH

The most dramatic change in the images used by Merleau-Ponty over the span of his career hinges on the introduction of the notion of the flesh.

Although mentioned once or twice in a few of his essays, this notion only comes to center-stage in the latter part of *The Visible and the Invisible*, especially in the final chapter and in the "Working Notes." As mentioned earlier, the reader is hardly prepared for the intensity with which this metaphor, along with correlative biological images, dominates the concluding pages of Merleau-Ponty's final work. His use of the term "flesh" follows a complex and opaque pattern, making it what may well be the most difficult of all Merleau-Ponty's notions to trace.

Actually, the first and best clue to the predominance of this image of the flesh in Merleau-Ponty's thought is provided in the introduction to his collection of essays entitled *Signs*. This lengthy and interesting gloss on the themes within that volume was written in 1960, during the same period he was working on *The Visible and the Invisible*. Amidst the familiar pattern of such images as "field," "fabric," "horizon," and "wake" and "wave," Merleau-Ponty rather suddenly begins speaking in various ways of the "flesh of the world," the "flesh of history," and the "flesh of my flesh" (pp. 15–20). For the first time he seems to switch from stressing individual embodiment to emphasizing our natural connection, through embodiment, with both physical and social reality.

This emphasis on the flesh as the connecting fabric or tissue that binds us to the world and to one another first appears in the *The Visible and the Invisible* in Merleau-Ponty's critique of Bergsonian intuitionism. More specifically, it occurs within his account of the reciprocal, enfolding and all-encompassing character of human language (p. 118). A bit farther on, he remarks that "the presence of the world is precisely the presence of its flesh to my flesh, that I 'am of the world' and that I am not it . . . there is this thickness of flesh between us and the 'hard core' of Being . . ." (p. 127).

On the first page of his last chapter, in a discussion of the visible and the invisible (to which we shall return before long), Merleau-Ponty locates the image of flesh at the center of his summary of the dynamic of perceptual activity in particular and cognitive activity in general. He says:

> What there is then are not things first identical with themselves, which would then offer themselves to the seer who is first empty and who, afterward, would open himself to them—but something to which we could not be closer than by palpating it with our look, things we could not dream of seeing "all naked" because the gaze itself envelops them, clothes them with its own flesh. (p. 131)

In the notation accompanying this passage, Merleau-Ponty also speaks of "flesh being offered to flesh" and of "openness through flesh" (p. 131).

Once more we see the cognitive process illuminated by thinking of the knowing subject and the known object, not as separate entities that confront and discover each other, but as sharing a common nature, as various aspects or dimensions of the same living tissue, by means of which cognition takes place. In other words, Merleau-Ponty repeatedly insists that by virtue of our fleshly embodiment we are both in the world and of the world; thus our knowledge of it is mediated by means of our participation in it and thus perhaps more easily grasped, as in the case of our knowledge of social reality, both cultural and personal. Such cognition is not "added to" our participation in the social world, but it is both the basis and natural result of this participation. Being and knowing are but two aspects of the same reality; they are co-constitutive.

In another passage Merleau-Ponty speaks of "The look which envelops, palpates, espouses the visible things . . . which knew them before knowing them . . . so that finally one cannot say if it is the look or if it is the things that command" (p. 133). He goes on to explain this magical relation between the knower and the known in terms of "tactile palpation where the questioner and the questioned are closer" than in vision.

> This can happen only if my hand, while it is felt from within, is also accessible from without, itself, tangible, for my other hand, for example. . . . Through this crisscrossing, within it of the touching and the tangible, its own movements incorporate themselves into the universe they interrogate, are recorded on the same map as it. (p. 133)

Such is the nature of the relation of the knower to the known by virtue of their common flesh.

Merleau-Ponty returns to this idea of the reciprocal commonality of the flesh of the knower and the known several times in this last chapter. At one point he speaks of it in terms of the paradox of distance and proximity inherent within the cognitive process:

> . . . this distance is not the contrary of this proximity, it is deeply consonant with it, it is synonymous with it. It is that the thickness of flesh between the seer and the thing is constitutive for the thing of its visibility as for the seer of his corporeity; it is not an obstacle between them, it is their means of communication. (p. 135)

In another place he speaks of it in terms of the body's bipolar character:

> We say therefore that our body is a being of two leaves, from one side a thing among things and otherwise what sees them and touches them . . . it uses its own being as a means to participate in theirs, because each of the two beings is an archetype for the other, because the body belongs to the order of things as the world is universal flesh. (p. 137)

When focusing his attention directly on the images of the flesh Merleau-Ponty shifts to talking about it ontologically rather than epistemologically. He says,

To designate it, we should need the old term "element," in the sense it was used to speak of water, air, earth, and fire, that is, in the sense of *general thing*, midway between the spatio-temporal individual and the idea, a sort of incarnate principle that brings a style of being wherever there is a fragment of being. The flesh is in this sense an "element" of Being. (p. 139)

He continues a bit further along:

If we can show that the flesh is an ultimate notion, that it is not the union or compound of two substances, but thinkable itself, if there is a relation of the visible with itself that traverses me and constitutes me as a seer, this circle which I do not form, which forms me, this coiling over of the visible upon the visible, can traverse, animate other bodies as well as my own. (p. 140)

In these passages it is clear that Merleau-Ponty is not only using the notion of flesh in a metaphorical sense, but is extending it in a rather surprising, cosmic direction. He seems to want to speak of the flesh of the whole of reality in a way analogous to the way we might speak of the flesh of the whole body, as that within which all that *is* inheres. In this sense there seems to be an incorporeal as well as a corporeal significance to the image. As Merleau-Ponty himself says: "The flesh is not matter, in the sense of corpuscles of being which would add up or continue on one another to form beings . . . it is not a fact or sum of facts 'material' or 'spiritual' . . . the flesh is not matter, is not mind, is not substance" (p. 139). In this way he seeks to distinguish his own view of the basic matrix of reality from traditional metaphysical theories.

If there is any ontology to which Merleau-Ponty's interpretation of the flesh bears a resemblance it might well be that of Alfred North Whitehead's "process philosophy." In the thought of both of these thinkers there is a crucial emphasis, not only on the actual process of cognition as reflective of the very structure of reality, but on the convergence or bipolar character of the physical and mental or spiritual dimensions of that structure. The following remarks of Merleau-Ponty clearly exhibit these emphases:

Once again, the flesh we are speaking of is not matter. It is the coiling over of the visible upon the seeing body, of the tangible upon the touching body, which is attested in particular when the body sees itself, touches itself seeing and touching the things, such that, simultaneously, *as* tangible it descends among them, *as* touching it dominates them all and draws this relationship and even this double relationship from itself, by dehiscence or fission of its own mass. (p. 146)

In the "Working Notes," which presumably served as a sort of annotated outline from which Merleau-Ponty worked when writing *The Visible and the Invisible*, we find an excellent summary of what he is and is not trying to do by means of the image of the flesh. He *is* attempting to say:

. . . that my body is made of the same flesh as the world, and moreover that this flesh of my body is shared by the world, the world, *reflects* it, encroaches upon it and it encroaches upon the world. . . . This also means: my body is not only one perceived among others, it is the measurement of all, *Nullpunkt* of all the dimensions of the world. (p. 248)

At the same time, he is *not* saying that the flesh of the world is "explained" by the flesh of the body. "The flesh of the world is not *self-sensing* as is my flesh—it is sensible and not sentient—I call it flesh, nonetheless . . . in order to say that is a *pregnancy* of possibles . . . it is by the flesh of the world that in the last analysis one can understand the lived body" (p. 250). The nature and significance of human existence is not, therefore, understood only, or even primarily, on the basis of our understanding of the world. It is, rather, by virtue of our own commonality with the world that we are enabled to understand ourselves, as well as the world, and to be understood by the world of others as well.

All of these aspects or folds of our mutual "enfleshment" with the world are drawn together by Merleau-Ponty, in the last chapter of *The Visible and the Invisible*, by means of the image of "intertwining." This metaphor unifies both those images connected with "woven fabrics" and "threads," on the one hand, and those pertaining to the tissues and leaves of the body, on the other. In this sense, it is a metaphor with which we are already quite familiar. There are, however, two particular "twists" that Merleau-Ponty gives to this image, in this his last chapter, which serve to enrich it considerably. The first involves transposing it from two dimensions to three, while the second develops it in relation to artistic, especially musical composition.

When speaking of the dual foci of the body, of its knowing and being known, Merleau-Ponty says:

My body as a visible thing is contained within the full spectacle. But my seeing body subtends this visible body, and all the visibles with it. There is a reciprocal insertion and intertwining of one in the other. Or rather, if as once again we must, we eschew the thinking by planes and perspectives, there are two circles, or two vortexes, or two spheres, concentric when I live naively, and as soon as I question myself, the one slightly decentered with respect to the other. (p. 138)

This shift to a three-dimensional model of intertwining reminds one of the double helix image mentioned earlier. In addition, it is carried out in this last chapter with the images of "coiling," "currents," "enveloping," and "clothing." In one place Merleau-Ponty speaks of the relation between the knower and the known as "an intimacy as close as between the sea and the strand" (p. 130).

In like manner, when speaking of the reality of intangible aesthetic significance as intertwined within the tangible aspects of a given artistic medium, Merleau-Ponty insists that "the medium is the message," that intangible meanings do not hover "above" the tangible particulars.

> It is not only that we would find in that carnal experience the *occasion* to think them; it is that they owe their authority, their fascinating, indestructible power, precisely to the fact that they are in transparency behind the sensible, or in its heart. Each time we want to get them immediately, or lay hands on them, or circumscribe them, or see them unveiled, we do in fact feel that the attempt is misconceived, that they retreat in the measure that we approach. The explication does not give us the idea itself; it is but a second version of it, or more manageable derivative. (p. 150)

These particular "intertwining" images lead us directly to the very center of Merleau-Ponty's final work, namely to the relationship between "the visible and the invisible." This two-sided image emerges as the high-water mark of the chapter entitled "The Intertwining—The Chiasm," and thus deserves specific attention before bringing to a close our consideration of the use of metaphor in Merleau-Ponty's various writings. This theme is every bit as complex and comprehensive as the others have been.

First a note of clarification. The term 'visible" is used by Merleau-Ponty in three different senses, only one of which is of special concern here. It occurs in discussions of visual perception and as a way of designating the whole of physical reality. While both of these are, in a sense, included in the third use of the term, they are not its primary focus. This third use pertains to the relationship between tangible (the visible) and intangible (the invisible) reality, to the way the latter is somehow already within and/or mediated by the former. It is to this relationship that we must now direct our attention.

Near the close of the concluding chapter of *The Visible and the Invisible* Merleau-Ponty zeros in on the theme announced in this title in the following fashion:

> We touch here the most difficult point, that is, the bond between the flesh and the idea, between the visible and the interior armature which it manifests and which it concerns . . . the relations between the visible and the invisible . . . and idea that is not the contrary of the sensible, that is its lining and its depth. (p. 149)

He takes his lead here from Marcel Proust's treatment of "musical ideas" as representative of intangible reality in general, wherein "this invisible, these ideas, unlike those of science, cannot be detached from the sensible appearances and be erected into a second positivity" (p. 149).

It is clear that in Merleau-Ponty's mind, a proper understanding of intangible reality is not a matter of getting beyond, or behind, or beneath tangible reality. Rather, it is a matter of, as the title of Owen Barfields' book would have it, "saving the appearances"; they alone mediate the intangible. Earlier on he spoke of how the visible both "veils and unveils" the invisible (p. 131), and in this context he introduces the image of a screen. Whereas generally we think of knowledge of reality as the result of removing the screen of ignorance or illusion, thereby allowing us to "dis-cover" the truth, "Here, on the contrary, there is no vision without the screening: the ideas we are speaking of would not be better known to us if we had no body and no sensibility; it is then that they would be inaccessible to us" (p. 150).

What Merleau-Ponty seems to be aiming at here is an understanding of the reality of the invisible as within the visible, as more or other than it without in any way being beyond it, as being a function of the tangible without being reducible to it. In this connection he frequently employs the image of simultaneously interpenetrating "dimensions" in order to convey the notion of mediation, of one dimension being experienced and known in and through the other. Here he speaks of the idea of the invisible as the all-inclusive level or dimension that endows the various aspects of the visible with meaning.

> The idea is this level, this dimension. It is therefore not a *de facto* invisible, like an object hidden behind another, and not an absolute invisible, which would have nothing to do with the visible. Rather, it is the invisible *of* this world, that which inhabits this world, sustains it, and renders it visible, its own and interior possibility, the Being of this being. (p. 151)

It is in the "Working Notes" for this chapter that Merleau-Ponty speaks most often, if somewhat cryptically, about the relation between the visible and the invisible. More specifically, it is there that he ties this sort of imagery to the notions of meaning and transcendence. The former notion is incorporated in the following manner:

> Meaning is *invisible*, but the invisible is not the contradictory of the visible: the visible itself has an invisible inner framework . . . and the invisible is the secret counterpart of the visible, it appears only within it . . . is presented to me as such within the world—one cannot see it there and every effort to *see it there* makes it disappear, but it is *in the line* of the visible, it is its virtual focus, it is inscribed within it (filigree). (p. 215)

Frequently, especially in the "Working Notes," Merleau-Ponty uses the visible-invisible imagery in connection with the metaphors of the "vertical," "depth," and "ground" by relating it to the notion of transcendence or Being. While this is not the place to go into the metaphysical ramifications of Merleau-Ponty's philosophy of embodiment (a task we shall at least address in Chapter 6), some indication of the import of this connection is surely in order. There is a straightforward sense in which Merleau-Ponty identifies the invisible with the transcendent when he speaks of it as the "vertical," the "depth," and the "ground" of the visible. Furthermore, he occasionally uses the terms "invisible" and "transcendent" interchangeably, as the ensuing quotations will make clear.

For Merleau-Ponty, however, the transcendent, the vertical, is always mediated by means of the horizontal, the mundane, and thus cannot be thought of or known apart from it. As he puts it:

> The essence, likewise, is an inner framework, it is not above the sensible world, it is beneath, or in its depth, its thickness. It is the secret bond . . . with transcendence I show that the visible is invisible, *that vision is in principle what convinces me by an appearance already-there that there is no room to seek a proximal being.* . . . This invisible of the visible is then what enables me to rediscover in productive thought all the structures of vision. . . ." (p. 220)

This concept of transcendence is quite distinct from those of traditional philosophy or theology, since for Merleau-Ponty it makes no sense to speak of the visible or the invisible as being ever, in any sense, separate from each other. Nonetheless the one inheres within the other, providing its meaning and structure, and can be experienced and known, albeit indirectly and tacitly.

The anti-metaphysical bent of Merleau-Ponty's way of dealing with the transcendent, of seeing it as a dimension of the here-and-now rather than as a world of its own, can be seen in the following remarks:

> . . . principle: not to consider the invisible as an *other visible* "possible," or a "possible" visible for another: that would be to destroy the inner framework that joins it. Moreover since this "other" who would "see" it—or this "other world" it would constitute—would necessarily be connected to our own, the true possibility would necessarily reappear within this connection. The invisible is *there* without being an *object*, it is pure transcendence, without an ontic mask. (p. 229)

This way of putting the matter constitutes a denial of the very meaningfulness of the idea of a transcendence that exists independently of our cognitive relation to the mundane world, since even this idea must arise within and as a result of our common cognitive activity.

Merleau-Ponty approaches this mediational relation between the visible and the invisible from a slightly different angle when he speaks of it in terms of the images of "absence" or "negativity." Under the heading, "The Invisible, the Negative, Vertical Being," he makes the following comments:

> A certain relation between the visible and the invisible, where the invisible is not only non-visible . . . but where its absence counts in the world (it is "behind" the visible, imminent or eminent visibility . . . as another dimension) where the lacuna that marks its place is one of the

points of passage of the "world." It is this negative that makes possible the *vertical* world, the union of the incompossibles, the being in transcendence, and the topological space and time in joints and member . . . and the male-female (the two pieces of wood that children see fitting together of themselves, irresistibly, because each is the possible of the other). (pp. 227–228)

Later on Merleau-Ponty returns to this image of negativity, managing to avoid the tortured intricacies of Heideggerian and Sartrean analysis, while nonetheless stressing the viability of the transcendent within the visible. He insightfully suggests that there is an error that lies beneath the error of conceiving of the invisible or transcendent dualistically, as "beyond" the mundane, as "spiritual" rather than as merely "physical." This is the error of first conceiving of the visible as an "objective positive," as a reality that exists independently of human experience and is capable of being understood by objective analysis (p. 258). When the visible and the invisible, the mundane and the transcendent, are initially conceived of as symbiotic dimensions of each other, the need to define the latter as the negation or denial of the former does not arise. The transcendent can encompass the mundane without being "beyond" it, in the same way the horizon encompasses the visual field without in any sense being "outside" of it. Merleau-Ponty expresses it this way: "This negation-reference is common to all the *invisibles* because the visible has been defined as dimensionality of Being, i.e. as universal, and because therefore everything that is not a *part* of it is necessarily *enveloped in it* and is but a modality of the same transcendence" (p. 257).

While it is true that for Merleau-Ponty it is philosophy, as interrogation, that is best suited to trace the invisible in the visible, it is also true that all levels of human existence and cognition are capable of such discernment, since it is their very ground or structure.

This discernment occurs in, through, and by virtue of our embodiment in and of the flesh of the world. As Merleau-Ponty says near the end of his "Working Notes":

My body *in* the visible. This does not simply mean: it is a particle of the *visible*, there is the visible and here (as variant of the there) is my body. No. It is *surrounded* by the visible. This does not take place on a plane of which it would be an inlay, it is really surrounded, circumvented. This means: it sees itself, it is a visible—but it sees itself seeing, my look which finds it *there* knows that it is here, at its own side—Thus the body *stands* before the world and the world upright before it, and between them there is a relation that is one of embrace. And between these two vertical beings, there is not a frontier, but a contact surface. (pp. 270–271)

Thus in a sense we have come full circle. We began our examination of Merleau-Ponty's use of metaphor by focusing on the role of embodiment as presented in *Phenomenology of Perception*. After tracing the implications of this axial notion to broader, cultural issues and themes in his essays, we concluded with an exploration of the metaphorical "explosion" that comprises his final work, *The Visible and the Invisible*. The powerful and interrelated images that animate these pages, especially that of the flesh as the symbiosis of the visible and the invisible, once again return us to the somatic quality of human existence and cognitive activity. In Part Two we shall turn our attention to the significance of Merleau-Ponty's characteristic use of the metaphoric mode for shaping an understanding of his view of language, metaphor, and philosophy, respectively.

PART TWO

THE MEANING OF
METAPHOR

4

LANGUAGE AS GESTURE

The previous chapters locate and trace the main metaphors used by Merleau-Ponty in his major works. The question before us now is, "What is the significance of his use of metaphor for understanding his views of language, metaphor itself, and philosophical activity, respectively?" The following chapters will focus on these three aspects of Merleau-Ponty's philosophy, each of which leads to the next. In this chapter consider the somatic basis and character of Merleau-Ponty's view of language, centered in the notions of embodiment and gesture. It may prove helpful to begin with a brief account of what he says language is *not*.

WHAT SPEECH IS NOT

From the outset, in his chapter on language in *Phenomenology and Perception* (Chapter 6), Merleau-Ponty stood opposed to what in analytical circles has come to be called the "picture theory" of meaning. According to this theory, language comprises a collection of words that *name* various objects, qualities, and relationships in the world. When put into statement or propositional form these names (or labels) are said to mirror the states of affairs comprising the world. If it is accurate, the proposition is judged to be "true," and if not it is judged to be "false." Thus, for example, the statement, "This book is green and belongs to Ralph" comprises the names "this book," "green," and "belongs to Ralph." If the logic or structure of this statement corresponds to the structure of the facts pertaining to the things it names, then it is a "true" statement—and if not, it is not.

Generally speaking, there are two main ways this theory can be applied to linguistic activity. On the one hand, it is sometimes claimed, especially by empirically minded thinkers, that the purpose of speech is to picture facts as they exist external to the speaker and hearer. Thus speech is about the "world" in the sense of seeking to represent the relationships among the various elements of sensory experience. In this view language is essentially optional and/or arbitrary in relation to the world; that is, how things "are" is entirely independent of speech. In short, according to this understanding of language, first we experience and know the world, and then, if we choose, we speak about it. So meaning is a function of representation, and truth is a matter of doing so accurately.

On the other hand, there are those who interpret the "picture theory" of meaning as pertaining to our efforts to express or represent our inner thoughts. Thinkers who follow a rationalist approach generally affirm the purpose of speech to be that of making our private thoughts public, of encoding our ideas and intentions into a conventional symbol system in order to communicate them to others. Here what is "pictured" are not facts in the world external to one's mind, but the very content and structure of the speaker's thoughts. Thus the statement, "This book is green and belongs to Ralph" represents the mind or belief of the speaker; this is its purpose and meaning. The truth of this statement or belief is dependent on the public facts concerning the book and Ralph in question, but its meaning is the thought of the speaker. When a statement is actually about the content of the speaker's mind, such as with the statement, "I believe this book is green and belongs to Ralph," then even its truth is a function of whatever is in the speaker's mind.

Once more, language is viewed as essentially optional and arbitrary to that which it is said to be about. We are interpreted as being capable of thinking our thoughts in and of themselves, quite apart from whether or not we choose to express them in speech. Thus, language is once again seen as an external "overlay" or artificial representation of mental activity. Human life is conceived as going on pretty much as we know it quite apart from language, only less complexly and efficiently. As Merleau-Ponty in *Phenomenology and Perception* (pp. 176–177) puts it: "The word is still bereft of any effectiveness of its own, this time because it is only the external sign of an internal recognition, which could take place without it, and to which it makes no contribution . . . it is thought which has meaning, the word remaining an empty container."

Over against both empiricism and intellectualism, Merleau-Ponty insists that both views rob language of its significance: "In the first case, we are on this side of the word as meaningful; in the second, there is certainly a subject, but a thinking one, not a speaking one" (p. 177). Language serves as the network of "intentional threads" that ties our thoughts and the physical world together within the common fabric of our embodied and interactive life together. Language is primordial in that it calls forth or constitutes both the world and our thought; it is the matrix or loom from within which both our physical and mental lives arise. Without speech neither we nor the world would be "human." But for the present, let us return to what language is *not*.

Not only is speech not a representation of the world or of internal thought, but thought itself, according to Merleau-Ponty, is not a representation of the things in the world. Under normal circumstances a person does not think first and then speak about the world. Rather, one simply speaks and thinks at the same time; or better yet, one thinks through one's speech. "We must recognize first of all that thought, in the speaking subject, is not a representation, that is, that it does not expressly posit objects or relations. The orator does not think before speaking, nor even while speaking; his speech is his thought" (p. 180). Thus our relationship to speech is much the same as our relationship to our bodies: we indwell language in the same way as we indwell our bodies, and through them both we indwell the world.

> I do not need to visualize external space and my own body in order to move one within the other. . . . In the same way I do not need to visualize the word in order to know and pronounce it . . . the word has a certain location in my linguistic world, and is part of my equipment. (p. 180)

There is a reductionistic thrust to nearly all linguistic philosophy as developed and practiced in English-speaking countries in the twentieth century. The assumption that the main function of speech is to represent the world naturally leads to the conclusion that language can be completely understood and explained as a mosaic of basic building blocks placed in various and frequently complex patterns. The fundamental mistake here, in Merleau-Ponty's view, is to suppose that ideally words have only one meaning, that a given sign "stands for" or designates one separate and identifiable feature of reality. This applies even to the language of philosophical activity.

> One can reduce philosophy to a linguistic analysis only by supposing that language has its evidence within itself, that the signification of the word "world" or "thing" presents in principle no difficulty, that the rules for the legitimate use of the word can be clearly read in a univocal significa- tion. But the linguists teach us that this is precisely not the case, that the univocal signification is but one part of the signification of the word, that beyond it there is always a halo of signification that manifests itself in new and unexpected modes of use, that there is an operation of language upon language, which even without other incitements, would launch language back into a new history, and makes of the word-meaning itself an enigma. (*The Visible and the Invisible*, p. 96; hereafter *VI*).

Another way to approach the issues involved in Merleau-Ponty's under-standing of what language is *not* is by way of the distinction between ends and means. Those who philosophize about the nature and function of speech from an empiricist perspective frequently do so by speaking of it as the means by which we achieve the desired ends of expressing thought and/or effecting actions in the world. On the other hand, those who theorize about language from what might be called the "poetic" perspective often overstress the "orphic" or creative function of language as a kind of end in itself, since the world is said to arise and align itself in relation to and as a result of speech.

Over against both of these opposing views, Merleau-Ponty stresses the symbiotic character of speech and signification:

> We must therefore say the same thing about language in relation to meaning that Simone de Beauvoir says about the body in relation to mind: it is neither primary nor secondary. No one has ever made the body simply a means or an instrument, or maintained for example that one can love by principle. And since it is no more true that the body loves all by itself, we may say that it does everything and nothing, that it is and is not ourselves. Neither end nor means . . . similarly, language is not meaning's servant, and yet it does not govern meaning. There is no subordination between them. Here no one commands and no one obeys. What we *mean* is not before us, outside all speech, as sheer signification, it is only the excess of what we live over what has already been said. With our apparatus of expression we set ourselves up in a situation the ap-paratus is sensitive to, we confront it with the situation, and our state-ments are only the final balance of these exchanges. (*Signs*, p. 83)

Yet another way by which Merleau-Ponty seeks to counteract the re-ductionist tendencies or the philosophical account of language is in terms of the distinction between wholes and parts. Not only do individual words and sentences not function as the individual building blocks out of which the mosaic of meaning is constructed, but meanings themselves do not comprise or encompass the overall significance of speech itself. As the Gestalt psychologists would have it, the whole of meaning is greater or other than the mere compilation of its parts.

> By coming back to spoken or living language we shall find that its expressive value is not the sum of the expressive values which allegedly belong individually to each element of the "verbal chain." On the contrary, these elements form a system in synchrony in the sense that each of them signifies only its difference in respect to the others . . . and as this is true of them all, there are only differences of signification in a language. The reason why a language finally intends to say and does say something is not that each sign is the vehicle for a signification which allegedly belongs to it, but that all the signs

together allude to a signification which is always in abeyance when they are considered singly, and which I go beyond them toward without their ever containing it. (*Signs*, p. 83)

In addition to his critique of the approach to language offered by linguistic analysis, Merleau-Ponty also engages in an examination and critique of Husserl's phenomenological approach to language. He suggests that although in his earlier works Husserl sought an "objective" vantage point from which to understand the world, including speech, in his later, more mature writings he came to admit the naïveté of such a program. Thus rather than bracketing meaning and significance off from the actual uses of language, and especially from its philosophical use, Merleau-Ponty argues that Husserl acknowledged that even the philosopher can only function from where he or she is situated, namely from within the web of meaning provided by language itself. In Husserl's own terms, the "phenomena of lived experience" can be known only in and through speech and embodiment; they cannot be made to stand alone, as it were, outside of our own "intentional consciousness" and relational activity.

Here is how Merleau-Ponty puts it:

When in the second part of his career Husserl returns to the problems of history, and especially to the problem of language, we no longer find the idea of a philosopher-subject, master of all that is possible, who must first put *his own* language at a distance in order to find the ideal forms of a universal language this side of all actuality. Philosophy's first task in respect to language now appears to be to reveal to us anew our inherence in a certain system of speech of which we make fully efficacious use precisely because it is present to us just as immediately as our body. Philosophy of language is no longer contracted to empirical linguistics as an attempt at total objectification of language to a science which is always threatened by the preconceptions of the native language. On the contrary, it has become the rediscovery of the subject in the act of speaking, as contrasted to a science of language which inevitably treats this subject as a thing. . . . The philosopher is first and foremost the one who realizes that he is situated in language, that he *is speaking*; and phenomenological reflection can no longer be limited to a completely lucid enumeration of the "conditions" without which there would no language. (*Signs*, p. 104)

One further gloss on what language is *not* according to Merleau-Ponty is provided by a consideration of the obvious point that meaning is not a private matter. Thus both the attempt to transcend the "subjective" point of view by providing a completely "objective" account of speech, and the effort to reduce the objective dimension of language to a merely personal, subjective phenomenon must be set aside. Language, after all, is and can only be something that arises and is carried on *among* speakers; in short, it is a social activity and can only be understood within the context of shared human activity. In other words, language, like all of human existence, is a relational reality and as such can only be approached holistically and dynamically. Meaning can be grasped, neither objectively nor subjectively, but only "intersubjectively."

Merleau-Ponty summarizes this point in the following fashion:

> Thus the proper function of a phenomenological philosophy seems to us to be to establish itself definitively in the order of instructive spontaneity that is inaccessible to psychologism and historicism no less than to dogmatic metaphysics. The phenomenology of speech is among all others best suited to reveal this order to us. When I speak or understand, I experience that presence of others in myself or of myself in others which is the stumbling-block of the theory of intersubjectivity, I experience that presence of what is represented which is the stumbling-block of the theory of time, and I finally understand what is meant by Husserl's enigmatic statement, "Transcendental subjectivity is intersubjectivity." To the extent that what I say has meaning, I am a different "other" for myself when I am speaking; and to the extent that I understand, I no longer know who is speaking and who is listening. (*Signs*, p. 97)

As we speak, and listen, then, we are not separated from each other like two prisoners tapping a code to each other through a wall. Rather, we are like two swimmers or dancers caught up in the waves and rhythms of a common medium, riding on and sharing in its patterns even as we contribute to and create them. In Yeats' image, we are unable to distinguish "the dancer from the dance," because as Heidegger put it, "we speak at home not only to *be* understood, but *because* we are understood."

It is against this backdrop of what speech is *not* that Merleau-Ponty develops his own account of what it *is*. His positive treatment of the nature of language may be understood as having two sides, each of which is the converse of the other. On the one hand, Merleau-Ponty considers human embodiment itself as a form of speech, while on the other hand he treats speech as a form of human embodiment. We shall now turn our attention to these two sides or aspects of the phenomenon known as language.

EMBODIMENT AS SPEECH

There is an inverse of J. L. Austin's famous title, *How to Do Things with Words*, which is every bit as important: "How to say things without words." We shall use the latter as the theme for this section of the present chapter, saving the former for the next section. There are, indeed, many ways to speak without using language *per se*, and Merleau-Ponty's philosophy of embodiment focuses this particular possibility. Our very way of being in the world (i.e. in and as a body) speaks volumes about the world and thus about the nature of speech as well. Our presence amid the spatial and temporal horizons constituted by our embodiment situates us within the field or world known by means of relational interaction. In this way our very existence already comprises a medium of communication; our embodiment functions as a form of speech. "The body is the vehicle of being in the world, and having a body is, for a living creature, to be intervolved in a definite environment, to identify oneself with certain projects and be continually committed to them" (*Phenomenology of Perception*, p. 82; hereafter *PER*).

To begin with, our body serves "as our means of communication with the world" (p. 92). Our consciousness is itself a holding "of inner communication with the world, the body and other people, to be with them instead of being beside them" (p. 96). To be more specific, one's very posture or position in space constitutes and expresses an "attitude" or angle of approach toward the world that tacitly says: "This is where and who I am, and this is what I am up to." "The word 'here' applied to my body does not refer to a determinate position in relation to other positions or to external coordinates, but the laying down of the first coordinates, the anchoring of the active body and an object, the situation of a body in face of its tasks" (p. 100). To be still more specific, our individual and concrete movements in time and space in relation to various objects and other persons clearly indicate what we take them as and how we value or devalue them. Our consciousness is always consciousness of something, and this vectorial thrust communicates our intentions as persons in the world.

The actual dynamics by means of which this sort of somatic communication functions is likened by Merleau-Ponty to those of artistic expression. The focal concept here is that of mediation or what some thinkers call "supervenience." "In a picture or a piece of music the idea is incommunicable by means other than the display of colours and sounds. . . . Just as the spoken word is significant not only through the medium of individual words, but also through that of accent, intonation, gesture and facial expression" (pp. 150–151). In other words, the meaning of the intangible reality comes to us in and through the particulars constituting the tangible reality that serves as a mediating medium. To put it a bit differently, these intangible realities are supervenient to or on their tangible counterparts in that they are more or other than them, while being unknowable apart from them. Conversely, the intangible reality or meaning is dependent on such tangible particulars without being reducible to them.

Merleau-Ponty extends this analogy between expression in the arts and that of the body in the following remarks:

> A novel, poem, picture or musical work are individuals, that is, beings in which the expression is indistinguishable from the thing expressed, their meaning, accessible only through direct contact, being radiated with no change of their temporal and spatial situation. It is in this sense that our body is comparable to a work of art. It is a nexus of living meanings, not the function of a certain number of mutually variable terms. (*PER*, p. 151)

Since it is as embodied selves that we take up our place at the axis of our world as experienced, the body itself serves as the chief means of expression, or "radiation," of the nature and meaning of human existence. Thus embodiment functions as a mode of communication, as a form of speech.

In his discussion of "The Body in its Sexual Being," Merleau-Ponty develops this notion of somatic signification in a slightly different manner. Here he speaks of embodiment as the very foundation of medium, or better still, the loom upon and within which our more commonly understood forms of communication arise and take on meaning. Because we all share similar embodiment, we "understand" each other as fellow humans, even when we do not understand each other's speech. In fact, it is because of this primordial, somatic comprehension that we are able to come to understand one another's natural or even artificial languages. This can be seen ever so clearly from the fact that all newborn infants are spoken to from the outset as if they understand speech, and it is only because of this that they eventually come to understand and engage in speech themselves. The fulcrum for this quantum leap from square zero to square one, linguistically speaking, is our common embodiment, our tacit awareness that the infant is "bone of our bone, flesh of our flesh," and vice versa.

Here is how Merleau-Ponty summarizes his point:

> If we therefore say that the body expresses existence at every moment, this is in the sense in which a word expresses thought. Anterior to conventional means of expression, which reveal my thoughts to others only because already, for both myself and them, meanings are provided for each sign, and which in this sense do not give rise to genuine communication at all, we must, as we shall see, recognize a primary process of signification in which the thing expressed does not exist apart from the expression, and in which the signs themselves induce their significance externally. In this way the body expresses total existence, not because it is an external accompaniment to that existence, but because existence comes into its own in the body. This incarnate significance is the central phenomenon of which body and mind, sign and significance are abstract moments. (*PER*, p. 166)

Linguistic communication, then, is a sort of "language within a language," since it originates within and can only be sustained by the embodied commonality of the human form of life. As Wittgenstein put it, "if a lion could speak, would we not understand him.

On the basis of the preceding understanding of the nature of bodily expression, Merleau-Ponty turns his attention (in his chapter on "The Body as Expressions and Speech") more directly to the nature of linguistic communication proper. He begins by drawing a parallel between the way in which we employ our body as a means of expressing our intentions in the world and the way we use speech as an instrument of action. "Thus speech, in the speaker, does not translate ready-made thought, but accomplishes it" (*PER*, p. 178). Both bodily and linguistic expression take on significance only within the context of action, providing a kind of "gestural meaning" through participation in shared tasks, and so on. Here, again, we encounter the parallel to aesthetic significance and communication:

> Aesthetic expression confers on what it expresses an existence in itself, installs it in nature as a thing perceived and accessible to all, or conversely plucks the things themselves—the person of the actor, or the colours and canvas of the painter—from their empirical existence and bears them off into another world. (p. 183)

This sort of analogy is extended by Merleau-Ponty to the analysis of emotional significance as communicated by bodily expression and gesture.

> One can see what there is in common between the gesture and its meaning, for example in the case of emotional expression and the emotions themselves: the smile, the relaxed face, gaiety of gesture really have in them the rhythm of action, the mode of being in the world which are joy itself. (p. 186)

So, too, with linguistic meaning; the significance of the words does not lie *behind* the words, but rather it lies *within* them in relation to behavior.

> The link between the word and its living meaning is not an external link of association, the meaning inhabits the word, and language is not an external accompaniment to intellectual processes. We are therefore led to recognize a gestural or existential significance in speech, as we have already said. Language certainly has an inner content, but this is not self-subsistent and self-conscious thought. What then does language express, if it does not express thoughts? It presents or rather it *is* the subject's taking up of a position in the world of his meanings. The term "world" here is not a manner of speaking: it means that the "mental" or cultural life borrows its structure from natural life and that the thinking subject must have its basis in the subject incarnate. (p. 193)

In this way Merleau-Ponty answers the traditional question concerning the relationship between languages, as "constituted systems of vocabulary

I do not see anger of a threatening attitude as a psychic fact hidden behind the gesture, I read anger in it. The gesture is not perceived. . . . The sense of the gesture is not given, but understood, that is, recaptured upon by an act on the spectator's part . . . the communication of comprehension of gestures comes about through the reciprocity of my intentions and gestures of others, of my gestures and the intentions discernible in the conduct of other people. (*PER*, pp. 184–185)

Again, Merleau-Ponty falls back on the reality of our common embodiment to explain our mutual understanding. Because we live in the same world in the same somatic fashion, we are granted a kind of *pre*-understanding or *proto*-understanding that enables us, indeed compels us, to move from square zero to square one, linguistically speaking. This movement is not a result of intellectual interpretation; rather,

communication between consciousnesses is not based on the common meaning of their respective experiences, for it is equally the basis of that meaning. The act by which I lead myself to the spectacle must be recognized as irreducible to anything else. I join it in a kind of blind recognition which precedes the intellectual working out and clarification of the meaning. (*PER*, p. 185)

Indeed, it is this very "blind recognition" that renders subsequent intellectual interpretation possible in the first place; the former is thus "logically prior" to the latter. Such understanding is possible because we, even as newborn infants, tacitly recognize ourselves in the other, and vice versa, through our common embodiment. We do not learn that we have such a shared somatic axis; rather, we are able to learn everything else (and at all!) because we have it. We do not move from sensory observation and inductive inference to the idea that there are other persons in the world. Instead, on the basis of our recognition of other persons imbedded in our common embodiment, we are enabled to perceive the world as such and to construct inferences and concepts about it. As Merleau-Ponty expresses it:

It is through my body that I understand other people, just as it is through my body that I perceive "things." The meaning of a gesture thus "understood" is not behind it, it is intermingled with the structure of the world outlined by the gesture, and which I take up on my own account. It is arrayed all over the gesture itself. . . . The linguistic gesture, like all the rest, delineates its own meaning. (*PER*, p. 186)

Merleau-Ponty builds his understanding of linguistic meaning, of speech proper (which will be taken up more directly in the next section) on the basis of this understanding of gestural meaning. For he sees speech as a highly articulate and conventionalized form of somatic behavior. "The spoken word is a genuine gesture, and it contains its meaning in the same way as the gesture contains it" (p. 184). The backdrop against which the

and syntax," and speech, as ongoing creative expression (p. 193). He views the former as "both the repository and the residue" of the latter. Each uses the other to constitute and develop itself. Every speaker speaks within already existing languages, but it is equally true that such languages are themselves the result of previous speech acts. Ultimately, neither comes before the other; they exist in a symbiotic, reciprocal relationship to each other, each depending on the other for its reality and continuation. The only real resolution to this "chicken-or-egg" dilemma, according to Merleau-Ponty, is to acknowledge the primordial character of language in relation to the human form of life. "Everything is both manufactured and natural in man, as it were, in the sense that there is not a word, not a form of behavior which does not owe something to purely biological being—and which at the same time does not elude the simplicity of animal life (p. 189).

This general motif of the axial quality of embodiment to human signification serves as Merleau-Ponty's point of departure for his approach to our knowledge of the physical world, other persons, and social reality as meaningful dimensions of human experience. Natural objects, for instance, are encountered *as such*, as comprehendable entities within our cognitive framework, by means of a kind of "semantics of perception."

The object which presents itself to the gaze or the touch arouses a certain motor intention which aims not at the movements of one's own body, but at the thing itself from which they are, as it were, suspended. And in so far as my hand knows hardness and softness, and my gaze knows the moon's light, it is as a certain way of linking up with phenomenon and communication with it. (*PER*, p. 317)

As has been noted previously, the metaphorical image is Merleau-Ponty's pivotal means of treating all forms of cognition, including that of physical reality.

He takes essentially the same tack when addressing the nature of the relationship between our selves and other selves, what he calls "The Human World." Language, both literally and figuratively, is the key to understanding our knowledge of other persons.

In the experience of dialogue, there is constituted between the other person and myself a common ground; my thought and his are interwoven into a single fabric, my words and those of my interlocutor are called forth by the state of the discussion, and they are inserted into a shared operation of which neither of us is the creator. We have a dual being, where the other is for me no longer a mere bit of behavior in my transcendental field, nor I in his; we are collaborators for each other in consummate reciprocity. Our perspectives merge into each other, and we co-exist through a common world. . . . In present dialogue. . . . (*PER*, p. 354)

Thus speech is to be understood once again as a kind of "language within a language," only this time the backdrop or framework is the interrelationship between individual persons, whereas previously it was that of a common embodied humanity.

Also, and perhaps especially, there is our perception and understanding of the broader and more complex aspects of social reality, what might be called "the cultural world." Language itself, as well as government, education, religion, and the like, is part of this level of social reality. Yet all of these are encountered and comprehended in and through our embodied activity.

> Our body, to the extent that it moves itself about, that is, to the extent that it is inseparable from a view of the world and is that view itself brought into existence, is the condition of possibility . . . of all expressive operations and all acquired views which constitute the cultural world. (*PER*, p. 388)

Hubert Dreyfus makes this same point, borrowing from Merleau-Ponty, in his book, *What Computers Can't Do* (pp. 248–255). He argues that the reason computers cannot be said to think is not because they do not have minds, but because they do not have active bodies whereby they can enter into the vast and vastly complex modes of behavior that constitute the human cultural world.

At the absolute center of Merleau-Ponty's understanding of embodiment as the axis around which all human linguistic activity revolves stands the notion of gesture. At the most fundamental or primordial level, language is a mode of physical behavior, whether in relation to the sound-producing mechanisms of our upper body or to the movements of our facial muscles, shoulders, arms, and hands. Even posture and gait, as well as sitting and standing (or refusing to do so), speak eloquently within various contexts. In the final analysis, the discernment of meaning, whether at the infantile or adult level, is dependent on our ability to comprehend the significance of physical sounds and movements in relation to broader behavior patterns and environmental settings. Merleau-Ponty speaks of "gestural meaning," which is imminent in speech (*PER*, p. 179).

Two obvious examples of the crucial role played by gestures in the expression and grasping of linguistic meaning are the child's acquisition of its native language and the adult's acquisition of a foreign language. In the former case, the infant begins to "read" the parent's facial expression, tone and inflection of voice, as well as body movements (touching, cuddling, etc.) from the moment of birth (or before!) without any knowledge or previous experience of vocabulary or rules of grammar whatsoever. An infant recognizes a smile, its mother's face and voice, and even responds to and imitates these phenomena within a matter of days. Soon, various

patterns of behavior, and even facial and tonal "games" are established (songs, patty-cake, etc.) that provide the warp across which the weft of language *per se* (i.e., vocabulary, syntax, etc.) is woven. The resulting fabric of speech thus comprises the interlocking of these patterns and developments, with gesture providing the anchor or fulcrum for the entire process.

In like manner, when we as adults take on the learning of a language other than our native tongue, especially in a context where this language is the primary or only means of communication, gestural meaning comes to the fore. Often we come to "understand" and even use an expression of whose literal or dictionary definition we are completely ignorant. We do this by keying off of the context and by reading tones, facial expressions, and bodily movements. All linguistic communication presupposes a more fundamental mode of understanding that, as Merleau-Ponty has repeatedly stressed, is provided by our common embodiment. Even though they are to a significant degree culturally determined, and thus we frequently "misread" them, gestures provide the pivot-point around which this primordial mode of understanding, and even the recognition and correction of misunderstandings, revolve. In this way, speech is a natural extension of embodied existence.

> The body converts a certain motor essence into vocal form, spreads out the articulatory style of a word into audible phenomena, and arrays the former attitude, which is resumed, into the panorama of the past, projecting an intention to move into actual movement, because the body is a power of natural expression. (*PER*, p. 181)

Permit me to offer an illustration of the crucial role of gesture in linguistic communication. A number of years ago on public television, Joseph Papp demonstrated the significance of gesture to expression in the following two ways. First, he asked a group of actors to deliver various lines striking a posture that was antithetical to the conventional meaning of the lines. Not only did this produce a strange response in the viewer, it caused a good deal of cognitive dissonance in the actors as well. Second, Papp presented a simple hand gesture while uttering a series of statements that provided different linguistic contexts for the gesture. Thus with little or no variation in the positioning of his hand, he was able to say such diverse things as: (1) "Everything is A-OK," (2) "What an exquisite jewel," (3) "Where shall I put this filthy sock?" (4) "What a lovely flavor of tea," (5) "There I was looking through the key-hole," and so on. Even the way one wears a pair of glasses, especially if you are a teacher, allows for a wide variety of significations!

So far we have been discussing the expressive dimension of gestural meaning. Let us now consider how such meaning is understood by the prehender. Here Merleau-Ponty says:

gesture of speech takes on meaning is, of course, silence; even as the backdrop for gestural meaning is inertness.

> We become unaware of the contingent element in expression and communication, whether it be in the child learning to speak, or in the writer saying and thinking something for the first time, in short, in all who transform a certain kind of silence into speech. It is, however, quite clear that constituted speech, operates in daily life, assumes that the decisive step of expression has been taken. Our view of man will remain superficial so long as we fail to go back to that origin, so long as we fail to find, beneath the chatter of words, the primordial silence, and as long as we do not describe the action which breaks the silence. The spoken word is a gesture, and its meaning, a world. (*PER*, p. 184)

Merleau-Ponty frequently explores the various ways in which speech can go wrong, as with aphasia, in order to discover what it means for it to go right, and thereby ascertain what is. The aphasic person has not simply lost the ability to remember or form associations between words and things. Rather, what is lost is a "sense of place" in the world, an ability to use language in the give-and-take of everyday life.

> We are therefore led to recognize a gestural or existential significance in speech. . . . It presents or rather *is* the subject taking up of a position in the world of his meanings. . . . The phonetic "gesture" brings about, both for the speaking subject, and for his hearers, a certain structural co-ordination of experience, a certain modulation of existence, exactly as a pattern of my bodily behavior endows the objects around me with a certain significance both for me and for others. (*PER*, p. 193)

Two final considerations. The first pertains to the origin of language. Merleau-Ponty never addresses this question head-on, but he seems to think that there was and is a kind of "gestural onomatopoeia," as well as a linguistic one, out of which meaning and significance are initially generated. We come into the world as mutually embodied beings with the capacity, even the "compulsion," for communication. Our embodiment and our capacity interact so as to serve as the symbiotic basis, through physical and audial gesture, for expression and understanding. "A contraction of the throat, a sibilant emission of air between the tongue and the teeth, a certain way of bringing the body into play suddenly allows itself to be invested with a *figurative significance* which is conveyed outside us (*PER*, p. 194). In this way linguistic communication arises or emerges from physical gestures that serve as the boundary condition for expression and meaning without serving to fully explain them. *How* this happens remains, in some sense, a mystery; *that* it happens is undeniable.

Second, the question of the open-ended character of meaning arises as well. How is it that language is never complete, that fresh significance

seemingly can be created endlessly? The embodied capacities for signification, as described above, are necessary, but they are not sufficient to explain
this phenomenon:

> Speech puts up a new sense, if it is authentic speech, just as gesture
> endows the object for the first time with human significance, if it is an
> initiating gesture. Moreover, significances now acquired must necessarily
> have been new once. We must therefore recognize as an ultimate fact this
> open and indefinite power of giving significance—that is, both of appre-
> hending and conveying a meaning—by which man transcends himself
> towards a new form of behavior, or towards other people, or towards his
> own thought, through his body and his speech. (*PER*, p. 194)

There is an inexhaustible quality built into human embodiment; each
behavioral permutation opens up fresh possibilities for further adaptations.
Thus language is open at both ends—new meanings will arise and others
will become obsolete, as long as human life continues.

SPEECH AS EMBODIMENT

It is now time to turn to the other side of the question and consider, in J. L.
Austin's words, how it is possible "to do things with words." Just as
embodiment is in itself a form of expression, so speech is in itself a form of
embodiment, or a way of *doing* things in the world. Having examined the
somatic dimension of language, we must now take up more directly the
nature of speech itself as it is acquired and employed in human existence.
The juncture point for both of these dimensions is, in Merleau-Ponty's
view, the *gesture* as both physical act and linguistic act simultaneously.
Exactly how this is so should become clear during the course of the
following discussion.

   The focus of the previous section was on Merleau-Ponty's initial explorations of the relationship between embodiment and speech. As such, it drew
most heavily from his early work in *Phenomenology of Perception*. In this
section the focus will be on tracing the refinement of his views as they
developed between this and his final work, *The Visible and the Invisible*. In
addition to several essays, most of which are contained in *Signs*, there is also
the fascinating volume, *Consciousness and the Acquisition of Language*. This
book comprises the notes from his lectures on various aspects of this topic
during the early 1950s, and will serve as an excellent point of departure for a
presentation of his views of the phenomenon of human speech.

   After a brief introduction, in which he contrasts the phenomenological
method of studying language to the rationalist ("reflexive") and empiricist
("inductive") methods, Merleau-Ponty provides a survey of the child's
psychological development as it pertains to speech. While the rationalist

tradition fails to give a helpful account of language because its inherent dualism prohibits it from identifying it either with mind or matter (as an object), the empiricist tradition can never get beyond the mere collection of data to the meaning thereof. Merleau-Ponty maintains that only a method that begins by acknowledging the logical and existential priority of meaning in all human life will be able to make sense of the phenomenon of speech.

During the first year, undoubtedly the most crucial period as well as the most difficult to study, the child is said to proceed from (1) facial mimicry through (2) the babbling stage to that of (3) vocal imitation. Mimicry has been established as far more specific and extensive than generally believed. Recognition of significant others and of basic embodiment are clearly involved. Babbling is universally the same, no matter the native culture or language, but soon focuses on indigenous sounds. Verbal imitation is effected audially rather than visually, since the child fixes its attention on the speaker's eyes, not on the mouth. Meaning is thus sought by the child. Moreover, since virtually all children are spoken to as if they will understand, it is clear that meaning is expected as well.

Imitation is, of course, absolutely crucial to the acquisition process. Of special significance is the fact that what is initially imitated are tones and inflections, not words. Thus the child is aware of the use of speech, what Austin termed its "illocutionary force," prior to its "meaning" in the lexical sense. Children will talk into play telephones, employing a wide variety of "speech acts" (giving orders, asking questions, laughing, etc.) well before they can use any specific words. Once again, meaning, in the sense of "significance," is what the child initially picks up and seeks to participate in. From the outset the child is "bathed" in language, and by means of vocal imitation it begins to swim in this all-pervasive medium by pretending to do so.

Another way in which children seek to participate in language through imitation during this proto-linguistic stage is by directly inserting themselves into adult conversation. At the dinner table, for instance, when everyone is talking and laughing, a child will often yell out a whole string of sounds and then burst out laughing. Such behavior clearly indicates an innate desire to be included in shared activity, to be acknowledged as a participant in the linguistic community. Of course, it should be noted that mere imitation is not sufficient to explain language acquisition, since adults may often imitate the child as much as the other way around. Only an underlying predilection for significance enables a child to override such potentially confusing phenomena in its effort to become a fully-fledged member of the human society.

Around one year of age the child utters its first "word." Merleau-Ponty deemphasizes the seemingly pivotal character of this event, preferring to stress its continuity with what has gone before and what will follow after. Unlike Helen Keller, for instance, most children do not progress dramatically in word acquisition after this event. Moreover, there remains a "magical" quality in the fact that the child's apprehension and use of language, the word, and what is signified seem inextricably bound together. In fact, the child's first and early words may be more their own creation than a repetition of adult words. Merleau-Ponty says, "The child possesses a syncretic view of the situation, which allows him to assimilate things in a different order" (*Consciousness and the Acquisition of Language*, p. 18; hereafter *CAL*).

This initial utterance of a "word" is followed, over the next six months or so, by the addition of a large number of other one-word utterances. It is important to note that these are in fact one-word sentences rather than simply names or labels. When a child says "Fire" or "Dog," for instance, it is not just designating an object. On the contrary, it is saying, in effect, "That is a fire," "There goes a dog," and so on. In addition, usually such statements carry with them a tone that indicates a request for approval, an acknowledgment on the part of the adult(s) present that the child has, indeed, used the symbol correctly. Once attained, the drives toward meaning and inclusion play an extremely important role in language acquisition.

Between 18 months and 3 years the child progresses to multi-word utterances ("Hot tea Mama," etc.), according to a rather wide range of patterns, depending upon various circumstances. The same can be said for the various stages up to five years of age, at which point the vast majority of children are fully reliable users for their native tongue, although there is a wide variation with respect to the degree to which speech is actually used for social intercourse. Piaget is said to believe that prior to five years of age a child does not use language primarily as a means of communication with others. Merleau-Ponty sides, rightly in my view, with David Katz in maintaining that young children can and frequently do carry on conversations among themselves and with adults prior to their fifth year.

Next Merleau-Ponty moves on to a close examination of the question of exactly how a child acquires the ability to distinguish and use phonemes, the nonreferential elements comprising language "beneath" the level of meaning. He follows R. Jakobson's analysis in that it suggests that phonemes provide a system of sounds that take on meaning as a function of their configuration. Thus signification emerges from a combination of patterns and functions. In this way Jakobson, and Merleau-Ponty, can account for aphasia:

> An aphasic can no longer pronounce certain words, even though he is neither agnosic, nor apraxic. His words are lost only insofar as they are

part of a whole. Jakobson here uses Husserl's comparison to a game of chess. One can consider the chess pieces either according to their matter, or according to their signification in the game. Language is attained not as an articulatory phenomenon, but as an element of a linguistic game. In aphasia it is not the innate instrument that is lost, but the possibility of using it in certain cases. (*CAL*, p. 25)

Merleau-Ponty goes on to suggest, following K. Buhler, that language has a threefold function: (1) to represent, (2) to express, (3) and to appeal to others. This model is similar to that of J. L. Austin's definition of the speech act as having three dimensions or forces: (1) the locutionary (referential), (2) the illocutionary (intentional), and (3) the perlocutionary (resultant) (*How to Do Things with Words*). Both Merleau-Ponty and Austin hold that the meaning of given utterance comprises all three forces.

The child's movement toward speech is a constant appeal to others. The child recognizes in the other another one of himself. Language is the means of effecting reciprocity with the other. This is a question of a vital operation and not only an intellectual act. The representative function is an aspect of the total act by which we enter into communication with others. (*CAL*, p. 31)

This way of putting the matter suggests that the business of communication must be a two-way street from the outset. Both the adult and the child seek meaning, and each brings to their dialogue as much as he or she gets. Merleau-Ponty offers the analogy of the highly creative writer, such as James Joyce,

who, at first, is not understood, but who little by little becomes understandable by teaching people to understand him. His gestures seem to point in non-existent directions; then little by little, some notions begin to find themselves a potential home in these gestures. In the same way, language ends up by coming alive for the child. At a certain moment, the whole set of indications, which draw toward an undetermined goal, call up in the child a concentration and reassimilation of meaning. . . . The totality of meaning is never fully rendered: there is an immense mass of implications, even in the most explicit of languages; or rather, nothing is ever completely expressed, nothing exempts the subject who is listening from taking the initiative of giving an interpretation. (*CAL*, p. 29)

The problem of imitation is far more complex, for it involves the whole problem of selfhood and our knowledge of other selves. It would seem that in order to imitate an adult's speech, a child must first be able to identify the other person and to identify him or her self as a distinct person. Merleau-Ponty traces various philosophers' efforts, especially those of Husserl, to explain how a child performs this difficult feat. In the end he agrees with P. Guillaume that initially positing either one's own selfhood or that of the other will always leave the gap between the two essentially unbridgeable:

Hence, to solve the problem, one must not eliminate the initial opposition. Theoretically, it is insurmountable. However, since it is not a logical relation but an existential one, the self could rejoin other people by rendering the *lived experience* more profound. The self must become bound up with a certain *situation*. We must link the very notion of ipseity to that of situation: the ego ought to be defined as identical with the act in which it projects itself. The self and others are conscious of one another in a common situation. (*CAL*, p. 49)

With the notion of the logical and existential priority of intersubjectivity firmly in place, Merleau-Ponty is in a position to readdress the possibility of imitation. He sees it based, not in the imaging of another's behavior in one's own, but of acting in order to effect or achieve the same result as the other purpose. It is through sharing goals and tasks that we come to know each other, and thus acquire language.

In short, one makes use of his own body not as a mass of sensations, doubled by a kineasthetic image, but as *a way of systematically* going toward objects. . . . Imitation can be explained to the extent that other people utilize the same means as we do in order to obtain the same goal; it cannot be explained otherwise. Guillaume indicates the imitation is founded on a community of goals, of objects. It is from this imitation of results that subsequently the imitation of others becomes possible. (*CAL*, p. 35)

After a brief discussion of the insights and oversights to be found in Piaget's attempts to trace the development of language in children over seven years of age, Merleau-Ponty provides an account of the positive implications of speech pathology (especially aphasia) for his own analysis of the acquisition of language. Here he relies heavily on the work of K. Goldstein. Finally, the book concludes with a consideration of the bearing of contemporary linguistics on philosophical issues such as those under consideration here. Here Merleau-Ponty acknowledges his indebtedness to the scientific labors of de Saussure. He concludes this work, returning to the notion of embodiment, with the following remarks:

One could say about language in its relations with thought what one says of the life of the body in its relations with consciousness. Just as one could not place the body at the first level, just as one could not subordinate it or draw it out of its autonomy . . ., one can say only that language makes thought, as much as it is made by thought. Thought inhabits language, and language is its body. This mediation of the objective and the subjective, of the interior and to the exterior—what philosophy seeks to do—we can find in language if we succeed in getting close enough to it. (*CAL*, p. 102)

Thus speech becomes embodied in a speaker on the basis of his or her gestural imitation of other members of the speaking community. Although the somatic dimension of speech and personhood is thereby revealed as crucial, it is not to be opposed or contrasted to consciousness. Rather, embodiment and consciousness are to be understood as two complementary dimensions of a unified reality, the former mediating the latter and the latter inhabiting the former. Signification and meaning arise within the dynamic matrix provided by the interaction of these two dimensions, in relational activity with other embodied consciousness. Gesture remains as the pivot-point or intersection wherein meaning, and thus language is born.

In his essay, "Indirect Language and the Voices of Silence," Merleau-Ponty begins with an account of de Saussure's phonemic analysis of speech as a way of explaining how children acquire speech. He stresses the simultaneity of their grasping of the "lateral" or syntactic relation between individual sounds and the semantic or referential signification.

> The whole of the spoken language surrounding the child snaps him up like a whirlwind, tempts him by its internal articulations, and brings him *almost* up to the moment when all this noise begins to mean something. The untiring way in which the train of words crosses and recrosses itself . . . finally sways the child over to the side of those who speak. (*Signs*, p. 41)

Merleau-Ponty likens speech to a "fold in the immense fabric of language," which "is understood only through the interaction of signs, each of which, taken separately, is equivocal or banal, and makes sense only by being combined with others" (*Signs*, p. 42).

It is the "opaqueness" or incompleteness of language that provides both the possibility for misunderstanding and for creating fresh meaning in speech: "All language is indirect or allusive—that is, if you wish, silence" (*Signs*, p. 43). Not only does speech achieve its significance against the backdrop of non-speech in general, but it remains alive by trading, as it were, on its own indirectness, through which it always leaves a great deal *unsaid*. What is meant is as much a function of what is not said as it is a result of what is said. Not only is the context of an utterance crucial to this indirect quality of language, and thus to its meaningfulness, but our nonverbal behavior also serves as a form of indirect communication. Once again, we encounter the fundamental role of embodiment in linguistic signification.

In the end Merleau-Ponty claims that this indirect or "silent" character of language, like that of painting or creative writing, is grounded in or pivots around gesture and embodiment, around what he terms "tacit language." "All perception, all action which presupposes it, and in short, every human use of the body is already *primordial expression*" (*Signs*, p. 67). He concludes that beneath spoken language there is "an operator or speaking language whose words live a little-known life and unite with and separate from one another as their lateral or indirect signification demands . . ." (*Signs*, pp.

75–76). This tacit language is a function of our gestural and behavioral interaction with each other and with our shared physical environment and common tasks. Speech is a form of embodiment.

In the essay, "On the Phenomenology of Language," Merleau-Ponty begins by examining Husserl's approach to language "as thought's body" (*Signs*, p. 84). He develops this notion of "corporeal intentionality." He says that "speech is comparable to a gesture because what it is charged with, expression, will be in the same relation to it as the goal is to the gesture which intends it . . ." (*Signs*, p. 89). The image of "sedimentation" is introduced in order to account for the "solidity" or fleshy character of speech as it moves dialectically between closure and open-endedness. An utterance means what it says and much more; the meanings that are grasped and acted upon in a given context provide the accumulating that gets structured into and by convention, while those that are "left over" as possibilities remain "in solution," waiting for future use and sedimentation.

> Sedimentation occurs, and I shall be able to think farther. Speech . . . is that moment when the significative intention (still silent and wholly in act) proves itself capable of incorporating itself into my culture and the culture of others—of shaping me and others by transforming the meaning of cultural instruments. It becomes "available" in time because in retrospect it gives us the illusion that it was contained in the already available significations, whereas by a sort of *ruse* it espoused them only in order to infuse them with new life. (*Signs*, p. 92)

Here again, speech exhibits its embodied character.

In his introduction to *Signs*, which contains the two essays discussed above, Merleau-Ponty returns to the parallel between speech and embodiment when he speaks of the connection between language and "intercorporeal communication."

> Language can vary and amplify intercorporeal communication as much as we wish; it has the same spring and style as the latter. In language too, that which was secret must become public and almost *visible*. In intercorporeal communication as in language, significations come through in whole packages, scarcely sustained by a few pre-emptory gestures. (*Signs*, p. 19)

Just as in our actions we express and embody our intentions in our nonverbal behavior, so in speech we express and embody them in our verbal behavior. Speech is both embodied language and embodied intentions, even as embodiment is both a form of speech and an expression of intentions.

Merleau-Ponty further developed this interpretation of language in his final work, *The Visible and the Invisible*. A consideration of this development will complete the present exploration of his approach to the nature of language in general. As has been noted several times, it is in his final work that Merleau-Ponty pursues the metaphor of the flesh in relation to our place within and interaction with the world of things and persons. Unsurprisingly, he employs this image in relation to the nature and use of linguistic activity as well. The connection between ourselves, the world, and others, and even between our own mind and body (intentions and behavior) is mediated through our peculiar way of being in the world, whereby everything and everyone is "bone of my bone and flesh of my flesh." We are placed within the world, others, and ourselves by means of embodiment and speech.

> Like the flesh of the visible, speech is a total part of the significations, like it, speech is a relation to Being through a being, and, like it, it is narcissistic, eroticized, endowed with a natural magic that attracts the other significations into its web, as the body feels the world in feeling itself. In reality, there is much more than a parallel or an analogy here, there is solidity and intertwining: if speech, which is but a region of the intelligible world, can also be its refuge, this is because speech prolongs into the invisible, extends unto the semantic operations, the belongingness of the body to being and the corporeal relevance of every being, which for me is once and for all attested by the visible, and whose idea each intellectual evidence reflects a little further. (*VI*, p. 118)

The main thrust of the above passage pertains to the "fleshly" character of speech, parallel to or actually of a piece with the somatic character of human existence. This "carnality," in both human language and activity, is the axis around which all our intentions and significations orbit; it is the matrix or loom by and from within which the patterns of our existence and experience are woven. In addition, it is this fleshly quality of human life and speech that mediates the intangible, "invisible" dimensions of Being and existence, albeit in and through the very fabric or folds of the tangible, "visible" dimensions. We shall return to this notion of mediated transcendence in the next two chapters.

For Merleau-Ponty, even to the very end of his career, speech was understood as a form of embodiment, as the incarnation of intangible intentionality in tangible activity. Moreover, this embodiment in speech constitutes an embodiment interwoven with that of other speakers as well. As Merleau-Ponty puts it:

> A discussion is not an exchange or a conformation of ideas, as if each formed his own, shows them to others, looked at theirs, and returned to correct them with his own. . . . Life becomes ideas and the ideas return to life, each is caught up in the vortex in which he first committed only measured stakes, each is led on by what he said and the response he received, led on by his own thought of which he is no longer the sole

thinker. No one thinks anymore, everyone speaks, all live and gesticulate within Being. . . . (*VI*, p. 55)

Understood in this way, language for Merleau-Ponty is a pivotal, perhaps *the* pivotal dimension within the embodied existence known as the human way of being in the world. Just as our bodies are our entry-point into the world of things and persons, so speech is the hinge upon which this entry-point swings, both to open reality to us and to allow us to insert ourselves into reality. Thus speech itself is an embodiment of embodiment, not something we have and make, but something that has and makes us (*VI*, p. 190). To put it a bit differently, speech, when understood as essentially gestural, mediates our embodiment in the same way that our embodiment mediates our consciousness and intentionality.

This mediational quality of language is duplicated in the nature of the relationship between meaning and the spoken or written word. Meaning is communicated in and through words, not merely represented or "symbolized" by them; it is embodied in, rather than hovering over or behind them. As Merleau-Ponty says: "The meaning is not on the phrase like the butter on the bread, like a second layer of psychic reality spread over the sound: it is the totality of what is said, the integral of all the differentiations of the verbal chain; it is given with the words for those who have ears to hear" (*VI*, p. 155). In the same way, speech itself is not added to our intentions or behavior as a kind of optional or arbitrary afterthought. Rather, it is the very stuff or "flesh" out of which we, *qua* human beings, are made and through which we live.

5

THE PRIMACY OF METAPHOR

It is now time to turn our direct attention to the question of the nature and function of metaphor in the philosophy of Merleau-Ponty. The broad and implicit context for approaching this question is, of course, his own use of metaphorical images as presented in Part One of the present study. The narrow and explicit context for the focus of this chapter is the contemporary exploration of metaphor that has come center-stage in recent philosophical discussion. This background will be the concern of the first section, and then we shall turn to a more thorough examination of Merleau-Ponty's view of metaphor itself.

MODELS OF METAPHOR

Contemporary models of metaphoric activity range along a continuum between the extremes of those who see it as primarily "decorative" and those who think of it as essentially "constitutive" in nature. The former espouse a substitutionary view, which implies that all cognitively meaningful uses of metaphor can be replaced by or reduced to a set of literal or factual propositions. The latter, on the other hand, contend that metaphoric thought and speech actually comprise the very substance of framework out of which both factual knowledge and literal signification obtain their meaning. In fact, reality itself, in so far as we know and experience it, is said to be constituted or created by the metaphoric mode of expression.

Representative of the substitutionary perspective, which largely dominates the empiricist tradition, is the position of Paul Edwards. Like the young Wittgenstein, as well as Bertrand Russell, Edwards argues that "whatever can be said at all can be said clearly; thus whereof we cannot speak, we must remain silent." In his own words: "But we know this (what common metaphors mean) because we can eliminate the metaphoric expressions, because we can specify the content of the assertion in the non-metaphorical language, because we can supply the literal equivalent . . ." (*Mind*, April 1965, p. 199). It must be acknowledged that this extreme view of the expendability of metaphorical expressions is shared by very few philosophers today, primarily because (1) it fails to provide an account of how literal speech itself arises and (2) it fails to do justice to the nonliteral character of highly scientific, let alone philosophical theory (including empiricism itself).

There are other thinkers whose views cluster at the same end of the continuum as Edwards' but who develop their thought in much more sophisticated fashion. Susanne Langer and Colin Turbayne are two such thinkers. The former has built an elaborate and powerful theory of the nature of artistic symbolization, but unfortunately it is based on accepting Edwards' fundamental dichotomy between representation and expression. This leads her to admit that the purpose of language is to mirror facts and thought, while that of art is to present feelings. Thus she concludes that "metaphor is not language," raising serious questions about its dispensability as well as its cognitivity (*Problems of Art*, p. 23). Turbayne begins by acknowledging the impossibility of doing without metaphor, but he argues we can achieve a certain degree of objectivity by continually reminding ourselves that a metaphor is "only a metaphor" and by frequently shifting and recasting our metaphors so as not to become enslaved by them. He concludes, quoting Bertrand Russell, that "the only safeguard is to be able, once in a while, to discard words for a moment and contemplate facts more directly through images" (*The Myth of Metaphor*, p. 100). Unfortunately, neither Turbayne nor Russell manages to explain how this metaphor-transcending feat is to be accomplished.

Far more helpful are those thinkers who stress what has been termed the "interactionist" interpretation of metaphoric activity, namely Max Black and Phillip Wheelwright. We shall examine their views in considerable detail. At the outset of his account of metaphor, Black offers several examples of metaphoric expressions and makes some general observations about them ("Metaphor" in *Models and Metaphors*). He suggests that most often one word or phrase in a metaphorical utterance strikes us as being used in an unusual or unfamiliar way. He thinks it helpful to call this word or phrase the "focus" of the metaphor and to refer to the remainder of the utterance as the "frame." The same focus may appear within different frames, thereby producing different metaphors. In addition, Black asserts that it is necessary to examine both the linguistic context and the social setting within which a metaphor appears in order to determine its meaning. As with all linguistic activity, metaphorical meaning very much depends on such variables as emphasis (as revealed through intonation, gesture, etc.) and intention (as revealed through accompanying deeds and results).

Next Black turns to an examination of the "substitution" view of metaphor, according to which a metaphorical expression is used in place of this literal equivalent—either for convenience or for ornamentation. Black criticizes this view on the basis that it fails to account for the richness and complexity of many metaphorical expressions. For the attempt to "translate" or reduce metaphors to their literal equivalent often is unsuccessful. Sometimes (frequently the more interesting and important times) a metaphorical expression is used not as a convenient or ornamental substitute, but as the most direct and pointed way to articulate an insight.

Nor can the substitution view be salvaged by falling back on a "comparison" view, wherein metaphor is explained as a truncated simile in which an implied comparison is substituted for an explicit one. For it is precisely this similarity that an incisive metaphor captures, frequently for the first time, and thus it will not do to explain the metaphor in terms of the similarity. Frequently similes follow after metaphors, and thus the latter can hardly be explained in terms of or reduced to the former.

> Metaphorical statement is not a substitute for a formal comparison of any other kind of literal statement, but has its own distinctive capacities and achievements. . . . It would be more illuminating in some of these cases to say that metaphor creates the similarity than to say that it formulates some similarity antecedently existing. ("Metaphor," p. 32)

Black draws upon the work of I. A. Richards in developing an "interaction" view of metaphor. According to this theory metaphor involves the use of a word or phrase in a context different from those within which it usually appears. By placing a fresh focus in an unfamiliar frame a speaker sets up an interaction between the associations that normally accompany each. Thus both our understanding of human nature and our conception of wolves are altered by the metaphorical expression "Man is a wolf." Of course, the primary thrust of the metaphor is directed at generating an insight about the former, with wolf associations reorganizing our conceptual as well as our emotional understanding of what it means to be human. "Any human traits that can without undue strain be talked about in 'wolf-language' will be rendered prominent, and any that cannot will be pushed into the background. The wolf-metaphor suppresses some details, emphasizes others—in short, *organizes* our view of man" ("Metaphor," p. 41).

Black concludes that although not all metaphors need to be classified as involving such interaction, the most powerful and effective ones are best thought of in this way because they will not submit to simple substitution or translation. Such attempts destroy the delicate balance that mediates the cognitive insight achieved by conceptual affective interaction. He maintains that when we attempt to reduce such metaphors to their "literal" meaning, the loss is not merely emotive but is as well "a loss of cognitive content. The translation fails to give the insight that the metaphor did" ("Metaphor," p. 46).

In a slightly different context Black draws a likeness between the use of metaphor in everyday speech and the use of models in scientific endeavor ("Metaphor," pp. 230ff). Here, too, he argues against those who maintain that models are simply picturesque and inexact ways of expressing insights that can, if the insight is true, be reduced or translated to more "rigorous" language. Black offers several key instances in which it is clear that highly productive insights have not been so reduced, even after much effort, and that practicing scientists take their models far more seriously than such a view would allow. Against those who concede that models and metaphors may be fruitful as heuristic devices but continue to insist that they must not be confused with the epistemological justification of scientific theories, Black maintains that effective metaphors also have an internal structure that "resonates" with the structure of the reality being dealt with. This is what makes them fruitful.

> We have seen that the successful model must be isomorphic with its domain of application. So there is a rational basis for using the model. In stretching the language by which the model is described in such a way as to fit the new domain, we pin our hopes upon the existence of a common structure in both fields. If the hope is fulfilled, there will have been an objective ground for the analogical transfer. For we call a mode of investigation rational when it has rationale, that is to say, when we can find reasons which justify what we do and that allow for an articulate appraisal and criticism. The putative isomorphism between model and field of application provides such a rationale and yields such standards of critical judgment. We can determine the validity of a given model by checking the extent of its isomorphism with its intended application. In appraising models as good or bad, we need not rely on the sheerly pragmatic test of fruitfulness in discovery; we can, in principle at least, determine the "goodness" of their "fit". ("Metaphor," p. 238)

Another helpful and somewhat similar analysis of metaphor is offered by Phillip Wheelwright. He begins by defining metaphor as a metamorphosis of meaning at a deep level, brought about by the interaction of what he terms "epiphor" and "diaphor." The former signifies the extension of meaning through comparison of similarities while the latter designates the creation of new meaning by juxtaposition and synthesis of dissimilarities. Both diaphor and epiphor are most effective when not treating obvious similarities or dissimilarities:

The best epiphors have freshness; they call light attention to similarities not readily noticed; they involve, in Aristotle's phrase, "an intuitive perception of the similarity of dissimilars.". . . the comparison comes as a shock which is yet a shock of recognition. . . . The essential possibility of diaphor lies in the broad ontological fact that new qualities and new meanings can emerge, simply come into being, out of some hitherto ungrouped combination of elements. (*Metaphor and Reality*, pp. 74, 85)

The internal relationship between epiphor and diaphor is complex. Sometimes they can be alternated so as to repeatedly attack a subject from different perspectives, while at other times one may be used within the context of the other. Wheelwright gives the following examples of metaphoric expression and comments upon them:

(1) My salad days,
    When I was green in judgment
(2) A bracelet of bright hair about the bone
(3) We have lingered in the chambers of the sea
    By sea-girls wreathed with seaweed red and brown

That there is epiphor in each of the instances is shown by the felt subterranean power to mean something more than the words actually say. That there is diaphor is evident from the utterly untranslatable character of each utterance—the role of epiphor is to hint significance, the role of diaphor is to create presence (*Metaphor and Reality*, p. 238).

Elsewhere Wheelwright approaches the notion of metaphor from a slightly different angle (*The Burning Fountain*). He suggests that metaphor may well be the paradigm of figurative or expressive language, which he distinguishes from "steno-language." The latter is an abstraction in which the logical and representational features of linguistic utterances are focused and idealized; rarely if ever is language devoid of the expressive dimension. Wheelwright characterizes this expressive dimension as employing such features as continuity between symbol and referent (as in onomatopeia), contextual variation, plural-signification (useful ambiguity), concrete universalization, indirection, "soft" focus, assertorial lightness (multivalued logic), and paradox.

The crux of metaphoric expressiveness lies, according to Wheelwright, in the semantic tension created by its epiphoric and diaphoric qualities.

The essence of metaphor consists in a semantic tension which subsists among the heterogeneous elements brought together in some striking image or expression. Poetic language implicitly crossweaves multiplicity-in-unity and unity-in-multiplicity; it is intensive because of the precarious balance between two or more lines of association which it invites the imagination to contemplate. (*The Burning Fountain*, p. 102)

Wheelwright seeks to distinguish metaphor from simile, not on the basis of grammar, but at the level of semantics or meaning. In simile two verbal expressions, each conveying an individual image, are joined. In metaphor, however, a single expression conjoins two or more images to produce a unitary meaning. Thus in the former the vehicle is plural and the meaning is singular, while in the latter the vehicle is singular and the meaning plural. Here again, however, Wheelwright stresses that the most effective expressive language results from the use of simile and metaphor together.

There are a number of important similarities between the views of Black and Wheelwright. One of the more important of these is the notion of interaction and/or tension lying at the heart of metaphor. Another is their shared conviction that metaphor is capable of carrying a deep cognitive significance that cannot be communicated in more "straightforward" language. Perhaps the most important differences between the views of Black and Wheelwright stem from their distinct angles of approach. Black is concerned with the place and meaning of metaphor in ordinary and scientific language, while Wheelwright focuses on the contrast between these two uses of language and the poetic-religious use. Their differences are not so much substantive as perspectival.

In spite of the superiority of the interactionist approaches of Black and Wheelwright over those taken up in Chapter 1, however, there remains at least one major problem area, more implicit than explicit, in their treatment of metaphor. While they go a long way toward undermining the pervasive positivist dichotomy between cognitive and emotive language (by stressing the polysignificatory and interactive character of language in general), they do not offer a concrete account of how metaphoric expressions do in fact carry cognitive meaning. What is needed is an epistemological schema for treating the inner logic of metaphor in a manner that displays its distinctive cognitive character.

Monroe Beardsley slices the linguistic pie quite differently. Beginning with the sentence, rather than the word, as the vehicle of meaning, he distinguishes between what a statement "states" and what it "suggests." For example, the statements (1) "A republic has been declared and the king has committed suicide," and (2) "The king has committed suicide and a republic has been declared," *say* the same thing but *suggest* quite different causal connections. It is precisely this suggestibility within ordinary discourse on which, according to Beardsley, the metaphoric mode capitalizes. He also stresses that understanding a literary work as a whole is simply an example "writ large" of the metaphoric dynamic on the sentence level (*Aesthetics*, p. 115).

In Beardsley's view the metaphoric mode invites the hearer to explore the possibilities of meaning inherent in the creative utterance without specifying in advance what these possibilities are. Two principles regulate this exploration, "fittingness," or selection, and plenitude. There are, to be sure, limits to the potential meanings of a given metaphoric utterance, but within those limits there exists, in the more powerful metaphors, a vast richness of meaning (*Aesthetics*, p. 128). The hearer must play off, according to the principles of fittingness, the meaning of the terms of the two main categories chosen against the principle of plenitude, by which meaning is multiplied in terms of the open-textured nature of speech. Metaphor exists on the threshold between established meaning and nonsense, continually turning the latter into the former. The hearer is invited to explore the various signification possibilities inherent within a given metaphorical utterance, even and perhaps especially those involving logical absurdity. By means of these dynamics metaphor can be said to "produce" meaning, and the possibilities for such production seem limitless and indispensable within the body of living speech.

In a journal article Beardsley discusses one important aspect of metaphorical significations that often goes unmentioned ("Metaphorical Senses," *Nous*, March 1978). Generally, if not almost exclusively, metaphors are examined in terms of the established meanings of the terms involved and the intentions of the speaker. Beardsley notes that attention must be paid as well to the empirical knowledge of the hearer, and to the possible discrepancies that may arise between such knowledge and that of the speaker. He deals with these factors in terms of what he calls "credence-properties," suggesting that the variability ratio between what the speaker believes is characteristic of a given object or category, and what a hearer believes, makes it helpful to speak (as dictionaries frequently do) of the various "metaphorical senses" of a term or expression.

Here again the strength of Beardsley's analysis resides in his acknowledgement of what might be termed the "flexibility zone" that surrounds each use of metaphorical speech. The transfer or conversion of meaning by means of metaphor, while sufficiently predictable to ensure communication, can only take place within a kind of indeterminacy on the part of both the speaker and the hearer. The significance of a metaphoric utterance, and indeed of metaphor in general, pivots on a reciprocal interaction between the terms and categories comprising the utterance *per se,* and between the beliefs, knowledge, and intentions of the speaker on the one hand and the beliefs, knowledge, and imagination of the hearer on the other hand.

There can be no question that throughout his analysis and exploration of the nature of metaphor Beardsley maintains that metaphorical speech can be cognitive in character. He argues, along with Black, that "translation" and "substitution" tactics do not do justice to the depth of meaning often carried by a metaphor. In fact, the specifically paradoxical structure of metaphoric expression defies such reductionistic moves, since one must grasp the meaning of the metaphor prior to and independently of substitutions and translations in order to make them. In the article referred to above, Beardsley defends the propriety of judging metaphorical utterances as "true" or "false."

> If the referent(s) of the subject of a metaphorical statement does in fact have all the properties of the intention of the metaphorical predicate, I see no bar to calling the statement "true." In many cases, of course, the referent(s) will have only some of those properties, so the statement will be false. Yet if many of the properties are there—those most important to that context—we may say the statement is "largely true"—(the way we would with a complex historical narrative that includes some errors but is right about the main things)—or, if one likes, "apt." It is an apt description of the Nixon administration to say that it was the high-water mark of the imperial presidency, though like most metaphors isolated from a context this also contains some untruths. ("Metaphorical Senses," p. 15)

In spite of the power and insight of Beardsley's exposition there remains a sense in which his account, like most of those already examined, fails to cut deep enough to do justice to the richness and centrality of metaphorical expression. Greater attention needs to be paid to the relation between language in general, and metaphorical language in particular, on the one hand and "the world" or reality on the other.

At the opposite extreme from those who contend that metaphoric expression is cognitively expendable cluster those thinkers who take a stand even more radical than that of the interactionists. There are those who maintain that in some deep, important sense metaphoric expression is constitutive of reality. The central thrust of this position is that the world of human experience is woven, at least partly, out of the structure of the language in which we speak and think—and that the metaphoric mode lies at the center of the cognitive process. In short, in this view metaphor is taken to be logically prior to so-called literal speech. I shall begin with a consideration of the view of Nelson Goodman. Next we shall turn our attention to the position of the French philosopher Paul Ricoeur on the relation between thought and reality.

In his important and highly provocative book, *Languages of Art*, Goodman takes a definite position on the relation between language and the world. He contends that far from being optional and arbitrary, language is constitutive of reality. Words and statements refer, to be sure, to the world, but not as mere labels and/or "pictures." Rather, language and reality participate in a mutually symbiotic relationship. More specifically, Goodman maintains that we are continually "remaking reality" by means of language, especially the metaphors, we use in dealing with it. At the deepest and broadest level our basic symbols determine the structure and character of our world.

Goodman's position is essentially the diametric opposite of that taken by Paul Edwards and other logical empiricists. They view language as a passive mirror of reality, while he views it as an active creator of reality. Edwards and others like him have what has been called the "luggage-tag" theory of language, while Goodman has what might be termed an "orphic" understanding of symbolism, since he sees language as bringing the world to life. At the same time Goodman seems to go beyond even the interactionists, discussed in the previous paragraph, in his stress on the primordial quality of symbols in relation to the world. For him symbols not only reveal and evoke insight into reality, but they create it as well.

It is clear that Goodman stands with the interactionists against the substitutionists in emphasizing the cognitive character of symbolic and/or metaphoric expression. He stands squarely against the cognitive/emotive dichotomy, so prevalent in contemporary thought, arguing, "In aesthetic experience the emotions function cognitively." In both science and art truth is determined on the basis of the "appropriateness" established between a given symbol system and the facts of experience broadly conceived. Moreover, metaphor is said to work by, and to be evaluated in terms of, the transference of meaning from one set or system of symbols to another. Goodman defines metaphor (metaphorically!) as "an affair between a predicate with a past and an object that yields while protesting . . . a happy and revitalizing, even if bigamous, second marriage" (*Languages of Art*, p. 69).

There is a pragmatist and nominalist thrust to Goodman's theory of language in general and metaphor in particular. While stressing the referential and cognitive character of symbols, Goodman nevertheless insists that they are our instruments for creating and engaging the world, and thus in no way can be said to reflect the nature of reality. Reality is linguistically constituted and is thus ontologically prior to symbols and/or metaphors. Such a posture resembles both the neo-Kantian motif of someone like Ernst Cassirer (in *The Philosophy of Symbolic Forms*) and the pragmatism of W. V. O. Quine (in *Word and Object*). The sort of nominalism involved is far from being flat, narrow, and impoverished. It is, rather, as complex and comprehensive as it is rich in cognitive potential.

The conventionalism and/or relativism seemingly inherent in Goodman's theory of the relation between language and reality is faced up to directly in his more recent book, *Ways of Worldmaking*. Therein he develops three main lines of support for his seemingly irreverent and imprudent affirmation of a kind of "linguistic relativity." He argues for and from (1) a metaphysical pluralism, (2) epistemological "relativism under rigorous restraints," and (3) a theory of symbolic expression as cognitive. A brief examination of each of these lines of support will provide an excellent basis for understanding the main force of Goodman's view of metaphor.

To begin with, Goodman takes as his axis the notion that all descriptions of or assertions about reality only have meaning within a conceptual and/or linguistic framework. Thus facts themselves only exist within a theoretic structure or symbolic system; they are always "theory laden" and not "pure."

> If I ask about the world, you can offer to tell me how it is under one or more frames of reference; but if I insist that you tell me how it is apart from all frames, what can you say? We are confined to ways of describing whatever is described. Our universe, so to speak, consists of these ways rather than of a world or of worlds. (*Ways of Worldmaking*, p. 3)

Goodman's view is not that we have multiple and alternative views of a single, actual world, but that we have multiple actual worlds that are constituted by the different visions and corresponding symbol systems developed within our various disciplines and dimensions of experience. These different worlds cannot and need not be reduced to one another or to a common ontological denominator. The worlds of science, art, philosophy, religion, and everyday discourse, to name several examples, neither describe the same world nor are they reducible to one another. The symbol systems appropriate to each are essentially self-contained and nontranslatable. Goodman contends that even the "stuffs" out of which our many worlds are made are themselves made alone within the worlds, not from nothing but from other worlds already on hand. Worldmaking is always a "remaking."

With respect to the question of the "truth" of our various efforts at worldmaking, Goodman affirms both the relativity and the rigor of epistemological criteria. Generally speaking, the standard tests of coherence with "unyielding beliefs and observations," internal consistency, simplicity, and comprehensiveness function as basic criteria. There are, however, no hard and fast lines between precepts and facts, no universally incorrigible "givens" that serve as the final test of truth. Nevertheless, there is always a difference between "rightness" and "wrongness," between what is fitting and what is not, in every worldmaking activity, whether it be science, painting, or philosophy. "A broad mind is no substitute for hard work."

> What I have said so far plainly points to a radical relativism; but severe restraints are imposed. Willingness to accept countless alternative true or right world-versions does not mean that everything goes, that tall stories are as good as short ones, that truths are no longer distinguished from falsehoods, but only that truth must be otherwise conceived than as correspondence with a ready-made world. Though we make worlds by making versions, we no more make a world by putting symbols together at random than a carpenter makes a chair by putting pieces of wood together at random. The multiple worlds I countenance are just the actual

worlds made by and answering to true or right versions. (*Ways of Worldmaking*, p. 94)

In the final analysis Goodman falls back on know*ing* as a judgment-making activity, as providing the bedrock for truth. Certain claims are accepted as true because they are judged by the person or persons involved to fit within a well-proved worldview. Worldviews, in turn, and even worlds themselves, are accepted or lived in because they are recognized as appropriate with respect to the task of worldmaking. Such acts of judgment are neither final nor entirely relative; rather they are the necessary fulcrum for all knowledge. The skills and commitments of the knowing subject(s) cannot be ignored as "mere psychology." Without the practice and authority of judgment makers, neither worlds nor knowledge thereof would exist.

> We have seen, on the contrary, that rightness of categorization, which enters into most other varieties of rightness, is rather a matter of fit with practice; that without the organization, the selection of relevant kinds, effected by evolving tradition, there is no rightness or wrongness of categorization, no validity of inductive inference, no fair or unfair sampling, and no uniformity or disparity among samples. Thus justifying such tests for rightness may consist primarily in showing not that they are reliable but that they are authoritative. (*Ways of Worldmaking*, p. 138)

Goodman brings the foregoing ideas on reality and truth to bear on the notion of metaphor in the following manner. In addition to his concern to stress the cognitive character of metaphoric speech, especially at the constitutive level of worldmaking, Goodman contends that the worlds made by and through the arts are every bit as "actual" as those made by physicists, historians, and behavioral scientists. Whereas metaphor may not be at the forefront in the latter (though its always at the fulcrum), it is clearly the main concern in the former. The worlds created by musicians, painters, and writers are "real," and thus the metaphoric moves whereby they are constituted serve as bearers of knowledge.

> Fiction, then, whether written or painted or acted, applies truly neither to nothing nor to diaphanous possible worlds but, albeit metaphorically, to actual worlds. Somewhat as I have argued elsewhere that the merely possible—so far as admissible at all—lies within the actual worlds. Fiction operates in actual worlds in much the same way as non-fiction. Cervantes and Bosch and Goya, no less than Boswell and Newton and Darwin, take and unmake and remake and retake familiar worlds, recasting them in remarkable and sometimes recondite but eventually recognizable—that is re-cogniz-able—ways. (*Ways of Worldmaking*, p. 104)

Goodman carries his "radical relativism under rigorous restraints" even to the point of applying it to his own views, to his own "outline of the facts concerning the fabrication of facts." The truth of philosophical accounts of "how things are" in various worlds and in worldmaking, as well as the truth of metaphilosophical versions of the nature of such philosophical accounts, is dependent on a flexible and relative application of such non-absolute criteria as coherence, consistency, and fittingness. When pressed to offer a justification of these criteria themselves, and of his own advocacy of them, Goodman replies that at such a bedrock level justification consists more of invitation and persuasion than of traditional argumentation.

> In such a context, I am not so much stating a belief or advancing a thesis or a doctrine as proposing a categorization or scheme of organization, calling attention to a way of setting our nets to capture what may be significant likenesses and differences. Argument for the categorization, the scheme, suggested could not be for its truth, since it has no truth-value, but for its efficacy in worldmaking and understanding. An argument would consist rather of calling attention to important parallels between pictorial representation and verbal denotation, or pointing out obscurities and confusions that are clarified by this association, of show-ing how this organization works with other aspects of the theory of symbols. For a categorical system, what needs to be shown is not that it is true but what it can do. Put crassly, what is called for in such cases is less like arguing than selling. (*Ways of Worldmaking*, p. 129)

Here again, Goodman stands out as an example of a thinker who maintains the constitutive character of metaphoric speech, especially at the level of justification of worldviews in general and of philosophical visions in particular. For Goodman the worlds in which we live are *made*, and they are made through the employment of concepts and metaphors under the watchful eye of certain flexible criteria. Even these criteria are justified and thus constituted by appeals to their usefulness in the process of worldmak-ing. Things are different in the view of Paul Ricoeur.

Ricoeur's encyclopedic and highly provocative study, *The Rule of Meta-phor*, undertakes to trace the history of the notion of metaphor from Aristotle to contemporary times. He begins by outlining and then critiquing the "substitution" theory of metaphor. The major difficulty with this theory is its assumption that the unit of meaning in language in general and metaphorical speech in particular is the word. Moreover, this assumption is commonly conjoined with the idea that words are essentially names. Such a point of departure inevitably leads to the view that at best metaphoric speech is "translatable" into "literal" speech and at worst it is merely "word salad." This approach to metaphor falls by the wayside when it is realized that the fundamental unit of speech is not the word but the sentence, and that so-called literal statements are themselves merely dead metaphors.

Ricoeur then moves to a consideration of "interactionist" views of metaphor, such as those of Black, Beardsley, and Emile Benveniste. For

Ricoeur the distinction between the substitution and interactionist views parallels that between semiotics and semantics in linguistic theory. The first members of each pair focuses on meaning as a function of isolated words within a syntactical system, while the latter stresses the necessity of relation and tension to the notion of meaning, especially with respect to metaphor. Ricoeur argues that the metaphorical mode creates meaning by engaging in what he terms "impertinent predication." The tension between traditional uses and utterances combined in a fresh manner gives rise to new insights into the world of experienced reality.

The heart of Ricoeur's analysis of this creative, impertinent predication lies in his treatment of the notion of resemblance and the function of the copula, *is*. Whenever we affirm a similarity between two or more aspects of our world, we by the same act simultaneously affirm various dissimilarities as well. Thus to say that chairs and table are similar in that they are both kinds of furniture is at the same time to say that they are different in some respects as well; otherwise, there would be no need, indeed no basis, for bringing them together at all, since they would be identical. In like manner, to say, as did Winston Churchill, that "Russia has dropped an iron curtain across Europe" is simultaneously to affirm a positive and a negative relationship between Russia's political policy immediately following World War II and the separation between actors and audience effected by a curtain. These are both similar and dissimilar. Thus the use of "*is*" always cuts in two directions at once, especially in metaphorical speech. For the fresh insight only comes to light as a result of the tension between these symbiotic meanings.

In addition to siding with the interactionists against the substitutionists, however, Ricoeur also follows Nelson Goodman in asserting the creative or orphic force of the metaphoric mode. In his chapter entitled "Metaphor and Reference" he draws on Goodman's "worldmaking" theory of metaphor and argues against the sophisticated yet latent positivism of the likes of Suzanne Langer and Northrop Frye. The former rejects, while the latter accepts, a dichotomy between cognitive and emotive meaning that relegates metaphoric utterances to an epistemological and metaphysical limbo. To experience a world of art as sad or warm is not the same thing as experiencing a person or room as such, but neither is it the same thing as feeling sad or warm oneself. There is some sort of real connection, albeit a metaphorical one, affirmed by the language clustering around such experiences. Indeed, the linguistic context even seems to provide the matrix or basis out of which these experiences arise. In short, there seems to be a sense in which it is proper to say that metaphoric speech constitutes our world:

> The expression (sad), therefore, is no less real than the colour (blue). The
> fact that it is neither verbal nor literal, but representational and trans-

ferred, does not make the expression any less "true," so long as it is appropriate. Expression is not constituted by the effects on the spectator. For I can perceive the sadness of a picture without being made sad by it. "Metaphorical importation" is able to make this predicate an acquired property; the expression is truly the possession of the thing. A painting expresses properties that it exemplifies metaphorically in virtue of its status as pictorial symbol. (*The Rule of Metaphor*, p. 238)

At this point, however, Ricoeur sees himself as parting company with Goodman because the latter is content to draw only nominalist conclusions from the foregoing affirmations. For Goodman the world is exclusively a function of the metaphors and models we devise, and whereas we can make and remake our world through our language we can never claim that we have, or are getting closer to, a description of the "real world." The fittingness of certain ways of speaking, to Ricoeur's mind, can hardly be fully explained in terms of internal linguistic consistency.

Does not the fittingness, the appropriateness of certain verbal and non-verbal predicates, indicate that language not only has organized reality in a different way, but also made manifest a way of being of things, which is brought to language thanks to semantic innovation? It would seem that the enigma of metaphorical discourse is that it "invents" in both senses of the word; what it creates, it discovers; and what it finds, it invents. (*The Rule of Metaphor*, p. 239)

Following Max Black, Mary Hesse, and Stephen Toulmin, Ricoeur goes on to explore the referential dimension of scientific models. In addition, he returns to the conflicting positions of Wheelwright and Turbayne on the question of the "truth" of metaphoric speech. Wheelwright grants too much to metaphor by implying that it has no cognitive limits, while Turbayne grants too little by insisting that metaphors are only metaphors. Ricoeur concludes that the paradox necessitated by the inescapable, twofold assertion within metaphoric speech—the "is" and the "is not"—suggests the acknowledgment of the referential quality of metaphor, and thus of its cognitive quality as well.

I do not say that this twofold critique proves the thesis. The internal critique only helps us recognize the assumptions and commitments of one who speaks and uses the verb *to be* metaphorically. At the same time, it underlines the inescapably paradoxical character surrounding a meta-phorical concept of truth. The paradox consists in the fact that there is no other way to do justice to the notion of metaphorical truth than to include the critical incision of the (literal) "is not" within the ontological vehe-mence of the (metaphorical) "is." In doing so, the thesis merely draws the most extreme consequence of the theory of tension. (*The Rule of Meta-phor*, p. 255)

Perhaps another way to put the epistemological thrust of Ricoeur's conclusion is in terms of Michael Polanyi's notion of "universal intent." Put generally, the point is that all linguistic affirmations seek, as a matter both of logic and fact, to state the truth ("how things are") about their chosen aspect of experienced reality (this statement itself is an excellent example). This is no less true of metaphoric speech than it is of non-metaphoric speech. In short, all affirmations intend to be taken as, directly aim at being, true universally. Even the statement "All truths are relative to a given culture (or individual)" is meant to be understood and agreed with as a universal truth claim. A case in point is B. F. Skinner's effort to describe "verbal behavior" exclusively as a function of operant conditioning, while at the same time proposing his description as a "true account of the facts. At the foundational level of their work, all scientists either affirm that their fundamental models are true (or more true than those of their competitors), or they undercut the value of their own efforts.

To put this point specifically in relation to the discussion of metaphor, Ricoeur is maintaining that Goodman's relativism with respect to the question of reference and/or truth in metaphoric speech is self-defeating. For any account of how it is that we make and remake our world(s) by means of our models and metaphors aims at being a *true* account. This is true even if the account itself is based in metaphor at the bedrock level, as Goodman's at least occasionally seems to be. At the deepest level a true insight about the nature of things is being affirmed, intended, as universally acceptable—and other accounts are being affirmed as in some sense inadequate. The only way Goodman, like Turbayne, can express his point of view (expecting to be understood and agreed with) is by drawing on an implicit claim that it is possible to aim at the truth. Without this claim the affirmation implodes itself.

Ricoeur's overall ontological position might be constructed in the following way. Although it may not be possible to claim that reality can be described directly, as with naive realism, it is not necessary to jump to the opposite extreme and take on a "linguistic idealism" that maintains that "the limits of my language are the limits of my world." Even if one prefers to label his position as a form of pragmatism, as Goodman seems to, it is neither necessary nor desirable to see this posture as entailing linguistic relativism. In making his case for the ontological significance of metaphoric speech, Ricoeur seems to take up the position that speech and reality are mutually constitutive of one another. Since as humans we are post-linguistic beings engaged in embodied existence, it makes no sense for us to speak *either* of reality in and of itself (Kant's long-lost noumena) *or* of linguistic meaning in and of itself (à la Humpty Dumpty). We use speech in relation to reality and we know reality in relation to speech.

A helpful model for understanding this view of the intrinsic relationship between language and reality might well be the symbiotic dynamic of a magnetic field. The poles that define this field are language and reality, and neither can exist, let alone be understood, apart from its relationship to the other. Ricoeur would seem to be maintaining that at this most fundamental level language is metaphoric, and that this metaphoric mode of speech is constitutive of reality, not in the sense that it totally determines it, but rather in the sense that the respective poles of a magnetic field can be said to constitute one another. Moreover, since the metaphoric mode is logically primitive in relation to our other linguistic modes, it is by means of metaphor that our deepest insight into reality can and must be expressed.

METAPHOR AND ART

After this rather lengthy survey we should be in a position to appreciate the approach offered by Merleau-Ponty. We shall begin by considering his treatment of artistic expression, especially as it is found in poetry, for it is in this context that we find the germ of Merleau-Ponty's understanding of the metaphoric mode. Such an approach is necessary as well as appropriate, since he nowhere directly confronts the notion of metaphor, let alone in the terms suggested by the contemporary philosophic discussion. Once having gained this vantage point, we shall be in a position to focus Merleau-Ponty's views in relation to the issues raised in the first section of the present chapter.

As early on as his preface to *Phenomenology of Perception*, Merleau-Ponty suggested an affinity between philosophy and art, especially with respect to the language they employ. There he spoke of the task of reflection as being neither a direct encounter with nor a withdrawing from the world, but rather as involving a slackening of "the intentional threads which attach us to the world," thereby bringing the nature and function of these threads of body and speech to our attention (p. xiii). This slackening process suggests a mode of thought and speech in between literal, propositional analysis on the one hand and the silence of mysticism on the other. Metaphor would seem to be the most likely candidate.

Merleau-Ponty concludes his preface by suggesting that both philosophy and art are activities whereby we "take up this unfinished world in an effort to complete and conceive it" (p. xx). We shall return to the implications of this remark for Merleau-Ponty's understanding of philosophy in the next chapter; it is sufficient at this point to establish the connection he makes between art and philosophy as activities involving creative, conceptual modes of expression. Later on he stresses the mediational or supervenient character of the arts, remarking how they communicate their meaning in and through the unique configuration of their constituent elements (p. 151). Here again the role of metaphor, as it presents the unfamiliar by means of the familiar, would seem to be implicit in this mediational character of the arts.

Throughout this major early work Merleau-Ponty emphasized the "over-extending" quality of all speech, how it means what it says while carrying the potential to mean much more. What he calls "originating speech," that is, language as it is actually and creatively used, "offers merely a resting-place in the unending process of expression, another thought which is struggling to establish itself, and succeeds only by bending the resources of language to some fresh usage" (p. 389). If this is true of everyday speech, surely it applies in spades to metaphor. Indeed for Merleau-Ponty, language extends beyond itself by "bearing" its meaning toward the world, by enabling one actually to "reach" the object about which one is speaking (p. 177); "Thus speech, in the speaker does not translate ready-made thought, but accomplishes it" (p. 178).

In all of his essays on aesthetics, which comprise a good deal of what might be termed Merleau-Ponty's early "middle works" (collected in *Sense and Non-Sense*), appearing as they did between *Phenomenology of Perception* and his posthumously published *The Visible and the Invisible*, he focuses on the mediational character of artistic expression. In the essay on "Cézanne's Doubt" he quotes favorably Cézanne's comment that in order to paint Balzac's description of the table setting it is necessary to paint the tangible particulars properly, allowing the intangible qualities to arise naturally. Any attempt to paint such intangibles directly will end in failure. These aspects can only be mediated by means of a visual metaphor rendered in paints on a canvas; the latter bear the meaning of the former, and in so doing they transcend themselves without being expendable.

This same mediational pattern is used by Merleau-Ponty when discussing the work of the novelist (in "Metaphysics and the Novel," *SNS*, pp. 9–25). He maintains that the metaphysical significance of human existence is not found in abstract theories about "vertical transcendence," but in the nitty-gritty of everyday life in this world. This results in a "horizontal transcendence" in which the meaning of human existence is mediated by means of concrete and relational activities. This meaning "cannot be expressed except in 'stories' and, as it were, pointed at" (*SNS*, p. 28). The art of film is also discussed in terms of Gestalt perceptual psychology, according to which the whole is often greater of more significance than the sum of its parts ("The Film and the New Psychology"). "The meaning of a film is incorporated in its rhythm. . . . The joy of art lies in its showing how something takes on meaning . . . by the temporal or spatial arrangement of elements" (*SNS*, p. 57).

This general theme is pinpointed even more specifically in the essays comprising Merleau-Ponty's later "middle works" (collected in *Signs*). In the essay, "Indirect Language and the Voices of Silence," he stresses the

> . . . opaqueness of language. Nowhere does it stop and leave a place for pure meaning; it is always limited only by more language, and meaning appears within it only set in a context of words. Like a charade, language is understood only through the interaction of signs, each of which taken separately, is equivocal or banal, and makes sense only by being combined with others. (*Signs*, p. 42)

This indirect, allusive character of language—which Merleau-Ponty designates as "silence"—is likened to that of painting and novel writing. In each of these cases what is expressed is both immanent within the specific elements employed and takes us beyond them: "language expresses as much by what is between the words as by the words themselves . . ." (*Signs*, p. 45).

Merleau-Ponty frequently refers to a "language within language," a "tacit language" upon which all expression depends and which is especially significant in artistic expression. Because speech takes place against the general backdrop of non-speech, and because there are always things left unsaid, as well as different ways something could have been said, Merleau-Ponty refers to this "tacit language" as a form of silence, or the absence of expression. This absence is itself a form of signification, and all communication depends upon our ability to "hear" these silences in and around speech. Here is how Merleau-Ponty makes his point:

> The case is no different for all truly expressive speech and thus for all language in the phase in which it is being established. Expressive speech does not simply choose a sign for an already defined signification, as one goes to look for a hammer in order to drive a nail or for a claw to pull it out. It gropes around a significant intention which is not guided by any text, and which is precisely in the process of writing the text. If we want to do justice to expressive speech, we must evoke some of the other expressions which might have taken its place and were rejected, and we must feel the way in which they might have touched and shaken the chain of language in another manner and the extent to which this particular expression was really the only possible one if that signification was to come into the world. In short, we must consider speech before it is spoken, the background of silence which does not cease to surround it and without which it would say nothing. (*Signs*, p. 46)

The important thing to bear in mind here is that, according to Merleau-Ponty, these surrounding, "silent" dimensions of meaning must themselves be understood in some tacit or implicit sense as and if the linguistic expression in question is to be comprehended. In a word, the entire fabric of language, which forms the background for any specific utterance, comes into play and must be acquired in order for any particular expression to carry signification. As with understanding a joke or a local idiom, so with all of speech, the meaning is more a function of the interactive field formed by common custom, nonverbal behavior, and intentionality than it is a matter of simple signification. What Merleau-Ponty terms an "expressive speech" both relies upon and extends beyond the structures and strictures of conventional linguistic communication.

It is this mediational and transformative quality of speech in general and artistic expression in particular that applies as well to our understanding of metaphoric language. Merleau-Ponty does not view language as comprising distinct levels or functions; rather, it is all "of a piece," with various emphases and connotations arising from fluctuating purposes and accomplishments. Thus there is, for him, no sharp line between literal and metaphoric speech—both are characterized by the mediational pattern inherent in the background/foreground structure of all language. Moreover, since the subsidiary, "silent" dimension is always the necessary framework within which even literal speech takes on meaning, all expression is, at the primordial level, mediational and thus metaphorical in character. Although he does not directly address the question of the nature and function of metaphor, Merleau-Ponty's view of language in general clearly entails a commitment to the primacy of the metaphoric mode in relation to every form of human linguistic activity.

That this is so can be seen from the way Merleau-Ponty concludes his discussion of the mediational parallel between painting and language, since it will

> lead us to detect beneath spoken language an operant or speaking language whose words have a little-known life and unite with and separate from one another as their lateral or indirect signification demands, even though these relations seem *evident* to us once the expression is accomplished. The transparency of spoken language . . . the property which it apparently has of extracting the meaning in its pure state . . . and its would-be power of recapitulating and enclosing a whole process of expression in a single act, are these not simply the highest point of a tacit and implicit accumulation of the same sort as that of painting? (*Signs*, pp. 75–76)

The terms "lateral" and "transparency," when used together with "indirect" and "tacit," clearly suggest the sort of meaning and communication characteristic of metaphoric speech, especially as analyzed and presented by "interactionists" such as Max Black and Phillip Wheelwright. While there exists a general equality among all forms and uses of language as such, with a potential for each to convey significance, in any given speech act and context there is always a vectorial relationship. That is to say, there is always a "from–to" pattern in speech in which the utterance in question derives its meaning from all the rest of language surrounding it. This vectorial pattern mediates the meaning of the specific statement. In this way all speech can be seen to exhibit the same structure as metaphoric communication, and vice versa.

For example, the statement "The door is open" derives its meaning from the context within which it is uttered, depending on the use to which it is put, by whom, to whom, when, where, and how. For instance, (1) as a declarative answer to an informational question, (2) as an imperative when said by an annoyed parent to a youngster who repeatedly leaves the outside door open, (3) as an invitation for discussion when uttered by a person in authority, (4) as encouragement when said by a friend who is urging you to take advantage of an opportunity, (5) as an example in a philosophical discussion, or (6) as a joke among the members of a philosophy class who are tired of the example. It should be noted that in instances (3), (4), and perhaps (6), the expression is being used in a metaphorical sense, thus "doubling" the vectorial mediation.

Finally, in his essay "On the Phenomenology of Language," Merleau-Ponty develops this idea of the mediational or metaphorical quality of all of language even further. Unsurprisingly, he does so in terms of several fresh metaphorical images of his own, a phenomenon the significance of which we shall consider in the next chapter. In the midst of his analysis of the gestural basis of speech, which parallels the somatic quality of thoughts and intentions, Merleau-Ponty argues that the supervenient character of linguistic signification establishes that while the semantic and syntactic particulars comprising language are necessary to the communication of meaning, they are never sufficient to explain or exhaust this meaning.

> The spoken word (the one I utter or the one I hear) is pregnant with a meaning which can be read in the very texture of the linguistic gesture (to the point that a hesitation, an alteration of the voice, or the choice of a certain syntax suffices to modify it), and yet is never contained in that gesture, every expression always appearing to me as a trace, no idea being given to me except in transparency, and every attempt to close our hand on the thought which dwells in the spoken word leaving only a bit of verbal material in our fingers. (*Signs*, p. 89)

Here again the images employed (pregnancy, transparency, etc.), as well as the point being made, clearly indicate a mediational or metaphorical understanding of the working of all human language. By means of the tangible we express and grasp the intangible, but are never able to encounter the latter apart from the former.

Perhaps no linguistic device more pointedly demonstrates this vectorial quality of speech than that of irony. When we deliberately say the opposite of what we mean, and expect to be understood, we are obviously relying on so-called extra-linguistic factors, such as context, tone, and facial expression to mediate our intentions. For example, some years ago a friend essentially said "I love you" with the words "Go to hell" when I offered to pay him for a book he had just given to me. In such situations, the meaning of an utterance is borne or transported by means of the use to which the words are put. It is more than interesting that in Greek the term *metaphor* means to transport or transfer something from one place to another. Thus the vectorial character of speech.

A bit further on in this same essay, Merleau-Ponty trades off of the ambiguity of the term "understood" in an enlightening manner. All understanding of what is said depends upon understanding many things that are left unsaid, so we understand an utterance to the degree that we grasp certain unspoken factors that simply must be "understood." He summarizes this point in the following fashion:

> So let us not say that every expression is imperfect because it leaves things understood. Let us say that every expression is perfect to the extent it is unequivocally understood, and admit as a fundamental fact of expression *a surpassing of the signifying by the signified which it is the very virtue of the signifying to make possible.* (*Signs*, p. 90)

Meaningful communication is always more than the particulars of language without ever being other or less.

Merleau-Ponty also makes this general point concerning the metaphorical quality of all speech in terms of his image of "sedimentation." It is the accumulation of common contexts and conventionalized linguistic uses that provides the springboard for the meaning of any particular utterance. This accumulation or sedimentation results from previous speech-acts wherein the meaning was active "in solution," what Merleau-Ponty calls "expressive speech." But in each new case, the given significative intention of the speaker both incorporates and carries beyond the previously established meanings. It uses and transforms these meanings, becoming freshly available "in turn because in retrospect it gives us the illusion that it has contained in the already available significations, whereas to infuse them with a new life" (*Signs*, p. 92).

What is here said of the transformative character of all speech, as it recoils upon conventional patterns and springs forward to fresh expression, can and must be said of metaphoric speech. The primary difference between "regular" speech and metaphor is not one of kind but of degree. In metaphor the extent or torque of the "twist" given the words involved, to borrow Monroe Beardsley's term, is more pronounced rather than being qualitatively distinct. Indeed, the last line from the above remarks by Merleau-Ponty suggests a useful definition of metaphor: in metaphor one's significative intentions are embodied in conventional locutions "only in order to infuse them with a new life."

METAPHOR AND REALITY

We are now in a position to return to the questions that served as the dual foci in the discussion of the various models of metaphor on the contemporary philosophical market. The first focus was the issue of the relationship between literal and metaphoric speech in relation to the problem of cognitivity. There is little question about where Merleau-Ponty fits into the spectrum of views with respect to this issue; he clearly sides with the "interactionists" in rejecting any and all forms of reductionism, according to which literal propositions must be substituted for metaphoric expressions if cognitivity is to be maintained: Merleau-Ponty flatly denies the dichotomy between these two "kinds" of language that lies at the heart of such views. Indeed, he even goes so far as to ground all speech in the metaphoric mode, granting signification to "literal" propositions only within the framework provided by context, convention, and creative intention. Explicit cognition, to the degree that it exists, arises out of tacit cognition.

The second focus in the discussion comprising the first section of this present chapter pertained to the relationship between language and reality in general, with specific reference to the role of metaphoric language. On the one hand, Merleau-Ponty seems to go beyond both Black and Wheelwright in affirming the creative as well as the expressive function of metaphor in relation to reality. He definitely stresses what has been called the "orphic" function of language in "singing the world's praises." For Merleau-Ponty the world is not simply "out there," waiting to be discovered and described. Rather, since we come to experience and know it through our interaction with it and each other, it *is* and must be as we encounter it. With Nelson Goodman we would contend that it makes no sense for us to speak of the world as it is "in itself," apart from its incorporation into our world, since this way of speaking itself only has meaning within our discussion of it and is thus part and parcel of the world as we know it.

At the same time it seems clear that Merleau-Ponty would not go as far as Goodman in suggesting that the world we live in is entirely of our making. It is more likely that he would agree with Paul Ricoeur that there is an intractable, unpredictable character to whatever it is with which we have to do, which in some sense sets limits for and contributes to the composition of our experience. Perhaps the symbiotic model suggested by Ricoeur's "is/is not" interpretation of metaphorical expressions would fit nicely with Merleau-Ponty's own understanding of the relationship between speech and reality. Our efforts to interact with and express the world through language can be thought of as combining with whatever is already there, including the results of our previous interactions and expressions, to form ever fresh worlds for yet further interactions and expressions. Metaphoric speech might be thought of as existing at the cutting edge of this ongoing process. Let us see how this is so.

The fundamental motif running throughout and forming the very axis of all of Merleau-Ponty's works is the concept of relationality. Thus, when approaching the questions of the role of the metaphoric mode in the general relationship between language and reality, it is no surprise to find this relational notion, in all of its diverse images, at the very center of his thought. The basic idea inherent in the concept of relationality is that everything, in both its being and its knowing, as well as its being known, is intricately connected with everything else. This suggests that metaphoric speech, as a dimension of human embodiment, must be understood as integral, not only to our prehension and understanding of reality, but to its very being and nature itself.

To my mind no passage in Merleau-Ponty's entire corpus of writings better focuses this relational axis of his thought than that found in his preface to *Phenomenology of Perception*. Let me here quote it once again and then comment upon it:

> Reflection does not withdraw from the world toward the unity of consciousness as the world's basis; it steps back to watch the forms of transcendence fly up like sparks from a fire; it slackens the intentional threads which attach us to the world and thus brings them to our notice. . . . (p. xiii)

We shall return to this crucial passage in the next chapter in order to consider its bearing on Merleau-Ponty's theory of the nature of philosophy in relation to phenomenological methodology. At this point our attention is directed to the character and role of the "intentional threads" through which we are related to the world.

Having previously rejected the possibility of obtaining a direct, "objective" knowledge of reality through science or philosophy, Merleau-Ponty here also rejects the viability of "subjectively" collapsing the world into a function of human consciousness, à la Bishop Berkeley, Immanuel Kant, or Jean-Paul Sartre. The gap between the subjective and the objective, between the knower and the world is overcome, in Merleau-Ponty's philosophy, by denying their separation at the outset. We are bound together with the world, both physical and social, and the world with us, by means of mutual

involvement and interaction through the "intentional threads" of embodiment and speech. Our knowledge of this relational reality is, therefore,
neither subjective nor objective, but "intersubjective," and is achieved by
means of "slackening," not dispensing with or tightening these threads.

Throughout the entire scope of his work, from perceptual psychology
and epistemology, to aesthetics, linguistics, and social philosophy, this
understanding of both the world and our knowledge thereof being relational and intersubjective plays a dominant role in Merleau-Ponty's philosophy. Moreover, the intentional threads of somatic and linguistic activity
are continually and systematically invoked in his exploration of these
various aspects of human existence. It is especially important to notice that
this applies with equal, perhaps special force to his treatment of language in
general and to his view of indirect, expressive speech, such as the metaphoric, in particular. Nowhere is this more clearly evident than in
Merleau-Ponty's final and appropriately most metaphoric writing, *The
Visible and the Invisible*. It is to this volume that we now turn our attention.

In the latter half of his final book, Merleau-Ponty continues to develop
the notion of "the intentional threads" through which we and the world
interact with each other. Against the general backdrop of his account of
human experience and knowledge taking place within an interrelational
field, surrounded by a flexible and porous horizon, he provides further
indication of what is meant by "slackening" the intentional threads.

> The effective, present, ultimate and primary being, the thing in itself, are
> in principle apprehended in transparency through their perspectives, offer
> themselves therefore only to someone who wishes not to have them but
> to see them, not to hold them as with forceps, or to immobilize them as
> under the objective of a microscope, but to let them be and to witness
> their continued being. . . . (*VI*, p. 101)

He goes on to speak of this slacking-off posture as one of dialogue and
interrogation, as an ongoing conversation rather than an accumulation of
information and conclusions.

A bit later on Merleau-Ponty pointedly relates this way of encountering
reality to linguistic activity. He says that what is needed is a way of speaking
that neither confronts reality directly nor backs away from it altogether.
Both speaking, in the traditional, objectifying sense, and silence, out of
reverence for reality as it is, seem inappropriate postures for the one who
would know the world and the means by which it is known. What is needed
is a linguistic mode that enables us both to engage reality and to allow it to
present itself. The interactive, open-ended character of the metaphoric
mode, which mediates the unfamiliar and intangible through the familiar
and tangible, is perfectly suited to this task:

One has to believe, then, that language is not simply the contrary of the truth, of coincidence, that there is or could be a language of coincidence, a manner of making the things themselves speak . . . it would be a language of which he (the knower) would not be the organizer, words we should not assemble, that would combine through him by virtue of a natural intertwining of their meaning, through the occult trading of the metaphor—where what counts is no longer the manifest meaning of each word and of each image, but the lateral relations, the kinships that are implicated in their transfers and their exchanges. (*VI*, p. 125)

Thus the indirect, "sidling up to" posture inherent in metaphoric thought and speech is in the final analysis the only appropriate approach to a reality that can only be known "through a glass, darkly." By means of exploring the connections and creative possibilities within the networks formed by our conceptual and somatic activity—the "lateral" relations—we can tease out the edges and patterns of reality. By changing the image we can allow the joints, not the bones, of reality to display themselves, albeit actively rather than statically. Perhaps the most fruitful image is still that of the dance, wherein the two partners (ourselves and the world) together choreograph reality as they interact through embodiment and linguisticality. Reality is thus a symbiosis between the knower and the known, as mediated through action and speech, especially through the metaphoric mode.

One further passage in Merleau-Ponty's final work warrants our attention. As if following up on the image of "through a glass, darkly," he casts the problem and possibility of the knowledge of reality in terms of a perceptual or linguistic screen that separates us from the world.

Here, on the contrary, there is no vision without the screen: the ideas we are speaking of would not be better known to us if we had no body and no sensitivity; it is then that they would be inaccessible to us. . . . It is not only that we would find in that carnal experience the *occasion* to think them; it is that they owe their authority, their fascinating, indestructible power, precisely to the fact that they are in transparency being the sensible, or in its heart. . . . Thus it is essential to this sort of ideas that they be "veiled with shadows," appear "under a disguise." (*VI*, p. 150)

It is the metaphoric mode that provides this transparency, since it alone simultaneously veils and reveals. Just as no set of literal propositions can suffice to "translate" a rich and appropriate metaphor, so reality cannot be set or parsed off from language or from the knower. Both meaning and reality, according to Merleau-Ponty, are somatically and linguistically constituted (not invented), and are thus mediated at the primordial level by gesture and metaphor, respectively.

In conclusion, there is one consideration that bears mentioning before moving on. The primacy of metaphor in Merleau-Ponty's philosophy is nowhere more forcefully and obviously demonstrated than in the simple but highly significant fact that he himself found it both impossible and unhelpful to carry out his own work apart from an exceedingly rich display of metaphoric images. Indeed, it is possible to argue that no other philosopher in the history of the Western tradition has relied so heavily upon the metaphoric mode as a means of developing and expressing his thought. It is safe to say that there is scarcely a page of Merleau-Ponty's works that is not replete with figurative images.

Moreover, it is clearly evident, both from numerous specific passages and from the general thrust of Merleau-Ponty's philosophy, that this reliance on the metaphoric mode was no mere accident or convenience. His images, especially the dominant ones, function as the very heart of his entire approach, as the foregoing chapters should make clear. In other words, the medium in which he found it necessary and helpful to forge his own insights is itself an instance of those insights; he displays and demonstrates the richness and effectiveness of his own philosophy in the manner in which he works it out. Thus it is appropriate to conclude that both in his method and in his thought Merleau-Ponty affirmed the primacy of the metaphoric mode.

The harmony between Merleau-Ponty's philosophy and his mode of expression serves as an excellent transition to the next and final chapter of the present investigations. For with an examination of his philosophy of language, with special reference to the role of metaphor, already before us, we can now direct ourselves to the question of the nature and function of philosophy according to Merleau-Ponty. Unsurprisingly, we shall find that his conception of philosophy is closely tied to and mainly guided by his understanding of the language employed therein. Here again, the metaphoric mode will come to the fore as axial in relation to philosophical activity. We can now consider how this is the case.

6

PHILOSOPHY AND METAPHOR

We come now to our final task. We shall explore the implications of Merleau-Ponty's prolific use of metaphor, together with his understanding of the nature of linguistic activity, for his view of the purpose and method of philosophy. I shall begin with a review of his position with respect to traditional versions of the philosophical enterprise, focusing on his account of the similarities and differences between himself and his mentor, Edmund Husserl. Next, I shall endeavor to pinpoint Merleau-Ponty's understanding of philosophy as revealed in his characteristic employment of metaphor. Finally, I shall trace his own implementation of this posture in relation to the notion of transcendence.

OBJECTIVITY AND DOGMATISM

In 1956 Merleau-Ponty edited an anthology of the works of a number of philosophers representing classical, oriental, Catholic Christian, and contemporary existential thought. His introduction to this volume was entitled "Everywhere and Nowhere," and is included in *Signs* under this title. This essay provides an excellent backdrop against which to appreciate the particular contours of Merleau-Ponty's own view of philosophy. He begins with an account of classical Western thought from Plato to Kant in which the distinction between the "outside" and "inside" approaches was paramount. Many thinkers, predominantly the ancient Greeks, sought to grasp and describe reality and truth objectively, from the outside, as it were, and this goal has always played an important part in the way Western philosophy is done.

In modern times, especially in Europe, many thinkers have sought to base philosophy on the internal thought processes of the mind, be they deductive, as with Descartes, or inductive, as with Hume. In addition, some modern thinkers have argued that "true" philosophy must be grounded in the socioeconomic history of human experience. About these various postures and their ensuing debates Merleau-Ponty has this to say:

> We do not have to choose between a false conception of "interior" and the false conception of the "exterior." Philosophy is everywhere, even in the "facts," and it nowhere has a private realm which shelters it from life's contagion. We need to do many things to eliminate the twin myths of pure philosophy and pure history and get back to their effective relationships. (*Signs*, p. 130)

With respect to the nature and value of Eastern thought, Merleau-Ponty contends that although it generally lacks the distinction between objectivity and subjectivity, which is so characteristic of Western views of philosophy, it has much to teach the West about the proper approach to comprehending reality and truth.

> One has the feeling that Chinese philosophers do not understand the very idea of understanding or knowing . . . that they do not have the intellectual genesis of the object in view or try to *grasp* the object, but simply seek to evoke it in its primordial perfection. And that is why they are suggestive; why commentary and what is commented upon, enveloping and enveloped, signifying and signified are indistinguishable in their work; why in their work concepts are as much allusions to aphorisms as aphorisms allusions to concepts. (*Signs*, p. 135)

Merleau-Ponty sketches the history of Christian philosophy in terms of the struggle between reason and faith. Either they seek the same goal through different methods, rational analysis or revelation, or they each offer truth about altogether different realities. In the former case, conflict is inevitable and in the latter conflict is impossible. In either case, the notion of a Christian philosophy seems out of the question. Merleau-Ponty concludes: "Will this always be the case? Will there ever be a real exchange between philosopher and Christian . . .? In our view this would be possible only if the Christian . . . were to accept without qualification the task of mediation which philosophy cannot abandon without eliminating itself" (*Signs*, p. 146).

Contemporary existentialist thought arose out of the dissatisfactions of many thinkers with the alternatively skeptical or dogmatic conclusions of traditional philosophy. In their place existentialist thinkers put "subjectivity" and proceeded to celebrate it. Since life must be lived in order for it to be understood, our understanding must be anchored in "lived experience"; thus Nietzsche, Kierkegaard, Sartre, and Heidegger. About this "discovery of subjectivity" Merleau-Ponty says:

Of course this is no discovery in the sense that America or even potassium was discovered. Yet it is still a discovery in the sense that once introduced into philosophy, "subjective" thinking no longer allows itself to be ignored. Even if philosophy finally eliminates it, it will never again be what it was before this kind of thinking. After all, that which is true . . . becomes as solid as a fact, and subjective thinking is one of these solids that philosophy will have to digest. (*Signs*, p. 154)

Last, Merleau-Ponty discusses briefly what he calls "concrete philosophy," which focuses on reality and truth by beginning with the lived experience of human existence and proceeding dialectically according to an open-ended question-and-answer format. He believes that this "phenomenological" perspective is what modern philosophy has been seeking in its various efforts to overcome the subjective–objective dichotomy on the one hand and the stalemate between skepticism and dogmatism on the other.

A concrete philosophy is not a happy one. It must stick close to experience, and yet not limit itself to the empirical but restore to each experience the ontological cipher which marks it internally . . . it will never regain the conviction of holding the keys to nature or history in its concepts, and it will not renounce its radicalism, that search for presuppositions and foundations which has produced the great philosophies. (*Signs*, p. 157)

Along the way to this conclusion, Merleau-Ponty remarks that logical positivism or analytical philosophy has been left out of his anthology because "all the philosophies we have just named speak a common language, and for logical positivism all their problems put together are meaningless" (*Signs*, p. 157). He acknowledges that if "concrete philosophy" does emerge as the preeminent form of philosophy, analytical thought will have to be understood as "the last and most energetic resistance" to its arrival. It should be noted at this point that it is indeed unfortunate that Merleau-Ponty did not distinguish between the hard–core analysts of the Vienna Circle and the more open-textured approach of the later Wittgenstein's "ordinary language" philosophy. In my own view there are many profound similarities between Wittgenstein's "linguistic phenomenology" and the "concrete philosophy" advocated by Merleau-Ponty.

It is, of course, well known that Merleau-Ponty received his inspiration and early philosophical guidance from the work of Edmund Husserl. Thus it is that he frequently casts his presentation of his own philosophical methodology in the form of a dialogue with Husserl's ideas. On the one hand Merleau-Ponty acknowledges that in his early work Husserl generally spoke in terms that not only placed him within the objectivist, dogmatic tradition of Western thought, but which often seemed to contradict his own commitment to the truth. This is especially true with respect to his simulta-

neous affirmation of (1) the importance of the phenomenological "bracketing" of all ontological and epistemological questions, and (2) the
fundamental character of the vectorial quality of all consciousness. Bracketing and intentionality would seem to be mutually exclusive motions since
the latter renders inoperative the search for the "pure phenomena" of lived
experience.

On the other hand Merleau-Ponty repeatedly claims that in his later work
Husserl saw the tensions within his own thought, and the notion of full
phenomenological "reduction," and became more concerned with the
dialogical reciprocity of relational interaction as the proper philosophical
method. This is not the place to enter into the complex question of whether
or not Merleau-Ponty has read Husserl correctly. Our concern here is with
Merleau-Ponty's view of philosophy, and thus we shall focus on his reading
of Husserl only as a means of exposing his own perspective. If Husserl did
not, in fact, mean what Merleau-Ponty says he meant, in Merleau-Ponty's
view he should have done so, and that is what helps render more clear
Merleau-Ponty's own understanding of the nature of the phenomenological
method in philosophy.

In his preface to *Phenomenology of Perception*, Merleau-Ponty seeks to
clarify his own approach in relation to that of Husserl. After providing a
brief history of how phenomenology, as a philosophical movement,
evolved out of the thought of nineteenth century thinkers and culminated in
the work of Husserl, Merleau-Ponty reviews the main themes of the
phenomenological method. His aim here is to zero in on why this approach
became a problem for itself and seems to have arrived at something of a
standstill. The whole of *Phenomenology of Perception* is, of course, offered as a
way of getting the movement going again by placing human embodiment
at the center of phenomenological method in particular and philosophy in
general.

To begin with, Husserl asserted that phenomenological method seeks to
describe the world as it is lived, apart from presuppositions and/or doubts
about its ontological status. We are already involved in the world before and
as we reflect on it, and this "intentionality of consciousness" must be
acknowledged at the outset of any genuine philosophical investigation. This
leads to the effort to isolate or bracket off the pure "essence" "facticity" of
reality from preconceived philosophical questions and answers, to "reduce"
philosophy to an account of the bare "phenomena of lived experience." The
essences sought here do not lie behind or beyond the phenomenal world, à
la Kant, but constitute that very world itself as it is known by means of our
interaction with it and with each other.

Although he is in general agreement with this philosophical agenda, there
are as well indications that he is aware of certain difficulties inherent within

Husserl's program, especially as it was expressed in the latter's early writings. Merleau-Ponty maintains that Husserl himself began to address these problems in his later work. Whether or not this is true, Merleau-Ponty himself acknowledges in this preface that "the most important lesson which the reduction teaches us is the impossibility of complete reduction" (*PER*, p. xiv). Since "all our knowledge of the world is gained from my own particular point of view" (p. viii), or from a person's primordial, intentional involvement in and with the world (both physical and social), it is neither possible nor necessary to dream of achieving some form of absolute objectivity.

Elsewhere Merleau-Ponty argues that Husserl, in his more mature work, acknowledged these limitations in the initial efforts of phenomenological analysis, and himself suggested a reformulation of the method.

> So the idea of philosophy as a "rigorous science"—or as absolute knowledge—does reappear here, but from this point on with a question mark. Husserl said in his last years: "Philosophy as a rigorous science? The dream is dreamed out. . . ." Husserl had understood our philosophical problem is to open up the concept without destroying it. (*Signs*, p. 138)

This notion of "opening up" concepts and reality without claiming to know them "objectively" becomes the key idea in Merleau-Ponty's understanding of phenomenological method. Only by accrediting the possibility of knowing the world without encompassing it can philosophy avoid the dogmatism of previous approaches.

This brings us, once again, to the image of "slackened threads" that Mealeau-Ponty introduces in his preface to *Phenomenology of Perception*. Because we are so totally involved in the world, indeed are constituted by our relationships with all the aspects comprising it, before we even begin our investigation of it, the idea of obtaining completely objective knowledge of the world simply makes no sense. We cannot sever the threads by means of which we are connected to the world, in which we live and move and have our being, in order to make an object of it. At the same time, however, this does not mean that we can gain no knowledge of reality or of the threads by means of which we are involved in it. We are not condemned to pure subjectivity and skepticism.

The crucial difference here is captured in the distinction between Husserl's concept of "bracketing" or "suspending" our natural involvement with the world in order to know it, on the one hand, and Merleau-Ponty's notion of "slackening" the threads so as to know both them and the world *as* we are engaged in interacting with and through them. Examples of how this process works come readily to mind. We often loosen our grip slightly on a steering wheel in order to get a feel for the stability and bent of the steering mechanism. In this process we often get a different perspective on the condition of the road as well. We do a similar thing occasionally with lines of authority, such as parents, teachers, and supervisors. We even do it with language and concepts when we employ them in order to get clearer about them. We are neither "bound" by them into ignorance of them, nor are we able to "rise above" them to some sort of pure knowledge.

By and through using these intentional threads, if we pay attention as we use them we can, then, come to a fruitful understanding of their nature and of the world with which we have to do through them. This is Merleau-Ponty's interpretation of the phenomenological method he inherited from Husserl. In my own opinion, this seemingly small but significant divergence from Husserl's way of putting things represents a fundamental improvement. Indeed, it seems to me that Merleau-Ponty has found a way to overcome most of the dilemmas that have been plaguing Western philosophy since its inception. He has found a way to avoid objectivism and dogmatism without falling into subjectivism and relativism.

On the basis of the content of the investigations carried out in *Phenomenology of Perception* it is possible to conclude that the main "threads" of which Merleau-Ponty speaks in his preface are the body and speech (*Signs*, p. 95). By means of our embodiment we are placed in and interact with those aspects of the physical environment comprising our experienced reality. Supervenient on this embodiment is the capacity to think and speak, and through these threads we are "placed" in and interact with those others, both as persons and as culture, that comprise our social reality. By directing our attention to these threads, without ever being able or needing to disengage ourselves from them, we can gain an understanding of them, ourselves, and the world (both physical and social) that is both helpful and adequate. The world, our world, does not exist independently of us—such a notion makes no sense—but we do not create it willy-nilly, either. Rather, by means of our mutual somatic and linguistic dance, we and the world are both brought into being.

Throughout the essays he wrote in the middle of his career, on aesthetics, politics, linguistics, and social theory, Merleau-Ponty continued to develop and implement this symbiotic model of the relationship between ourselves and the world. For example, after his lengthy analysis of the parallels between the rule of tacit or indirect expression in language and the arts of painting and creative writing, Merleau-Ponty suggests that philosophy too is, at best, a mode of thinking and speaking that evokes and weaves reality as much as it reveals it. In all signification, philosophy included, we are in contact with reality "only by using language and not by going beyond language" (*Signs*, p. 82). In like manner, when concluding his discussion of

Husserl's account of the dynamics of linguistic communication as parallel to those of somatic signification, Merleau-Ponty suggests that phenomenological philosophy exhibits a similar pattern. In all these cases, the understanding that results from participation in the given activity is indirect and is neither "objective" nor "subjective," but is "intersubjective" (*Signs*, pp. 92–97).

Things are no different when Merleau-Ponty moves on to considering the relationship between sociology and philosophy. In spite of some claims to the contrary, it is clear that the cultural relativism that sociological knowledge attributes to all cognitive activity, including philosophy, applies as well to sociology itself. This does not result in complete skepticism, however; what it does is underscore the interdependency of all knowing. The knowing subject is situated in relation to the world, including other subjects, and together, through reciprocal interaction, an ever growing, changing field of knowledge arises amid them. Such knowledge, as intersubjective, neither transcends nor is reducible to the physical, social, and historical factors comprising the context within which it arises. Moreover, these "limitations" are not to be regretted but simply acknowledged as the matrix necessary to what is meant by human knowledge.

> Since we are all hemmed in by history, it is up to us to understand that whatever truth we may have is to be gotten not in spite of but *through* our historical inherence. Superficially considered, our inherence destroys all truth; considered radically, it founds a new idea of truth. As long as I cling to the ideal of an absolute spectator, of knowledge with no point of view, I can see my situation as nothing but a source of error. But if I have once recognized that through it I am grafted onto every action and all knowledge which can have a meaning for me, and that step by step it contains everything which can *exist* for me, then my contact with the social in the finitude of my situation is revealed to me as the point of origin of all truth, including scientific truth. And since we have an idea of truth, since we are in truth and cannot escape it, the only thing left for me to do is to define a truth in the situation. (*Signs*, p. 109)

THE METAPHORIC MODE

The first thing to establish at this point in our discussion is that the metaphoric mode is anything but incidental to Merleau-Ponty's understanding of philosophy. Indeed, it is no exaggeration to say that it lies at the very center of his overall philosophy in general and his view of philosophical activity in particular. Another way to put this is to say that it is no accident that Merleau-Ponty's writings, especially his major works, literally wallow in metaphor. In fact, he seems almost incapable of thinking at the deepest level without the copious use of metaphoric images; and this is precisely what one would expect on the basis of the foregoing account of his philosophical method and conclusions. Let us see exactly how this is the case.

In simple terms, the crucial feature of the metaphoric mode is the effort to comprehend an unfamiliar, frequently intangible aspect of reality in terms of, or in relation to, more familiar, tangible aspects. This symbiotic, vectorial process lies at the very center of Merleau-Ponty's understanding of human existence, experience, knowledge, language, art, and politics. At each and every turn he insists that relationality and intersubjectivity, embodiment and dialogue, indirection and mediation are the primary characteristics of the human way of being in and coming to grips with the world, both physical and social.

Perhaps the most helpful way to imagine the metaphoric mode is in terms of creating an arena in which one is both invited and challenged to engage an aspect of reality that is to some degree alien to one's usual patterns of thought and life. Merleau-Ponty has not only developed a philosophy that makes room for, indeed requires, this mode of understanding and existence, but he has expressed and implemented it in this mode as well. The content and form of Merleau-Ponty's philosophy strongly support and reinforce each other in a highly appropriate fashion. His images continuously and consistently create an horizon within which we are led to a deeper, broader, and richer comprehension of and interaction with ourselves in relation to the world of things and others.

Consider his portrayal of human existence and cognition in terms of somatic relationality. Not only do we come to know the world around us by means of our participation in it, but this very participation is both possible and necessary because we are at once one with the world and each other ("flesh of our flesh") while being capable of transcending the world and others through reciprocal interaction. Both this ontological condition and existential situation, as well as the correlative cognitive process, partake of the mediational character of the metaphoric mode, of being in and knowing various aspects of reality in and through being in and knowing other aspects.

Consider, as well, Merleau-Ponty's philosophy of language. Indeed, here we have seen that not only is the metaphoric mode important in the communicative enterprise, it constitutes the very matrix out of which language in general is created. All meaning is mediated in and through context, tone, and gesture, whether it be expressed in ordinary, scientific, or symbolic discourse:

> Strictly speaking, therefore, there are no conventional signs, standing as the simple notation of a thought free and clear in itself, there are only

words into which the history of a whole language is compressed, and which effect communication with no absolute guarantee, dogged as they are by incredible linguistic hazards. (*PER*, p. 188)

What we call "literal" speech is made up primarily of "dead" metaphors, creative figures of speech that have been domesticated through conventional (over?) use.

Consider, finally, Merleau–Ponty's account of artistic creation and appreciation. Even this form of expression must rely upon the mediation of intangible aspects of experience and reality in and through its tangible particulars. The characters and events of a story, the tones and rhythms of a piece of music, the lines and colors of a painting, all serve to express and communicate richer, more significant aesthetic qualities in an *indirect* manner; these intangible qualities are mediated through or supervenient upon the more tangible ones. Recall Merleau-Ponty's quotation of Cézanne's remarks about his desire to paint Balzac's table scene:

I know now that one must try to paint only: "the plates and napkins rose symmetrically," and "the light-coloured rolls." If I paint "crowned," I'm finished, you see. And if I really balance and shade my napkins and rolls as they really are, you may be sure that the crowning, the snow, and all the rest of it will be there. (*PER*, p. 198)

This mediational or metaphoric quality of all of speech is brought out forcefully by Merleau-Ponty in his essay, "Indirect Language and the Voices of Silence." There he speaks of language as "opaque," "indirect," and "allusive," while characterizing meaning as "lateral" or hidden "between the words." "As far as language is concerned, it is the lateral relation of one sign to another which makes each of them significant, so that the meaning appears only at the intersection of and as it were in the interval between words" (*PER*, p. 42). Merleau-Ponty intensifies this characterization of all speech as metaphoric by stressing the fact that linguistic meaning is as dependent on what is not said as it is on what is said, at both the empirical and poetic levels. Not only do the context, tone, purpose, and pattern of our speech help to carry its significance, but the silence behind and between our locutions often communicates significantly. "The absence of a sign can be a sign, and expression is not the adjustment of an element of discourse to each element of meaning, but an operation of language upon language which suddenly is thrown out of focus toward its meaning" (*PER*, p. 44).

The majority of the essay in question is devoted to exploring the similarities between speech and art, especially painting and novel writing. Merleau-Ponty insists that both modes of expression rely on an unexpressed or "tacit" level of meaning in their efforts to communicate or signify. Without the commonality of our embodiment in the physical world and our "enfleshment" with each other, without our shared needs, dreams, and tasks linguistic activity would never arise, let alone take on meaning. It is, according to Merleau-Ponty, this "lateral" meaning that gives linguistic activity its apparent "transparency" and clarity. Only through the indirectness of the metaphoric mode, serving as the matrix of linguistic signification, can direct speech achieve its clarity and transparency (*PER*, pp. 75–76).

All of this brings us to the main thrust of the current chapter, namely that for Merleau-Ponty philosophy itself is essentially a metaphoric enterprise. In the final third of his last work, *The Visible and the Invisible*, Merleau-Ponty addresses the issue of the nature of philosophical inquiry directly, though he continues to speak of it metaphorically and as a metaphoric activity. He begins by distinguishing philosophical questions both from those to which "objective" answers are sought and from those that can be "solved" by means of a speculative "awakening of consciousness." As he indicated in the preface to *Phenomenology of Perception*, Merleau-Ponty here insists that philosophical reflection aims, not at an exhaustive account of the "stuff" of the universe, not at a merely creative but subjective "approximation" of it, but rather at allowing the "joints" of the universe to be revealed in and through using them.

> The effective, present, ultimate and primary being, the thing itself, are in principle apprehended in transparence through their perspectives, offer themselves therefore only to someone who wishes not to have them but to see them, not to hold them with forceps, not to immobilize them as under the objective of a microscope, but to let them be and to witness their continued being—to someone who therefore limits himself to giving them the hollow, the free space they ask for in return, the resonance they require, who follows their own movement, who is therefore not a nothingness the full being would come to stop up, but a question consonant with the porous being which it questions and from which it obtains not an *answer* but a confirmation of its astonishment. (*VI*, pp. 101–102)

From this it would seem to follow that the language of most interest to philosophy is that which, in Wittgenstein's idiom, is not "idling," but which is actively engaged in getting things done in the world. Such speech "opens upon" reality and conveys "the life of the whole and makes our habitual evidences vibrate until they disjoin" (*The Visible and the Invisible*, p. 102). In like manner, the language most appropriate to philosophy would be that which would allow reality to display itself without being forced to do so. Clearly it is the metaphoric mode that is called for at this point. As Merleau-Ponty says:

> Hence it is a question of whether philosophy as reconquest of brute or wild being can be accomplished by the resources of the eloquent lan-

guage, or whether it would not be necessary for philosophy to use language in a way that takes from it its power of immediate or direct signification in order to equal it with what it wishes all the same to say. (*VI*, pp. 102–103)

It is clear from the above quotation that it is the metaphoric use of speech that Merleau-Ponty advocates for the philosophical enterprise, and his own philosophical language both demonstrates and substantiates this claim. It is especially important to note that Merleau-Ponty speaks here of a specific *use*, not *kind*, of language. The metaphoric mode is not a specialized form of speech, but involves a particular usage of ordinary and/or specialized speech. It is also significant that he characterizes this mode as one that is mediate and indirect, one that says what it has to say in and through what appears to be transparent speech while at the same time denying this transparency—indeed, while trading on it!

Merleau-Ponty concludes this section of *The Visible and the Invisible* by returning to the passage in which Claudel speaks of the ultimate meaning of life by means of a description of a man going about his daily tasks.

> From time to time, a man lifts his head, sniffs, listens, considers, recognizes his position: he thinks, he signs, and, drawing his watch from the pocket lodged against his chest, looks at the time. *Where am I? What time is it?* Such is the inexhaustible question turning from us to the world. . . . (p. 103)

Both existentially and literally the images in this passage mediate a cosmic significance through the mundane. Both the man in question, as a symbol of all human beings, and Claudel find a double significance in such terms as "position," "watch," "chest," "time," and "where." Through them the everyday, the tangible and the ultimate, the intangible are united by means of the metaphoric mode. The human activities themselves and the author's images mediate a richer, more comprehensive dimension of reality.

A bit further on this dual function of the metaphoric mode is offered as the crucial tool or posture through which philosophy can be realized. The philosopher must focus on a special use of language.

> It would be a language of which he would not be the organizer, words he would not assemble, that would combine through him by virtue of a natural intertwining of their meaning, through the occult trading of the metaphor—where what counts is no longer the manifest meaning of each word and of each image, but the lateral relations, the kinship that are implicated in their transfers and their exchanges. (p. 125)

Here Merleau-Ponty explicitly identifies the metaphoric mode as most appropriate to philosophical activity.

The term "intertwining" in the above quotation serves as a natural bridge between this section and the final section of *The Visible and the Invisible*. For the image of intertwining, along with "the flesh," "the visible and the invisible," and "the chiasm," is central to Merleau-Ponty's final reflections on the relation between philosophy and the world. Moreover, each of these final images serves to bring out the pivotal role played by the metaphoric mode in Merleau-Ponty's understanding of philosophy. Perhaps if we take these images up one at a time we shall be able to elucidate further the contours of Merleau-Ponty's view of philosophy and metaphor.

The title and theme of Merleau-Ponty's final project, *The Visible and the Invisible*, point directly to the mediational character of our experience of reality, as well as of the metaphoric mode. Strictly speaking, the phrase should read "the invisible *in* the visible," since this is the central theme of Merleau-Ponty's ontology and epistemology. The world is structured dimensionally, with the richer and more comprehensive (i.e., the intangible or invisible) dimensions emerging from and within the less rich and less comprehensive (i.e., the tangible or visible) dimensions without being reducible to them. Similarly, these intangible or invisible dimensions are known mediationally by means of our interaction with the tangible or visible ones.

The mediational structure of the world and our knowledge of it render the metaphoric mode of expression highly appropriate, even necessary. Only by means of a mode of speech that allows a person to speak of one aspect of reality *as* one speaks of another can this mediational structure be disclosed and discerned. In short, the mode of expression must resonate with that which it seeks to express, and the metaphoric mode does justice to the way in which the "invisible" dimensions of reality are mediated through the "visible." This is what Merleau-Ponty means, in the passage quoted above, where he speaks of "the occult trading of the metaphor" as the means of expression appropriate to philosophical investigation.

The image of "the flesh" is used by Merleau-Ponty to signify the commonality of human experience and form of life necessary to make shared knowledge and communication possible. Our common human embodiment serves as the "language beneath language," as the place of "intersection" or overlap between individual persons, which unites our diversity and makes a spoken language both possible and necessary. In this way the metaphor of flesh also serves as an excellent image of the metaphoric mode, since it too involves the overlapping of seemingly disparate terms and phrases, thereby uniting what appears to be distinct and separate meanings. As Merleau-Ponty himself says:

Once again, the flesh we are speaking of is not matter. It is the coiling over of the visible upon the seeing body, of the tangible upon the touching body, which is attested in particular when the body sees itself, touches itself seeing and touching the things, such that, simultaneously, *as* tangible it descends among them, *as* touching it dominates them all and draws this relationship and even this double relationship from itself, by dehiscence or fission of its own mass. (*VI*, p. 146)

This incarnational understanding of our relation to the physical world and to each other is equally appropriate to Merleau-Ponty's view of the nature of linguistic communication at the deepest, metaphorical level. The flesh becomes word and the word becomes flesh.

In his "Working Notes," which are included at the end of *The Visible and the Invisible*, Merleau-Ponty frequently speaks of "the flesh" (see especially pp. 248–259). He concludes his consideration of the incarnational character of human existence and experience by connecting it with the indirect or metaphorical function of speech in general and with the purpose of philosophical activity in particular. He says:

> Show that philosophy as interrogation (i.e. as disposition, around the this and the world which *is there*, of a hollow, of a questioning, where the this and the world must *themselves* say what they are—i.e. not as the search for an invariant of language, for a lexical essence, but as the search for an invariant of silence, for the structure) can consist only in showing how the world is articulated starting from a zero of being which is not nothingness, that is, in installing itself on the edge of being, neither in the for Itself, nor in the Itself, at the joints, where the multiple *entries* of the world cross. (*VI*, p. 260)

The image that dominates the final pages of *The Visible and the Invisible* is that of the title of the fourth chapter, "The Intertwining—The Chiasm." This image centers the true character of both our interactive relation to the world and the multidimensional function of the language most appropriate to the task of philosophy. By means of the notion of intertwining, which ties in nicely with many other images, such as fabric, weaving, tissues, Merleau-Ponty draws together his emphasis on the interpretation that exists between all aspects and dimensions of reality, rendering them capable of being experienced and known. The physical world and human beings are, at the center, intertwined through embodied interaction. Moreover, it is by means of this intertwining that the intangible, "the invisible" quality of reality is mediated in and through the tangible, "the visible" quality. This image of threads twisted together into a common fabric speaks as well of the way linguistic meaning works.

> The meaning is not on the phrase like the butter on the bread, like a second layer of "physic reality" spread over the sound," it is the totality of what is said, the integral of all the differentiations of the verbal chain; it is given with the words for those who have ears to hear. (*VI*, p. 155)

The specific nature and function of metaphorical speech is expressed nicely in the image of the chiasm, which only appears for discussion in the "Working Notes" at the end of the book. The fundamental idea conveyed by this image is that of reversal, the dialectic or paradox whereby two seemingly opposed or distinct realities trade places and are thereby transformed and united without yielding their own independence (p. 199). One thinks here of the biblical notions of two persons becoming one in marriage, of losing one's life in order to save it, and of the trinitarian formula of "three persons in one being"—or perhaps better yet, of the principles of yin and yang united in dynamic harmony without losing their individuality.

> By reason of this mediation through reversal, this chiasm, there is not simply a for-Oneself for-the-Other antithesis, there is Being as containing all that, first as sensible Being and then as Being without restriction. . . . Chiasm, instead of the for-the-Other: that means that there is not only a me-other rivalry, but a co-functioning. We function as one unique body. (*VI*, p. 215)

The image of chiasm is applied directly to the phenomenon of language by Merleau-Ponty when he speaks of the dialectic between speech and silence at the center of the child's acquisition of language. Silence and speech endow each other with meaning; apart from the other neither can be meaningful. Merleau-Ponty introduces the image of the finger of a glove that is turned inside out to illustrate this notion of reversibility. Both the inside and the outside pivot on the tip of the finger, and both exist and are known only in relation to each other. Language, too, turns on this reversibility, this ability of speakers and hearers to communicate in and through, and in spite of, their diversity by means of their commonality.

It strikes me that this image of chiasm is especially appropriate to the metaphoric mode, since they both embody the notions of duality within unity and of reversibility. A metaphoric image means two things at once, depending on which way it is being read. Like the finger of a glove, a metaphor can be read from the "outside" literally, or from the "inside," figuratively. Also, because of conventional usage, a given metaphor may have its figurative meaning transformed into its literal meaning. Metaphor, like irony, reverses the thrust of a given expression, thus changing everything without changing anything; one says one thing and means another, and expects to be understood! Earlier on Merleau-Ponty spoke of the language most appropriate to philosophy as metaphoric, "where what counts is no longer the manifest meaning of each word and of each image, but the lateral relations, the kinships that are implicated in their transfers and their exchanges." (*VI*, p. 125) Here we see the image of chiasm fleshed out, as it were.

Merleau-Ponty applies the image of chiasm directly to philosophy when he says:

> The idea of chiasm . . . starting from there, elaborate an idea of philosophy: it cannot be total and active grasp, intellectual possession, since

what there is to be grasped is a dispossession—it is not *above* life, overhanging. It is beneath. It is the simultaneous experience of the holding and the held in all orders. *What* it says, its *significations*, are not absolutely invisible: it shows by words. Like all literature. It does not install itself in the reverse of the visible: it is on both sides. (*VI*, p. 266)

Once more we see the crucial significance of the notion of dynamic overlapping or intertwining, where language shuttles back and forth, amid the threads of the warp of our embodied world, creating patterns of meaning within the weft of our life together. Philosophy brings understanding of this process and these factors, according to Merleau-Ponty, neither by standing objectively above them, nor by losing itself subjectively within them, but by practicing in them and reflecting through them at one and the same time. This paradoxical posture is maintained by means of thought and speech that partake of "the occult trading" of the metaphoric mode.

> We are invited to discern beneath thinking . . . another thought which is struggling to establish itself, and succeeds only by bending the resources of constituted language to some fresh usage. . . . Language outruns us, not merely because the use of speech always presupposes a great number of thoughts which are not present in the mind and which are covered by each word, but also of another reason, and a more profound one: namely, that these thoughts themselves, when present, were not at any time "pure" thoughts either, for already in them there was a surplus of the signified over the signifying. . . . (*PER*, pp. 389–390)

PHILOSOPHY AND THE TRANSCENDENT

Throughout the full span of his writings, Merleau-Ponty makes frequent use of the notion of transcendence, and yet he never speaks directly or at length about it. Our final task in this exploration of his thought in relation to the metaphoric mode is to engage this notion and trace its ramifications within Merleau-Ponty's overall philosophy. My central contention is that the concept of transcendence serves as an excellent centering image for the main themes constituting the broad sweep of Merleau-Ponty's thought. Moreover, this notion itself, in Merleau-Ponty's understanding of it, embodies the significance and rationale of the metaphoric mode of thought and expression, as well.

The place to start our consideration of Merleau-Ponty's view of transcendence is with his pivotal remark concerning the nature of philosophical activity in the preface to *Phenomenology of Perception*:

> Reflection does not withdraw from the world towards the unity of consciousness as the world's basis; it steps back to watch the forms of

transcendence fly up like sparks from a fire; it slackens the intentional threads which attach us to the world and thus brings them to our notice. . . . (p. xiii)

Let us begin with a brief summary of the "forms of transcendence" as they are displayed within Merleau-Ponty's account of our knowledge of the world, other persons, and ourselves. We shall then focus on the pattern of transcendence, as revealed in these *forms*, and finally conclude with a consideration of the notion of transcendence as understood theologically.

At the axis of human existence and experience stands the body; this is the fulcrum of Merleau-Ponty's entire philosophy. The first orbit of significance is our encounter with the physical environment by means of fully embodied, synaesthetic perception. As we interact with the things around us, we eventually discern, if only tacitly, that while we can never fully separate ourselves from them, we are, nonetheless, in some sense distinct from them. Although he does not use the term "transcendence" in the following passage, the dynamic described therein pinpoints the symbiotic character of our embodied perceptual relation with the physical world.

> The theory of the body image is, implicitly, a theory of perception. We have relearned to feel our body; we have found underneath the objective and detached knowledge of the body that other knowledge which we have of it in virtue of its always being with us and of the fact that we are our body. In the same way we shall need to reawaken our experience of the world as it appears to us in so far as we are in the world through our body, and in so far as we perceive the world with our body. But thus by remaking contact with the body and with the world, we shall also rediscover ourself, since, perceiving as we do with our body, the body, is a natural self and as it were, the subject of perception. (*PER*, p. 206)

Merleau-Ponty employs the notion of transcendence much more frequently when speaking of our relation to and knowledge of other selves. Here the key term is "intersubjectivity," and it is crucial to every aspect of our social existence, from language and sexuality to economics and art. The merely physical relationship is transformed into a sexual one, in the fullest sense of the term, when through the intersubjectivity of "the flesh" we actually make "contact" with another person.

> We shall give the name transcendence to this act in which existence takes up, for its own purposes, and transforms such a situation. Precisely because it is transcendence, existence never utterly outruns anything, for in that case the tension which is essential to it would disappear. (*PER*, p. 169)

This concern to show that whatever is transcendent does not exist independently of or go beyond that which is imminent appears often in Merleau-Ponty's discussions. For him, the transcendent and the immanent are always dual realities, symbiotically related as are the poles of an electromagnetic field. While the transcendent is "more" than what it transcends, and thus cannot be reduced to it, it is never "other" than what it transcends, in the sense of existing independently of it. In his discussions of Marxist "economic determinism," for instance, Merleau-Ponty insists that while "every cultural phenomenon has, among others, an economic significance, . . . history by its nature never transcends any more than it is reducible to, economics" (*PER*, p. 173).

In the same way, speech emerges out of bodily behavior so as to create language, without ever really becoming separate from it.

> The meaning of the gesture is not contained in it like some physical or physiological phenomenon. The meaning of the word is not contained in the word as a sound. But the human body is defined in terms of its property of appropriating, in an indefinite series of discontinuous acts, significant cores which transcend and transfigure its natural powers. This act of transcendence is first encountered in the acquisition of a pattern of behavior, then in the mute communication of gesture: it is through the same power that the body opens itself to some new kind of conduct and makes it understood to external witnesses. (*PER*, p. 193)

Even our experience and knowledge of other persons, in the social world, as transcendent to our own reality, without being separate therefrom, is seen to follow this symbiotic, relational pattern. The so-called problem of other minds is only a problem for those who begin by defining persons as essentially disembodied minds that could exist atomistically, completely independent of one another.

> The central phenomenon, at the root of both my subjectivity and my transcendence towards others, consists in my being given to myself. *I am given*, that is, I find myself already situated and involved in a physical and social world—*I am given to myself.* . . . We must therefore rediscover, after the natural world, the social world, not as an object or sum of objects, but as a permanent field or dimension of existence: I may well turn away from it, but not cease to be situated relatively to it. (*PER*, pp. 360, 362)

The same reciprocal dynamic that instantiates the transcendent reality of the natural and social worlds in relation to myself also establishes my own transcendent identity in relation to these worlds. In both cases, it must be remembered, this is transcendence with a difference, namely "symbiotic transcendence."

> The acts of the *I* are of such a nature that they outstrip themselves leaving no interiority of consciousness. Consciousness is transcendence through and through, not transcendence undergone . . . but active transcen-dence. . . . It is the deep-seated momentum of transcendence which is

my very being, the simultaneous contact with my own being and with the world's being. (*PER*, pp. 376, 377)

Merleau-Ponty develops the concept of self-consciousness in relation to such phenomena as space, time, and freedom according to the same relational pattern of symbiosis. These are experienced as real features of the world in which we live, dimensions that transcend us and yet are immanent within our everyday experience. They are encountered in the give and take of history, as the past is remembered and the future is anticipated here and now in the present.

As my living present opens upon a past which I nevertheless am no longer living through, and on a future which I do not yet live, and perhaps never shall, it can also open on to temporalities outside my living experience and acquire a social horizon, with the result that my world is expanded to the dimensions of the collective history which my private existence takes up and carries forward. The solution of all problems of transcendence is to be sought in the thickness of the pre-objective present, in which we find our bodily being, our social being and the pre-existence of the world, that is, the starting point of "explanations," in so far as they are illegitimate—and at the same time the basis of our freedom. (*PER*, p. 433)

The notion of transcendence also appears, unsurprisingly, in Merleau-Ponty's infrequent discussions of religion. In "Indirect Language and the Voices of Silence" he distinguishes between traditional "vertical" and modern "horizontal" transcendence, speaking against the former and in favor of the latter. In so doing he strikes a surprisingly contemporary note that harmonizes very well with important themes in contemporary Christian theological thought. He insists that we must not

forget that Christianity is, among other things, the recognition of a mystery in the relations of Man and God, which stem precisely from the fact that the Christian God wants nothing to do with a vertical relation of subordination. He is not simply a principle of which we are the consequence, a will whose instruments we are, or even a model of which human values are only a reflection. There is a sort of impatience of God without us, and Christ attests that God would not be fully God without becoming fully man. . . . Transcendence no longer hangs over man: he becomes, strangely, its privileged bearer. (*Signs*, pp. 70–71)

In putting the matter of theological transcendence this way, as horizontal rather than vertical, Merleau-Ponty seems to be taking a position not unlike that of Alfred North Whitehead. Both seek to find a place for God between the traditional, hierarchical dualism of orthodox supernaturalism on the one hand and a pantheistic, monistic naturalism on the other. Whitehead's view is called "panentheism" in order to stress the idea that God is actually *within* the world (and the world in God) without being reducible to the world. Merleau-Ponty's view might best be termed "naturalistic theism." And both Merleau-Ponty and Whitehead emphasize the crucial role of humans as co-creators with God in the process of enabling good to overcome evil in concrete, historical situations.

Merleau-Ponty approaches this topic in a slightly different, but closely related manner in his essay, "Faith and Good Faith." There he focuses the notion of horizontal transcendence in terms of the Incarnation. He says:

> The Incarnation changes everything. Since the Incarnation, God has been externalized. He was seen at a certain moment and in a certain place, and He left behind Him words and memories which were then passed on. Henceforth man's road toward God was no longer contemplation but the commentary and interpretation of that ambiguous message whose energy is never exhausted. In this sense, Christianity is diametrically opposed to "spiritualism." It reopens the question of the distinction between body and spirit, between interior and exterior. (*SNS*, pp. 174–175)

The Word becoming flesh means, for Merleau-Ponty, that the reality and work of God must be found with and through human beings.

In this vein it is again not surprising that Merleau-Ponty's understanding of the Christian scriptures, especially the Gospel stories, centers in their metaphoric character. The form of the stories befits their content, in that both the Incarnation and the scripture are mediational realities in which intangible Truth is disclosed and discerned in and through tangible aspects of human life. In the following remarks, Merleau-Ponty connects the sacramental quality of Jesus' parables to the teaching of bodily resurrection:

> The parables of the Gospel are not a way of presenting pure ideas in images; they are the only language capable of conveying the relations of religious life, as paradoxical as those of the world of sensation. Sacramental words and gestures are not simply the embodiment of some thought. Like tangible things, they are themselves the carriers of their meaning, which is inseparable from its material form. They do not evoke the idea of God; they are the vehicle of His presence and action. In the last analysis the soul is so little to be separated from the body that it will carry a radiant double of its temporal body into eternity. (*SNS*, p. 175)

Here we see all of the key themes of Merleau-Ponty's philosophy focused in relation to the Christian gospel. The cruciality of the body, the embodied character of meaning, both existential and linguistic, and the metaphoric quality of talk about the transcendent are all integrated in these brief remarks about the significance of the Incarnation. Especially relevant for our present concern in this section is his reaffirmation of the sacramental power of the metaphoric mode, in which language is not used to represent or merely symbolize an intangible aspect of reality, but is used, rather, to exemplify or embody its own meaning—to be an instance of that which it is about.

This last point casts a great deal of light on Merleau-Ponty's own philosophizing and writing, since he himself employs an extraordinary number of metaphoric images in the process of expressing his own ideas. As he himself would undoubtedly point out, these images do not explain or stand for his ideas, they *are* his ideas. In other words, the content of Merleau-Ponty's philosophy requires the metaphoric format, not only because of the nature of his particular theory of meaning, but also because at the center all language is tethered to the metaphoric mode. To invert the early Wittgenstein, "Whatever can be said at all must ultimately be said indirectly; whereof we cannot but speak, we must speak metaphorically."

If we now review the foregoing summary of Merleau-Ponty's remarks about the notion of transcendence, three main characteristics become evident. First, since Merleau-Ponty views reality as structured dimensionally, transcendence must be understood as a richer, more comprehensive dimension of natural human experience, rather than as an interruption thereof. Second, this means that the transcendent dimension's reality is mediated in and through the other dimensions of human experience, being thus "horizontal" rather than "vertical." Third, our awareness of the transcendent is a result of our interaction with it as it is embodied in the various aspects of the other dimensions of our lives. Thus, all transcendence must be "incarnational."

Finally, the locating and exploring of all those forms and levels of transcendence in human experience of the world is, for Merleau-Ponty, the task of philosophy. Thus, philosophy is itself a mediational and interactive process by means of which the "joints" of reality, the transcendent, are allowed to disclose themselves. Philosophy is not transcendental in the sense of being a "superior" form of cognition or about a "higher" level of reality. Rather, it is transcendental by virtue of its efforts to embody and reveal the multifarious forms of mediation inherent within experienceable reality by way of its conceptual interaction with them. It slackens, but never stiffens or releases, the "intentional threads" by means of which we are connected to the world. This slackening calls to our attention the contours and timbres of the fields and horizons within which we are embodied.

The expressive mode most appropriate to this slackening process is clearly metaphor. Merleau-Ponty's own inability to carry on the philosophic enterprise apart from copious images, as well as his unquestionable ability to employ these in an extremely insightful way, attest to his own commitment to the primacy of the metaphor as crucial to philosophical activity. Moreover, his explicit statements concerning the essential character of the "lateral" meaning and "occult trading" inherent in the metaphoric mode make it abundantly clear that he believed that philosophy is in fact impossible apart from this mode of thought and expression. In the end Merleau-Ponty would agree with Aristotle when he said that "to be master of the metaphor is the greatest thing by far."

CONCLUSION

In the Introduction to this consideration of Merleau-Ponty's use and theory of metaphor I sought to establish the importance of such an undertaking. On the one hand, anyone at all familiar with Merleau-Ponty's writings cannot help being struck by the frequency and richness of his images. More than most philosophers he chose to express himself, or could not avoid expressing himself, in metaphor. Indeed, it is fair to say that he did his best thinking in these images. Not only is this true of his major early work, *Phenomenology of Perception*, but it remains true of his other works, especially and more intensively, his final, unfinished work, *The Visible and the Invisible*.

At the same time, and on the other hand, those who are familiar with the interpretive literature dealing with Merleau-Ponty's philosophy may also be aware that no serious or extended treatment of the metaphorical character of his mode of thought and expression is available. Most interpreters have been content to explicate Merleau-Ponty's *message* quite apart from his *medium*, as if his philosophy stands on its own, entirely separable from the images he employed in expressing it. Such an approach reveals a subtle but quite traditional view that the role of the metaphorical mode is "decorative" or "substitutional"—a view that Merleau-Ponty himself clearly rejects, since it flatly contradicts his central notion of the axial character of embodiment, whether existential or linguistic. I trust that the investigations in the foregoing pages have made this abundantly clear.

Even those interpreters who focus on Merleau-Ponty's theory of language for the most part fail to consider the radical and far-reaching implications of his tethering of all speech to gestural, and thus to somatic, significance. If linguistic meaning necessarily orbits around and is embodied in physical and social behavior, then the notion of metaphor becomes specifically crucial in developing an understanding of linguistic meaning. Despite this seemingly obvious ramification of Merleau-Ponty's philosophy of language, no special attention has been given to it by those interpreters who focus on this general aspect of his thought. Thus the rationale for the explorations of the preceding chapters.

152

We began in Chapter 1 with a consideration of the images used by Merleau-Ponty in his first major work, *Phenomenology of Perception*. We found an amazing number and variety of these images there, falling roughly into three main categories: (1) those that draw on some aspect of the environment, especially spatiality and habitation, (2) those that are drawn from organic life, especially physiological and regenerative processes, and (3) those taken from human creative activity, such as artistic and mechanical endeavors. These seminal images remain a vital feature of Merleau-Ponty's speech and thought throughout the development of his philosophy in his ensuing works.

In Chapter 2 we traced those metaphors employed by Merleau-Ponty in his aesthetic, political, and humanistic essays. Many of the images introduced earlier continue to appear, but others are added as well. With respect to the arts, he is especially fond of images that stress the incarnational or mediational quality of aesthetic significance. His discussions pivot around what is left "unsaid" in works of art, around indirection and "silence." With respect to political issues, Merleau-Ponty explains his somatic orientation in terms of history and intersubjectivity by means of such images as "anchorage" and "tunneling toward each other." In relation to cultural reality, theatrical images suggesting both "centrifugal" and "centripetal" forces are introduced, as are those of "bipolarity" and "osmosis." Even religion is recast in terms of "horizontal" rather than "vertical" transcendence.

Chapter 3 was devoted primarily to Merleau-Ponty's final, unfinished work, *The Visible and the Invisible*. At the outset he turns his attention to understanding itself, seeking to revise the traditional images of objectivity, such as "externality" and "manipulation," and the reactionary images of subjectivity, such as "internality" and "self-transcendence." He does this chiefly by means of his own image of "the flesh," which is both internal and external, while remaining "porous." Next he seeks to redefine philosophical activity by means of the images of "interrogation" and "chiasm," as a continuous asking, answering, and re-asking of all the basic questions about human existence. Philosophy, for Merleau-Ponty, seeks to "show rather than say" the "hollows" and the "joints" of Being. Metaphorical thought and speech are seen as indispensible to this process because only in them can the necessary chiasm or reversal of meaning be encountered, which alone displays the richness of Being and existence. Metaphor supplies the two-directional "doubling up" required for philosophical activity. It is, indeed, the very "flesh" or "intertwining" of thought, speech, and life. In this way the invisible can be seen to be incarnated in the visible.

The chapters comprising the second part of our explorations were centered on the nature of language, metaphor, and philosophy, respectively.

Merleau-Ponty was seen, in Chapter 4, as tethering language to bodily gesture. Embodiment is not only the true medium of expression, but is itself a form of speech, since it tells us about both the physical and social worlds, as well as about ourselves, by fixing our place in relation to them. Language is viewed as a fundamental mystery by Merleau-Ponty, since it seems to require itself in order to account for itself; like silence, language acquires its significance only in relation to its own absence. This mystery is the "hinge" that connects us with each other and with the world.

In Chapter 5 metaphor was found to be the fulcrum of all speech for Merleau-Ponty. His entire view of language as a mode of embodiment is folded back on and intensified by his concrete employment of and musings about metaphor as a mediational "transparency" in which the "sedimentation" of meaning is continually kept "in solution" so that the signified may always be surpassed by fresh signifying. As such, metaphor for Merleau-Ponty is clearly both cognitive and constitutive of reality. That is, it is both capable of being true, albeit indirectly, and symbiotically creative of the worlds that together we find and build for ourselves. Through the metaphoric mode alone we are able to "slacken the threads" by means of which we interact with each other and our physical environment, thus bringing to light both the world and our understanding of it.

Last, in Chapter 6, we brought all of the foregoing considerations to bear on Merleau-Ponty's overall view of philosophy itself. Against the standard traditional definitions of philosophical activity, he advocates a "concrete" approach that may be characterized as "linguistic phenomenology." By virtue of, and by means of our interrogation of, the threads that web us together in relation to the world, namely embodiment and speech, we are capable of understanding the world, each other, and ourselves. For Merleau-Ponty philosophy can only yield knowledge of "brute or wild being" in a mode that allows but does not force it to display itself. In metaphor alone is meaning intrinsically incarnate, for here alone is the reversibility of signifying and signification clearly exemplified. Thus it is the metaphoric mode that best mediates the transcendent, whether it be construed in terms of the self, others, or ultimate value. For in metaphorical understanding we are able to encounter a "more" that neither reduces to nor goes beyond our incarnational existence.

The central motif throughout all of Merleau-Ponty's work is, of course, embodiment. What we have discovered, by means of our consideration of the foregoing dimensions of his thought, is that the metaphoric mode is the natural extension and expression of this dominant motif. By means of our bodies we are situated in relation to both our physical and our social surroundings. Language is the incarnation of our being in social reality. Moreover, since all speech is inherently metaphoric, being indirect and open-textured by nature, metaphoric meaning is but the other side, or linguistic manifestation, of our embodiment. This, I take it, is Merleau-Ponty's view.

I believe it will prove both interesting and instructive to bring this conclusion to a close by relating the results of our investigation to the reflections offered by Eva Feder Kittay in her exceedingly thorough and insightful book, *Metaphor: Its Cognitive Force and Linguistic Structure*. Although she works almost entirely within the analytical tradition, and expresses her insights in that mode, the results and ramifications of her work are quite parallel to, even suggestive of, those of Merleau-Ponty.

Kittay develops what she terms a "perspectival" theory of metaphor, in which it is seen as arising from

> the placing of an object in two perspectives simultaneously. From this juxtaposition results a reconceptualization, sometimes permanent, more frequently transient, in which properties are made salient which may not previously have been regarded as salient and in which concepts are reorganized both to accommodate and to help shape experience. (p. 4)

Such a theory, not unlike the "interactionist" views of Black, Wheelwright, and Beardsley, as well as the "predicative" view of Ricoeur, requires that we think of "language as an expressive medium, which . . . allows us to say that we think *in language*, just as the artist expresses herself *in paint*; that we understand that language is not merely a conduit . . . for our thoughts" (p. 5). This way of putting the matter coincides nicely with what Merleau-Ponty says about speech, as well as with the actual images he uses.

More significantly, Kittay affirms the essentially cognitive function of metaphor even in scientific thought.

> When science is seen as a human activity rather than as a repository of ultimate truths, and cognition generally is seen as a creative shaping of our conceptions of the world, the creative, imaginative play of metaphor is seen as characteristic not only of poetry, but also of science. When language is seen not only as the medium of making picture-like true statements about the world but as a tool for communicating, expressing and creating—a chief element in [to use Goodman's term] "world-making"—the role of metaphor must be accounted for in a theory of language. . . . By illuminating the creative contribution of mind and language to knowledge, the study of metaphor will, in turn, force revisions of our basic views of language and thought. (pp. 9–10)

By shifting the focus of linguistic meaning away from words and propositions and toward contextual usage and fields of semantic signification, Kittay is able to avoid the inevitable pitfalls of the traditional dichotomy between literal and metaphoric utterances. Instead, she distinguishes between first- and second-order meaning:

The position to be worked out in this book is that metaphors necessarily break some semantic rules, however subtly, but only to be subject to a new set of conditions whereby they are metaphors as opposed to mistakes or other deviant language. The semantic rules which metaphors break are the ones governing first-order discourse. These are rules governing discourse in which we are to assume that the applied timeless meanings are coincident with the utterance-type's occasion meaning. Where there is an indication . . . that there is a divergence between the two, we no longer have first-order discourse, for second-order meaning emerges just when there is a divergence between some applied timeless meaning and an utterance-type occasion meaning. The utterance is then governed by second-order rules. (p. 50)

This distinction fits surprisingly well with Merleau-Ponty's image of chiasm or semantic reversal, in which communication results from twisting one linguistic pattern into another so as to produce a different, albeit richer level of meaning.

With respect to the question of whether metaphorical or nonmetaphorical language is primordial, Kittay suggests a three-layered model in which metaphor both generates and plays off of conventionalized meaning.

Language arises out of a metaphorical displacement of a meaning, desire, or purpose on to a sign. The metaphorical move collapses into literality and conventionality—necessarily so if we are to have a viable working language—but language must be able to use new metaphoric displacements and metaphorical organizations to bring new meaning and concepts into language. Thus metaphor is both first and last—both primary process and second-order meaning. (p. 121)

Here, too, there is a clear parallel between Kittay's view and that of Merleau-Ponty, as the considerations of Chapter 5 amply demonstrate.

Both meaning and truth are, for Kittay, whether on the first- or second-order level, a function of use, context, and referential field. Thus for her, as well as for Merleau-Ponty, all language has embodied physical and social activity as its axis. By means of our interactions with nature, as well as with other persons and institutions, in accomplishing certain tasks, we construe and construct our common worlds. The fulcrum for all such linguistic activity is our placement within the field and horizon relative to material reality, and our common "enfleshment" relative to social reality, provided by our bodies. Kittay likens this perspective to the image of various arrangements that can be given to the furniture in a room.

Truth in our analogue world, then, has something to do with given realities such as gravity, the solidity of walls, the construction of doors and windows, etc. (read laws of nature, natural climatic and environmental conditions, societal regularities, and restrictions of a more fundamental sort), much to do with the furniture (read objects and concepts of objects) which we have found, constructed, arranged, and rearranged, and something to do with what we need, want, desire, and believe about the furniture and its arrangement. Meaning has to do with the service-ability of the objects and their arrangement—where utilization includes satisfying not only needs but desires, aesthetic considerations, or any reasonable or intelligible goals. Reference has to do with those objects that are placed about the room and utilized according to the "meaning." A conceptual scheme is a chosen ordering which will both reflect and shape what we take as true and meaningful, although the fact of alternate schemes need not be precluded by a given arrangement. (p. 320)

Kittay concludes her book by providing a rather extensive development of this "metaphor for metaphor" in terms of furniture arrangement. She suggests that various friends and guests who visit her home could, for diverse purposes, rearrange her furniture, some more radically than others, so as to create different patterns of meaning, truth, and reality. Here is her final paragraph:

Language and our concepts, in their "proper" and metaphorical arrange-ments, like the room and its furnishings in our metaphor, are things we live among. They change with time, need, desire, and whim. They both reflect and shape our beliefs and desires. They are rarely as tidy as we might like, although we can glory in the disorder—knowing that our room and our language have a lived-in character. Some order, at least one intelligible to ourselves and to those with whom we share our space and our words, none the less remains crucial. And a systematic tolerance of a "disorder" that can be shown to be purposeful and intelligible is equally essential, if we are to remain in touch with the well-springs of our creativity and to keep our surroundings and our minds adaptable to the changing circumstances of our lives and our world. Understanding the workings and the meaning of this latter "disorder" is as much a part of understanding meaning and language as is understanding the "proper order." It is within a carefully conceived "chaos" that metaphors attain an irreducible cognitive content and their special meaning. (p. 327)

It is entirely appropriate that Kittay concludes her analysis of the structure and force of the metaphoric mode by offering a "metaphor for metaphor." More significantly, the specific image she offers, that of rearranging the furniture in a room, is especially relevant to our exploration of metaphor in the work and thought of Merleau-Ponty. This image revolves around the mediational character of the relation between physical embodiment and social significance. Not only does the latter arise out of the interaction inherent within the former, but it can only be understood by means of an understanding of the former as well. At the same time, however, it must be acknowledged in keeping with Merleau-Ponty's overall philosophy that social and linguistic significance cannot be reduced to an account of physical embodiment. The one emerges in relation to but without being exhausted by the other. In the end, for both Kittay and Merleau-Ponty, metaphor, like the other fundamental mysteries of life, can never be fully explicated. In Wittgenstein's idiom, "Explanations must come to an end; otherwise they would not be explanations."

BIBLIOGRAPHY

PRIMARY SOURCES CITED

These abbreviations have been used in documenting the most frequently cited of Merleau-Ponty's works:

CAL   *Consciousness and the Acquisition of Language*
PER   *Phenomenology of Perception*
SNS   *Sense and Non-Sense*
VI   *The Visible and the Invisible*

Merleau-Ponty, Maurice. *Adventures of the Dialectic.* Translated by J. Bien. Evanston, IL: Northwestern University Press, 1973.

———. *Consciousness and the Acquisition of Language.* Translated by H. J. Silverman. Evanston, IL: Northwestern University Press, 1973.

———. *The Essential Writings of Merleau-Ponty.* Edited by Alden L. Fisher. New York: Harcourt, Brace, and World, 1969.

———. *Phenomenology of Perception.* Translated by Colin Smith. Atlantic Highlands, NJ: Humanities Press International, Inc., 1963.

———. *In Praise of Philosophy.* Evanston, IL: Northwestern University Press, 1963.

———. *The Primacy of Perception.* Edited by J. M. Edie. Evanston, IL: Northwestern University Press, 1964.

———. *The Prose of the World.* Edited by Claude Lefort. Translated by J. O'Neill. Evanston, IL: Northwestern University Press, 1973.

———. *Sense and Non-Sense.* Translated by H. L. and P. A. Dreyfus. Evanston, IL: Northwestern University Press, 1964.

———. *Signs.* Translated by R. C. McCleary. Evanston, IL: Northwestern University Press, 1964.

———. *The Visible and the Invisible.* Edited by Claude Lefort. Translated by Alphonso Lingis. Evanston, IL: Northwestern University Press, 1968.

SECONDARY SOURCES CITED

Arnheim, R. *Visual Thinking.* London: Faber, 1969.

Austin, J. L. *How to Do Things with Words.* Cambridge: Harvard University Press, 1960.

Bannon, J. *The Philosophy of Merleau-Ponty*. New York: Harcourt, Brace, 1967.

Barfield, O. *Poetic Diction*. Middletown, CT: Wesleyan University Press, 1973.

Beardsley, M. *Aesthetics*. New York: Harcourt, Brace, 1958.

Black, M. *Models and Metaphors*. Ithaca, NY: Cornell University Press, 1962.

Cassirer, E. *The Philosophy of Symbolic Forms*. New Haven, CT: Yale University Press, 1953.

Dreyfus, H. *What Computers Can't Do*. New York: Harper and Row, 1979.

Edie, J. Foreword to Merleau-Ponty's *Consciousness and the Acquisition of Language*. Evanston, IL: Northwestern University Press, 1973.

Gadamer, H. G. *Philosophical Hermeneutics*. Berkeley, CA: University of California Press, 1976.

———. *Truth and Method*. New York: Crossroad, 1984.

Geertz, C. *The Interpretation of Cultures*. New York: Basic Books, 1973.

Gibson, J. J. *The Perception of the Visual World*. New York: Houghton-Mifflin, 1966.

Gier, N. *Wittgenstein and Phenomenology*. Albany, NY: State University of New York Press, 1981.

Gill, J. H. *Wittgenstein and Metaphor*. Washington, D.C.: University Press of America, 1980.

Goodman, N. *Languages of Art*. Indianapolis, IN: Bobbs-Merrill, 1968.

———. *Ways of Worldmaking*. Indianapolis, IN: Hackett, 1978.

Johnson, M. *Philosophical Perspectives on Metaphor*. Minneapolis, MN: University of Minnesota Press, 1981.

———. *The Body in the Mind*. Chicago, IL: University of Chicago Press, 1987.

Kittay, E. F. *Metaphor: Its Cognitive Force and Linguistic Structure*. Oxford: Clarendon Press, 1989.

Kuhn, T. *The Structure of Scientific Revolutions*. Chicago, IL: University of Chicago Press, 1970.

Kwant, R. *The Phenomenological Philosophy of Merleau-Ponty*. Pittsburgh, PA: Duquesne University Press, 1963.

———. *From Phenomenology to Metaphysics*. Pittsburgh, PA: Duquesne University Press, 1966.

Langan, T. *Merleau-Ponty's Critique of Reason*. New Haven, CT: Yale University Press, 1966.

Langer, M. *Merleau-Ponty's "Phenomenology of Perception."* Tallahassee, FL: State University of Florida Press, 1989.

Langer, S. *Problems of Art*. New York: Scribners, 1957.

Lanigan, R. *Speech Act Phenomenology*. The Hague: Martinus Nijhoff, 1977.

Mallin, S. *Merleau-Ponty's Philosophy*. New Haven, CT: Yale University Press, 1979.

Mays, W., and S. Brown. *Linguistic Analysis and Phenomenology*. Lewisburgh, PA: Bucknell University Press, 1970.

Nelson, J. *Embodiment*. Minneapolis, MN: Augsburg, 1980.

Palmer, R. *Hermeneutics*. Evanston, IL: Northwestern University Press, 1969.

Panikkar, R. *Myth, Faith, and Hermeneutics*. New York: Paulist Press, 1979.

Polanyi, M. *Knowing and Being*. Chicago, IL: University of Chicago Press, 1969.

Quine, W. V. O. *Word and Object*. New York: Wiley, 1960.

Ricoeur, P. *The Rule of Metaphor*. Toronto: University of Toronto Press, 1977.

Rorty, R. *Philosophy and the Mirror of Nature*. Princeton, NJ: Princeton University Press, 1979.

Turbayne, C. *The Myth of Metaphor*. New Haven, CT: Yale University Press, 1962.

Wheelwright, P. *The Burning Fountain*. Bloomington, IN: Indiana University Press, 1968.

———. *Metaphor and Reality*. Bloomington, IN: Indiana University Press, 1962.

Wittgenstein, L. *Philosophical Investigations*. New York: Macmillan, 1953.

Zaner, R. *The Problem of Embodiment*. The Hague: Martinus Nijhoff, 1964.

INDEX